ON THE SQUARE WITHIN THE WALLS OF SALADIN'S CITADEL.
30th August, 1915.
The Mocattam Hills and Napoleon's Fort in the distant background.

(*Frontispiece.*)

THE 28TH

A RECORD OF WAR SERVICE WITH THE
AUSTRALIAN IMPERIAL FORCE,
1915-1919

VOLUME I.
EGYPT, GALLIPOLI, LEMNOS ISLAND,
SINAI PENINSULA

By COLONEL H. B. COLLETT, C.M.G., D.S.O., V.D.
FIRST C.O. of the Battalion

WITH FOREWORD *by* THE ARCHBISHOP OF PERTH,
CHAPLAIN-GENERAL TO THE FORCES

The Naval & Military Press Ltd

Published by
The Naval & Military Press Ltd
5 Riverside, Brambleside, Bellbrook
Industrial Estate, Uckfield, East Sussex,
TN22 1QQ England
Tel: +44 (0) 1825 749494
Fax: +44 (0) 1825 765701
www.naval-military-press.com
www.military-genealogy.com
www.militarymaproom.com

In reprinting in facsimile from the original, any imperfections are inevitably reproduced and the quality may fall short of modern type and cartographic standards.

CONTENTS.

FOREWORD: By The Most Rev. C. O. L. Riley, O.B.E., D.D., LL.D.,
V.D., Archbishop of Perth, Chaplain-General to the Forces. IX.
PREFACE ... ... XI.
CHRONOLOGY ... ... XIII.

CHAPTER I.
THE GENESIS.

W.A. in the South African War—The outbreak in 1914—Karrakatta and Blackboy Hill—The first units to embark—Scheme for raising new brigades—The 28th Battalion authorised—Enrolment of personnel—Selection and appointment of Officers and N.C.Os.—Specialists wanted—Equipping—Hard training—An accident—Hours off duty—Visit from H.E. the Governor—Medical precautions—The March through Perth—Final preparations for departure for the Front. **Page 1.**

CHAPTER II.
EN ROUTE.

Embarkation 9th June, 1915—The crowds along the route and at Fremantle—Farewell to Australia—The " Ascanius "—Quarters and messing—Other troops on board—Statistics—Training at Sea—Lectures—Stowaways—Competitions in tidiness — Entering the Tropics — Amusements—The Canteen—The Master—The East African Coast—The Red Sea—Strange rumours—Arrival at Suez—First contact with the Egyptians.
Page 15.

CHAPTER III.
FIRST STAY IN EGYPT.

Disembarkation and train journey to Abbasia—The Land of Goshen—Description of the Camp—Early difficulties—Institutes—The newsvendors—Tidings from Gallipoli—Unrest in Egypt—The local command and garrison—Inspection by Sir John Maxwell—Mobilisation of the 7th Brigade—Training in the Desert—Night marches—The Zeitun School—Formation of the 2nd Australian Division—Difficulties in feeding the troops—Clothing for the Tropics—In quarantine—Sickness—Pay and currency—Mails and the Censor—Amusements—Riots—The military Police—Chaplains. **Page 28.**

CHAPTER IV.
FIRST STAY IN EGYPT (continued).

Distractions—A march through Cairo—Leave—In the bazaars—Gharri and donkey rides—Esbekieh Gardens—The Kursaal and the Casino—Shepheard's Hotel—Guides—Sightseeing—The Pyramids and Sphinx—Memphis—Sakkara—The Tombs of the Sacred Bulls—The Cairo Museum—The Citadel and other Saracenic remains—Some beautiful mosques—Old Cairo—The Nile—The Egyptian aristocracy—Garrisoning Saladin's Citadel—A nephew of the Senussi—The trials of a soldier—Souvenir hunting—Visitors from Home—News of the August advance—Warned to proceed overseas—Entraining. **Page 45.**

CHAPTER V.

GALLIPOLI.

Some account of the Gallipoli Peninsula—The naval and military operations—Anzac Day—Arrival at Alexandria—Embarking on the " Ivernia "—Prejudices—Through the Grecian Archipelago—The " Southland "—In Mudros Bay—Closing the mail—In touch with the " Aragon "—Transhipping to the " Sarnia "—The last stage—The first glimpse of battle—Impressions—Landing in the " beetles "—Waterfall Gully—The first casualty—Contact with the 4th Brigade—Move to the Apex—Description of the position—Holding the salient—Condition of the trenches—Artillery support—Telephones—Dugouts—The New Zealanders—Attitude of the enemy—Sniping with field guns—Bombs, mortars, and catapults—Broomstick bombs. **Page 58.**

CHAPTER VI.

GALLIPOLI (continued).

First night in the trenches—Cleaning up—Shell fire—Generals Birdwood and Godley—No Man's Land—View from the Apex—Casualties—Pick and shovel—Sleep—Turkish demonstration—Divine service—Visit of Sir Ian Hamilton—Private Owen's escape—Company reliefs—Mining and tunnelling—Salvage—Patrols—Our guns—Propaganda—Espionage. **Page 77.**

CHAPTER VII.

GALLIPOLI (continued).

Poison gas—Targets for the guns—A general—A false alarm—" The one shall be taken — "—Relieved by the 25th Battalion—The fly pest—Sickness—Bully beef and biscuits—Rum—Scarcity of water—Cooking—Gathering fuel—Supply and transport—" Dunks." **Page 90.**

CHAPTER VIII.

GALLIPOLI (continued).

Lower Cheshire Ridge—Description of new position—A break in the weather—Trenches—Tunnels—Timber and iron—Sniping—Ruses—The Mohammedan festival—Arrival of reinforcements—Promotion from the ranks—Formation of bombing section—Change in command of Brigade—Canteen stores—Pay—A miss—Aeroplanes—Relieved by the 4th Brigade—Taylor's Hollow—Beach fatigues—Soldiers as sailors—News—Mails from Australia—Diversions—The naturalist—The beauties of land, sea, and sky. **Page 102.**

CHAPTER IX.

GALLIPOLI (continued).

Move to Happy Valley—Visit of Lord Kitchener—Unsettled weather—Humanity—A proposed stunt—The " close season for Turkey "—The blizzard and its dire consequences—Increased enemy gun fire—The arrival of the German heavies—Russell's Top—Three tiers of tunnels—Death of the three majors—News of the evacuation—The main body leaves the Peninsula—The Die-hards—Work of the Machine Gun Section—The last man. **Page 120.**

CHAPTER X.

LEMNOS ISLAND.

Landing in the Bay—A sick battalion—Sarpi camp—The arrival of the beer—Resting, recuperating, and re-fitting—Z Valley camp—Members selected for distinction—Touring Lemnos—General description of the island—The inhabitants—Kastro—Primitive agriculture—Mt. Therma—Crowded shipping—The arrival of the billies—Christmas Day—A conspiracy—The concert—The New Year—Leaving for Egypt. **Page 137.**

CHAPTER XI.

BACK TO EGYPT.

Alexandria—Arrival at Tel-el-Kebir—The transport rejoins—A deal in tents—Kitchen trouble—A camp for two divisions—The battle of 1882—Short rations—Inspection by Sir Archibald Murray—Leave to Cairo—The postal service—Training for savage warfare—Reinforcements—General Paton—Transfers to the Camel Corps—Rumours of a Turkish advance—Move to the Sinai Peninsula—The desert—Road and pipe line—Camels—Ferry Post—The defences of the Suez Canal—Passing shipping—Lumping and navvying—Secret service agents—Dangers to shipping in the Canal—Ismailia—Gambling—Cerebro-spinal meningitis—A visit from the High Commissioner in Egypt. **Page 148.**

CHAPTER XII.

PREPARING FOR FRANCE.

Three new divisions—Another 60,000 Australians—Transfers to new units—Changes in establishments—Promotions—Talk of the Western Front—Undesirables—Unfits—The khamsin—Assembling at Moascar—Final preparations—Train to Alexandria—The "Themistocles"—The menace of submarines—Through the Mediterranean—Malta—Approaching Marseilles—Entering the harbour—The end of the first phase. **Page 162.**

APPENDICES.

		Page.
A.	List of Units raised and recruited by Western Australia	171
B.	Roll of Honour	172
C.	Casualties whilst with the Mediterranean Expeditionary Force	174
D.	Roll of Original Officers of the Battalion	175
E.	Roll of Officers promoted from the Ranks between the 9th June, 1915, and 21st March, 1916	177
F.	Roll of Reinforcement Officers who joined the Battalion between 9th June, 1915, and 21st March, 1916	178
G.	Civil Occupations of Original Members of the Battalion who embarked as Officers or were subsequently promoted to Commissioned Rank	178
H.	Nominal Roll of Original Members of the Battalion who embarked at Fremantle on H.M.A.T. "A11" ("Ascanius"), 9th June, 1915, and on "Boonah," 12th July, 1915	180
I.	Nominal Roll of Members of Reinforcements who joined the Battalion in the Field prior to the 21st March, 1916	201
J.	Honours conferred on Original Members of the Battalion	218

LIST OF MAPS AND PLANS.

Cairo and Environs	Facing page	52
The Great Pyramid	Page	48
Portion of Gallipoli Peninsula, showing Allied Lines	,,	59
The Trenches at "The Apex"	,,	69
The Front Line on Cheshire Ridge	,,	103
Lemnos, Imbros, Tenedos, and Samothrace	,,	117
The Trenches on Russell's Top	,,	127
The Country adjacent to Tel-el-Kebir	Facing page	148
The Australian Position in Defence of the Suez Canal, 1916	Page	155
The Australian Lines on Gallipoli	Facing page	170

LIST OF ILLUSTRATIONS.

On the Square within the Walls of Saladin's Citadel	Frontispiece.	
Blackboy Hill Camp	Page	3
Some of the Original Officers	,,	5
The Regimental Signallers	,,	9
The Machine Gun Section	,,	9
The March through Perth	,,	11
The March through Perth: the Crowd in St. George's Terrace	,,	12
The Farewell at Fremantle	,,	17
H.M's. Australian Transport "A11"	,,	21
Two very young Soldiers	,,	25
Abbasia Camp	,,	31
The Adjutant and "Tim"	,,	31
Brigadier-General J. Burston, V.D.	,,	35
Lieut.-Colonel C. R. Davies, O.B.E.	,,	35
Major J. Kenny, A.A.M.C.	,,	39

List of Illustrations—continued.

	Page
Captain J. J. S. Scouler	39
The Wall of the Citadel	47
View of Cairo from the Citadel Walls	51
The Moqattam Hills	51
The Citadel	55
Chunuk Bair	63
Williams' Pier, where the 28th landed	66
The Apex	71
At the Apex: using the periscope rifle	74
"The Farm"	74
In the Front Line at the Apex	78
Excavating a "Bivvy" in the support trenches	79
View from Baby 700	83
Major J. A. Campbell Wilson	91
Captain J. Gettingby: The Quartermaster	92
Sergeant C. R. Field	96
Regimental Quartermaster-Sergeant R. G. Sexty	97
The Chailak Dere	106
View of the Aghyl Dere	107
"A" Company getting ready to move from the Reserve Position at Cheshire Ridge	111
The Q.M.'s Store of "A" Company at Cheshire Ridge	112
The Sari Bair Ridge	121
Headquarters of "C" Company, Happy Valley	125
The Great Traffic Trench	125
A Conference on Walker's Ridge, December, 1915	129
The view from Russell's Top looking into Malone Gully	131
Captain G. D. Shaw, M.C.	135
Captain T. O. Nicholls, M.C.	135
The Camp at Sarpi, Lemnos Island	141
The Shipping in Mudros Bay, 1915	141
On the Battlefield of Tel-el-Kebir, January, 1916	151
Ferry Post, showing the Suez Canal	158
Ferry Post: the landing place on the East bank	158
The Camp of the 28th at Ferry Post	160
The Suez Canal: a liner in the fairway	160
Private H. A. Franco, M.M.	164
The Pioneer-Sergeant at work	165
The 2nd Division crossing the Canal en route to Europe	169
The "Themistocles" at Alexandria	169

FOREWORD.

By The Most Rev. C. O. L. Riley, O.B.E., D.D., LL.D., V.D., Archbishop of Perth, Chaplain-General to the Forces.

I have been asked to write a short Foreword to the History of the 28th Battalion. I do so with very great pleasure, for two reasons—Firstly, because I have known Colonel Collett for many years, and, secondly, because I approve of the History.

The present volume is the first of several that will attempt to record the doings of those bodies of magnificent volunteers who went from Western Australia and of whose achievements the country is so justly proud. The Trustees of the Public Library, Museum, and Art Gallery of Western Australia, as the custodians of the archives of the State, have thought that those archives would be greatly lacking were a history of our part in the World War not included. With that object in view, the Commonwealth and State Governments have been approached and, largely through the assistance of the Premier, the Hon. Sir James Mitchell, K.C.M.G., and of the Minister for Education, the Hon. H. P. Colebatch, M.L.C., a practical commencement is now made with the narrative which concerns the 28th Battalion.

In the following pages we are not treated to long dissertations on military tactics, nor to clear proofs of how the writer could have concluded the war in half the time it really did take, if only the High Command had carried out suggestions made by one who knew all about it. You will find nothing like that in this book. Colonel Collett evidently asked himself: "What do the friends of the men of the Battalion want to know?" They want to know what the men did and what the Battalion did. What was the daily life of the man in the training camp; on the transports; in the war areas, and in the trenches. Of those who fell, they want to know, if possible, how and when they fell and where they were buried. Of those who were wounded, they want to know what they were doing when they "stopped a bullet," and how they were afterwards treated in hospital or in "Blighty." The public want a brief outline of the great doings of the Battalion, and all these things are plainly and proudly told by the writer.

I have often been in camp with Colonel Collett and know how thoroughly he did his work there. I am sure that all the men of the Battalion, their friends, and the public generally, will thank him for the loving care and labour he has devoted to a task which must have been to him a glorious record, and yet, at times, one full of sadness as he recalled to mind the "passing out" of friend after friend.

C. O. L., PERTH,
Chaplain-General A.I.F.,
C. of E.

PREFACE.

In the pages which follow an attempt has been made to give some account of how a Western Australian battalion was raised, organised, trained, and lived. How and where it travelled, some of the things it did and saw, and the nature of its environment. That is a large area to cover, and I am only too conscious that the result achieved is far from perfect.

This volume is confined to the period which terminated with the arrival of the 28th Battalion at Marseilles. That first phase of the unit's history was not so unimportant as might be thought. Although the following years were marked by a series of great events, in which the Battalion took a glorious part, yet there was a sameness in the surroundings and a monotony of routine which was conspicuously absent amongst the changing scenes and varied incidents of the earlier months of service. In those beginnings was moulded the high character for which the unit was ever afterwards esteemed. The trial by battle, hardship, and disease had not found its members lacking, and a fine spirit of comradeship had rapidly developed. With a high *morale* it arrived on the historic battlefields of Europe.

The few opinions offered in the course of the narrative are my own. They have not been formed lightly. Any individual charged with the care and direction of a body of his fellows must, of necessity—if he be worth his salt—study causes and effects.

Certain names have been mentioned in the text. Doubtless there are others equally worthy, but with the material I have had at my disposal it has been impossible to do due justice to all. There does exist a wealth of incident and anecdote which should be exploited but which, for obvious reasons, has not been available to me, and although I have made a general appeal to all ex-members to contribute to this record, a perfectly natural diffidence has held the hands of the great majority. For sins of omission and commission I beg the forgiveness of those with whom I had the great honour of serving and for whom, as comrades, men, and soldiers, I have the greatest respect and admiration.

The sources of information upon which I have had to mainly depend have been:—A very imperfect Official War Diary; my own letters; my memory; and a few contributions from former comrades. These last have been received from Major E. G. Glyde, Captains A. M. P. Montgomery, A. S. Isaac, N. W. Sundercombe, G. D. Shaw, T. O. Nicholls, and C. C. Flower. But more particularly am I indebted to Lieut. J. T. Blair, who placed at my disposal a considerable quantity of material which he had been at great pains to collect whilst in London.

As regards photographs and maps: Valuable prints and drafts have been supplied by the Trustees of the Australian War Museum. Mr. C. E. W. Bean, the Australian War Correspondent and Official Historian, has very kindly lent me photographs from his private collection. Mr. E. L. Mitchell and Mr. W. Owen, both of Perth, have generously given unrestricted permission to reproduce from their negatives, and certain members, and relatives of members, have also contributed interesting specimens. For the map of the Australian Corps' Front on Gallipoli, and the plans and diagrams referring to Cairo, Tel-el-Kebir, and the Pyramid, I have especially to thank Captain E. A. E. Andrewartha of the Australian Staff Corps.

The publication of the Nominal Rolls of Members of the Battalion has been made possible largely through the assistance of Major J. M. Lean, M.B.E., the Officer in Charge of Base Records, Melbourne.

For historical data, descriptive matter, and a few other essentials, I have also consulted the following works:—Barrett and Deane ("The A.A.M.C. in Egypt"); Callwell ("The Dardanelles Campaign and its Lessons"); Ellis ("Story of the 5th Division"); Hamilton ("Gallipoli Diary"); Masefield ("Gallipoli"); "Military History of the Campaign of 1882 in Egypt" (official); Nevinson ("The Dardanelles Campaign"); Schuler ("Australia in Arms"); Sladen ("Oriental Cairo"); Woods ("Washed by Four Seas"), and several others the names of which I cannot now recall. I am also under a great obligation to J. S. Battye, Litt.D., B.A., LL.B., the General Secretary of the Public Library, whose invaluable advice has guided me through a pleasing but arduous task.

Public Library,   HERBT. B. COLLETT.
  Perth, W.A.,
    June, 1922.

CHRONOLOGY OF THE 28th BATTALION, A.I.F.

1914.
August 4.—Declaration of War.

1915.
April 1.—Formation of the 7th Infantry Brigade approved and Establishments issued.
16.—Orders issued in Western Australia for formation of 28th Battalion of Infantry at Blackboy Hill. Necessary action taken the same day.
23.—Lieut.-Colonel H. B. Collett appointed to command.

May 12. ⎱ "A" and "B" Companies proceeded to Rockingham for
13. ⎰ advanced training. Returned 22nd May.
27.—Visit and inspection by His Excellency the Governor of Western Australia, Major-General Sir Harry Barron, K.C.M.G., C.V.O.

June 3.—The King's Birthday. March through Perth, fully horsed and equipped, with 1st Reinforcements.
6.—First Reinforcements embarked on H.M.A.T. "Geelong" at Fremantle. Sailed next day.
7.—Visit and inspection by O.C. 7th Infantry Brigade—Colonel J. Burston, V.D.
9.—The Battalion, less Transport details, embarked at Fremantle on H.M.A.T. "Ascanius" (A 11). Ship steamed out the same evening.
24.—East coast of Africa sighted—south of Ras-Jard-Hafun.
26.—Entered Red Sea.
29.—Suez sighted.
30.—Advance party landed and proceeded to Cairo.

July 2.—Battalion disembarked and proceeded by train to camp at Abbasia.
5.—Inspection by Lieut.-General Sir John Maxwell, General Officer Commanding in Egypt.
12.—Sergeant Faulkner and Transport details embark at Fremantle on H.M.A.T. "Boonah." Ordered that horses remain in Australia.

August 4.—Formation of 2nd Australian Division in Egypt.
8.—Transport details rejoin the Battalion.
17.—March to and occupation of Citadel of Cairo. First draft of reinforcements arrived and was taken on strength.
30.—Evacuation of Citadel and march to Aerodrome Camp, Heliopolis.

September 1.—Embarkation orders received. Transport to remain in Egypt.
3.—Entrained at Qubba Station.
4.—Arrived at Alexandria. Embarked on H.M.T. "Ivernia." Left harbour.
8.—Arrived off Lemnos Island.
9.—Entered Mudros Bay.

CHRONOLOGY OF THE 28TH BATTALION, A.I.F.—*continued*.
1915.
September 10.—Transhipped to s.s. "Sarnia" and proceeded in direction of Gallipoli Peninsula. That night landed at Williams' Pier and bivouaced in Waterfall Gully. Attached to New Zealand and Australian Division.
11.—First casualty. Private F. T. Mitchell wounded. Moved up Chailak Dere and bivouaced between Bauchop's Hill and Little Table Top—Rose Hill.
12.—"Apex" salient taken over from New Zealanders. First casualty in action. Lieut. F. E. Jensen dangerously wounded. He died a few hours later.
13.—First visit by Corps and Divisional Commanders.

October 4.⎱ Relieved by 25th Battalion. Moved to Lower Cheshire
5.⎰ Ridge.
30.—"B" Company relieved by "A" Company 26th Battalion.

November 1.—"C" Company moved to Taylor's Hollow.
2.—"D" Company moved to Taylor's Hollow.
3.—13th Battalion took over sector. 28th Battalion concentrated in Taylor's Hollow as Divisional Reserve. For next five weeks main body engaged on works and Beach fatigues.
12.—Moved to Happy Valley as support to 26th Battalion. Thus rejoined 2nd Division.
13.—Visit of Lord Kitchener.
24.⎱
27.⎰ Period of silence. Australians withhold their fire.
27.⎱ Peninsula visited by a blizzard. Heavy snow and ex-
29.⎰ treme cold.

December 4.—"A" Company went into line on Russell's Top.
6.—"D" Company went into line on Russell's Top.
7.—Head-quarters and "B" Company proceeded to Russell's Top.
8.—"C" Company joins Battalion.
11.—Received orders to embark on day following.
12.—Relieved by 20th Battalion. Embarked, less M.G. Section, on "Osmanieh" after dark.
13.—Landed on Lemnos Island and marched to camp at Sarpi.
15.—Marched to Z Valley, South Camp.
20.—Lieut. G. D. Shaw and Machine Gun Section left Gallipoli Peninsula with last of troops, 3.30 a.m. Rejoined Battalion same day.
31.—Advance Party left for Egypt.

1916.
January 6.—Embarked on H.M.T. "Ausonia."
7.—Left Mudros Bay at 7.30 a.m.
9.—Entered Alexandria Harbour.
10.—Disembarked and proceeded by train to camp at Tel-el-Kebir. Transport rejoined Battalion.
15.—Inspected by General Sir Archibald Murray, Commanding in Chief in Egypt.

CHRONOLOGY OF THE 28TH BATTALION, A.I.F.—*continued.*

1916.

February 3.—Moved by train to Moascar. Thence marched to Staging Camp—east bank of Suez Canal and opposite Ismailia. 7th Brigade in Divisional Reserve.

6.—Moved back to Ferry Post to garrison Inner Defences of Canal. Relieved 30th Battalion.

28.—Major C. R. Davies proceeded to Tel-el-Kebir to command 58th Battalion. Major A. W. Leane became 2nd-in-Command of 28th Battalion.

March 8.—Relieved by the New Zealanders. Crossed Suez Canal to Moascar Camp.

13.—Transport details and horses entrained for Alexandria. Embarked on H.M.T. "Minneapolis" next day.

15.—Battalion entrained for Alexandria.

16.—Arrived at Alexandria at 6.30 a.m. Embarked on H.M.T. "Themistocles." Left harbour same evening.

19.—Arrived off Valetta, Malta. Received orders as to route.

21.—Arrived in Marseilles Harbour.

The 28th:

A Record of War Service,

1915-1919.

CHAPTER I.

THE GENESIS.

The outbreak of the South African War in 1899 brought to the surface, in the people of Australia, that innate love of the Old Country which so marks the British race in whatever part of the world its members may happen to reside. Each Colony made an offer of men who were anxious to serve side by side with their kinsmen of the Regular Army. These offers were accepted—not because the men were needed at that time, but for the reason that statesmen recognised the existence of an era in the development of the dominions overseas that demanded the admission of their inhabitants to a share in the responsibilities attached to the maintenance and promotion of the welfare of the Empire. The reverses to the British arms which occurred during the opening months of the campaign roused in Australia a spirit of intense loyalty and patriotism, which was exemplified by renewed offers of assistance to the Government in London. These offers received an early response, with the result that across the Indian Ocean was maintained a steady stream of troops during the whole two and a half years of operations.

Western Australia readily took up a share of the burden and played her small, though not unimportant, part. Her contribution in troops consisted of 64 officers and 1,167 other ranks, together with 1,179 horses. On a population basis this effort was greater than that of any of the other Australian States. In casualties the various units (one infantry and nine mounted infantry) suffered a loss of 40 by death and 86 by wounds. That the services rendered were valuable, worthy of the State, and highly creditable to the individuals, may be gathered from the fact that the following honours were awarded:—1 V.C., 2 C.B.'s, 7 D.S.O.'s, 8 D.C.M.'s, and 3 additional Mentions in Despatches.

When Europe burst into the flame and smoke of war in August, 1914, Australia was unified in Government and a nation in sentiment

—but still a British nation. Her offers of assistance had been expected and were graciously and gratefully accepted. The Western Australians once more responded and, this time, in their thousands. Again the quota was exceeded—reinforcements being supplied even for Eastern States' units—and in all some 32,028 soldiers and nurses enlisted for service overseas during the period of 1914-1918.* Over 6,000 of these laid down their lives for Australia and the Empire, and many thousands more were wounded and maimed.

The 28th Battalion was one of three battalions wholly recruited and organised in Western Australia. It did not take the field in time to participate in the earlier days on Gallipoli, but showed its mettle in many a subsequent hard fight. Its deeds, and those of the other units which left these western shores, gained the unstinted admiration of the remainder of the Australian Imperial Force and constitute no mean record.

The contingents for South Africa were trained on the military reserve at Karrakatta. There there was a rifle range and sufficient space for the exercise of small bodies of troops. When, in 1914, it became obvious that larger numbers would be involved, a search was made for a greater and better camp site and training area. Eventually this was found at Blackboy Hill, which is situated about a mile east of Bellevue and quite close to the Eastern Railway. This area had been used by the Citizen Forces during the annual training of that year and found very suitable for dismounted work. The camp site is a rounded knoll of some few acres in extent, possessing the advantages of good natural drainage, a liberal number of shady trees, and firm soil underfoot. The surrounding country is broken by the foothills of the Darling Range and intersected by roads, fences, and—here and there—small watercourses. However, sufficient level ground is available to suit ordinary purposes and, altogether, the locality lends itself admirably to the training of infantry in platoons.

Here, then, when the first attested men were called up, were pitched the tents and marquees to shelter the troops. At the outset conditions of life were rough. The limited trained staff available, and the absence of many of the services recognised as essential in order to make military administration efficient, harassed the newcomers and caused a waste of time, together with considerable dislocation in the training. Later on, under successive camp commandants, conditions much improved. Efficient services were installed and competent men were trained to work them. Eventually Blackboy Camp came to be known throughout Australia as one of the most complete and comfortable.

---

* *See* Appendix A.

BLACKBOY HILL CAMP.
Photos. lent by Mr. E. L. Mitchell, Perth.

The camp was rapidly filled and, as units moved out, filled again. Before the end of February, 1915, there had proceeded overseas the 10th Regiment of Light Horse, the 8th Battery of Field Artillery, the 11th Battalion, the major portion of the 16th Battalion, and one company of the 12th Battalion; together with various technical and administrative units and detachments.

Recruits continued to pour in, and the men forthcoming were more than sufficient to supply the reinforcing drafts which were sent forward monthly. During February the Australian Government decided to raise further Light Horse Regiments and the 5th and 6th Brigades of Infantry. The 5th Brigade was to be furnished by New South Wales with one battalion (20th) from Queensland. Victoria was to supply the 6th Brigade, with two companies each from South and Western Australia to form the 24th Battalion.

The two companies ("C" and "D") of the 24th Battalion were immediately formed from the depôt units in camp and commenced to equip and train.

Hardly had this been done when Headquarters announced the raising of even another brigade of infantry—the 7th. On the 1st April the establishments for this were issued. One and a half battalions (25th and 26th) were to be supplied by Queensland; half a battalion (26th) by Tasmania; and one battalion each by South Australia (27th) and Western Australia (28th). Added to this was a brigade staff of five officers and 21 other ranks to be raised from all districts. This new proposal necessitated some re-arrangement in respect to the 5th and 6th Brigades. The responsibility for the 20th Battalion reverted to New South Wales. Victoria likewise undertook to provide sufficient men for the 24th Battalion.

The Commandant of Western Australia, therefore, found himself called upon to raise and equip a complete new unit consisting of 32 officers, 994 other ranks, and 63 horses, together with two machine guns, nine bicycles, and 13 transport vehicles.*

On the 16th April definite instructions were issued to the Officer Commanding at Blackboy Camp to organise the new battalion from the troops then under canvas. Action was immediately taken, and what were formerly "C" and "D" Companies of the 24th Battalion became "A" and "B" Companies of the 28th. Two new companies were formed from the depôt units, and the whole four were then moved to separate lines and placed under the temporary command of Captain L. B. Welch, who had 2nd Lieut. C. H. Lamb to assist

---

* This establishment was maintained until early in 1916, when modifications were made during the Battalion's stay at Ferry Post. Further material changes took place from time to time in the two years and eight months of the unit's campaign in France and Belgium.

SOME OF THE ORIGINAL OFFICERS.

Photo, lent by Mr. E. L. Mitchell, Perth.

him as Adjutant. Other officers from the depôt helped in the organisation and administration.

On the 23rd April Lieutenant-Colonel H. B. Collett was appointed to the command. This officer had formerly commanded the 11th Australian Infantry Regiment and the 88th Infantry Battalion (both of the Citizen Forces) in Perth, and had had considerable experience in military training, administration, and organisation. His first consideration was the selection and appointment of officers and non-commissioned officers, and the formation of the specialist detachments which were to be an integral and important part of the Battalion.

In the selection of officers little discretionary power was allowed the Commanding Officer. A Selection Board, appointed by the Minister for Defence, and sitting at Perth, recommended appointments. Very often this was done without a full knowledge of the candidate or of his qualifications. Under such circumstances some friction was bound to occur between the Board and the Commanding Officer. Eventually, however, it was possible, by means of compromise and adjustment, to gather together a reasonably sound team of officers. Major C. R. Davies, an officer of the 84th (Goldfields) Infantry, and a barrister of Boulder, became Second-in-Command. Captains A. W. Leane, L. B. Welch, and J. A. C. Wilson were promoted to the rank of Major and appointed to companies. A fifth major—F. R. Jeffrey—was transferred from Victoria and took "B" Company. This last-named officer, like the Second-in-Command, had seen service in South Africa, and had recently returned from England, whither he had conducted a draft of Imperial Reservists. A number of junior officers were found from the N.C.Os. attending a school of instruction for candidates for commissions. In the following years most of these men did exceedingly well. One of them commanded the Battalion during the major portion of 1917.

The selection and appointment of non-commissioned officers was a process of a different kind. With a large body of men unused to military formations and methods, the urgent need was to find other men who had had some slight experience and could teach the raw material routine and system and show it its place in the ranks. It did not, however, follow, that the same men, with their slight experience, were so equipped mentally and physically as to render them efficient leaders and commanders in the field. Another factor to be borne in mind was that from the ranks of the N.C.Os. would, in the future, be drawn the men to fill the gaps caused by casualties in the commissioned ranks. The qualities expected of an officer were personality, moral as well as physical courage, education, health, and a sporting disposition. The education sought was not necessarily academic, but such as indicated a capacity for rapid thought and for expression in speech and writing, together with a knowledge of men and their ways.* A high standard was thus set, and this being considered, all wearers of stripes were deemed to hold their rank temporarily—confirmation being dependent on their acquiring efficiency and displaying the desired qualifications. This method of appointment held good until after the Battalion's arrival in Egypt, and resulted in the collection of a most admirable body of subordinate leaders. Many of these same N.C.Os.—as officers—afterwards earned great distinction for themselves and for the unit. They were indeed the "backbone of the army."

The formation of the specialist detachments was rendered comparatively easy by the presence in the ranks of much excellent material. The Signallers were taken in hand by 2nd Lieut. J. J. S. Scouler, formerly attached to the Australian Intelligence Corps, who had passed through a signalling course in Victoria. He quickly gathered round him a body of enthusiastic young men whose efficiency subsequently became the envy of the other battalions and the admiration of the Division. The team for the two Maxim guns was organised and partly trained by Captain H. B. Menz. About the middle of May, however, 2nd Lieut. G. D. Shaw was appointed to the Section, and later commanded it most efficiently until the date it was absorbed into the 7th Machine Gun Company at Ferry Post, about the beginning of March, 1916. From the *personnel* of the original unit quite a large number of officers for the Machine Gun Corps was afterwards drawn. 2nd Lieut. T. D. Graham was appointed Transport Officer, and had little trouble in getting suitable men to look after and drive his horses and vehicles. He was fortunate in having to assist him Sergeant F. L. Faulkner, who had served with transport in India.

Captain John Kenny was attached as Regimental Medical Officer. On him devolved the responsibility for selecting and organising the Army Medical Corps details and the Stretcher Bearers. Both detachments were extremely useful. The Pioneers were chosen, and an excellent body of tradesmen secured. Numbering ten, they were placed under the immediate control of Sergeant J. W. Anderson—a Scotsman who afterwards became one of the best known members of the Battalion.

The warrant ranks were filled by the appointment of Sergeant J. Gettingby as Regimental Sergeant-Major; Sergeant R. G. Sexty as Regimental Quartermaster-Sergeant; Sergeants B. A. Bell, P. T. C. Bell, W. S. Appleyard, and H. M. Cousins, as Company Sergeants-Major; and Sergeants S. Jones, N. Graham, J. R. Gunn,

---
* See Appendix G.

and C. J. Piper as Company Quartermaster-Sergeants. With two exceptions, all these warrant officers subsequently attained commissioned rank.

2nd Lieut. C. H. Lamb was confirmed in the appointment of Adjutant and eventually received promotion to the rank of Captain. Upon him devolved a mass of detail work. This he handled with energy, skill, and success, and had very willing help from the Orderly Room Clerks—Sergeants E. C. Francisco * and S. S. Thompson.

A few other special appointments were made: Armourer-Sergeant L. C. Lewis to do minor repairs to the arms; Sergeant-Drummer W. T. Hocking to train the buglers and drummers; and Sergeant-Cook T. R. Graham to supervise and instruct in the kitchens. Shortly after embarkation Sergeant-Shoemaker F. Cox was allotted the work of looking after the footwear.

No chaplains were appointed to the Battalion, but four were gazetted to the Brigade. One of these, the Very Rev. Dean D. A. Brennan, of the Roman Catholic Denomination, and lately stationed at Narrogin, reported at Blackboy Camp. For many months he was attached to the 28th and shared its life in Egypt, Gallipoli, France, and Belgium.

The process of selection for the various appointments and duties took time. In the meanwhile the work of organising the platoons and companies continued, and much care was devoted to the training and equipping. For the first fortnight or so equipment came along very slowly. The Ordnance Stores were practically empty. Fresh supplies had to be obtained from the Eastern States, or collected from the Citizen Force units. It was not until within a few days of embarkation that all demands were met. This condition of affairs was bound to have an adverse effect on training, but, on the whole, much progress was made, and the unit soon began to take form and become easier to administer and handle. The number of officers available gradually increased, and two warrant or non-commissioned officers of the Instructional Staff were attached to each company in order to assist. The latter did exceedingly valuable work. A special class was formed for the purpose of instructing in their duties those men who aspired to wear stripes. In the training of sections and platoons, emphasis was laid on the necessity for obtaining a condition of physical fitness, and acquiring a thorough knowledge of the use of the rifle, the bayonet, and the spade. Physical exercises were followed by short marches of one or two hours' duration. After passing the elementary tests, companies, in turn, proceeded to Osborne Rifle Range and

---

* Afterwards Captain (temporary Major) E. C. Francisco, 50th Battn.

THE REGIMENTAL SIGNALLERS.

MACHINE GUN SECTION.

Photos. lent by Captain G. D. Shaw.

fired the recruits' course of musketry. A satisfactory figure of merit was obtained. For the more advanced training it was intended to move the Battalion to a camp at Rockingham. During the second week in May two companies proceeded there and the camp was established under the command of Major Davies. However, on account of the rumoured early embarkation, these companies had to be recalled, and the whole unit was once more concentrated at Blackboy Hill. Training proceeded energetically, with the result that officers, and other ranks within the companies, quickly settled down—daily becoming more and more accustomed to their tasks.

The health of the members was good. Very few cases of infectious disease, and fewer cases of serious illness, were reported. The situation of the camp, together with the insistence on the cleanliness of the lines and person, had a beneficial effect in this direction. Unfortunately one death occurred. Private F. W. Hopkins fell into an unprotected clayhole and was drowned. A few of these excavations existed on the western edge of the training area, and were a menace to those taking a short cut from the railway station at night time. All ranks submitted to vaccination and inoculation. This was unpleasant, but the medical history of the war has since demonstrated the value of the measures.

Discipline was fairly satisfactory from the outset and rapidly improved. At the commencement every member was given to understand that a high sense of duty and a strong *esprit-de-corps* were essentials for success. Both these traits were later very fully developed, and the regard that 28th men always had for their battalion was a subject of frequent comment in the A.I.F.

In all the preliminary work of organisation and training, the Commanding Officer had the great advantage of the sympathy, practical support, and advice of the District Commandant—Colonel J. H. Bruche. This help was invaluable, and resulted in the establishment of sound methods and the promotion of happy relations with mutual confidence between all ranks.

Although training and other duties absorbed long hours, leave was given daily after the tea hour and until near midnight. Half-holidays were also observed on Wednesdays and Saturdays. Leave from Saturday afternoon to Sunday evening was granted, too, on a liberal scale. Before embarkation every man was entitled to four days' leave in order to give him a final opportunity of attending to his private affairs. This was taken by many. In the camp itself efforts were made to amuse those who stayed in during the evening. In this respect the Y.M.C.A. did most by providing a large marquee wherein concerts and other forms of entertainment were given

THE MARCH THROUGH PERTH.
3rd June, 1915.

Photo. lent by Mr. E. L. Mitchell, Perth.

THE MARCH THROUGH PERTH.
3rd June, 1915.
The crowd in St. George's Terrace.

Photo. lent by Mr. W. Owen, Perth.

almost nightly. A post office and writing room—with free stationery—were also established by these voluntary helpers. Surrounding the camp were numbers of booths and shops where necessaries could be purchased and harmless refreshments obtained. Friends and relations frequently visited the camp during the idle hours.

His Excellency the Governor, Major-General Sir Harry Barron, K.C.M.G., C.V.O., showed great interest in the unit, and on the 27th May attended at the camp and addressed the members in an informal manner after the evening meal. He told them of his own experiences in the army, and, in a way that was greatly appreciated, tendered much wholesome advice.

Towards the end of May it was known that the day of embarkation was closely approaching. Efforts were made to complete the final issues of kit and clothing, and furnish the seemingly endless number of documentary records required by the Defence Department. A final and close inspection of the *personnel* was carried out. All men in the Battalion had been pronounced "fit." Vaccinations and inoculations had been duly performed. Yet there still remained in the ranks a number of men who, for various reasons, were unfit to go abroad as soldiers. Others there were whose family affairs were causing them anxiety and necessitated delay in their departure. Again, others—a few only—felt their ardour waning as the days of their stay at Blackboy grew fewer. In all these instances the men concerned were either discharged or transferred back to the depôt units. The Battalion was the better for the changes.

June 3rd was the anniversary of the Birthday of His Majesty the King. The 28th, together with certain other troops from the training camps, was to march through Perth and, in doing so, be inspected by the Governor and the District Commandant. In preparation, the riding horses and wheeled transport went to Perth the previous night and parked at the Drill Hall. The Battalion itself proceeded to the city by train, and by 10.30 on the morning of the 3rd had formed up in James Street. It then marched by Beaufort, Barrack, Hay, and Bennett Streets; thence along St. George's Terrace, returning to the Railway Station by Milligan, Hay, and Barrack Streets, and re-entraining for Blackboy Hill. The Governor took the salute from a point opposite Government House. The Battalion presented a fine spectacle, and received a magnificent reception from the enormous crowds that thronged the thoroughfares. The newspapers, in subsequently describing the proceedings, referred to an unprecedented muster of the public and an extraordinary display of enthusiasm. The people were evidently proud of their new unit, and the men had pride in themselves.

During the first week in June, definite information was received as to the transports allotted and the dates of embarkation. By the 6th June everything was ready. On that day the 1st Reinforcements, consisting of 99 rank and file under the command of Lieut. J. F. Quilty, went on board the transport "Geelong," which had arrived in Fremantle the day before and carrying the 27th Battalion. Dean Brennan also embarked, having been ordered for duty with the South Australians during the remainder of their voyage. Sergt. F. L. Faulkner, together with the 11 drivers and 53 horses of the Regimental Transport, was to follow by a boat the date of sailing of which had not then been fixed.

At this time orders were received to detach Major F. R. Jeffrey temporarily to act as Second-in-Command of the South Australian unit. He duly reported and another officer, Lieut. P. E. Jackson, was sent on shore in exchange. In consequence of this alteration, Captain W. G. Stroud was given the temporary command of "B" Company.

On the afternoon of the 7th June, the Brigadier of the 7th Brigade, Colonel J. Burston, V.D., accompanied by his Staff Captain, Captain M. J. G. Colyer, visited the camp and made the acquaintance of this portion of his command. The Brigadier, who had been personally known to the C.O. for some years, expressed his pleasure at what he saw of the unit and of its promise for usefulness and efficiency.

THE 28th: A RECORD OF WAR SERVICE, 1915-19.   15

CHAPTER II.

EN ROUTE.

The riding horses, transport wagons, and heavy baggage, having been sent to Fremantle the previous day, shortly after noon on the 9th June the Battalion proceeded in two trains to the port. Although officially the date and hour of departure had not been disclosed, certain indications had conveyed that information to the public. The consequence was a series of demonstrations along the route. The engines in the railway yards made loud and prolonged noises in imitation of barnyard inhabitants, flags and handkerchiefs were waved, and many cheers given to speed the Battalion on its way. On Victoria Quay was a large concourse of people for the purpose of bidding farewell to relatives and friends. This somewhat interfered with the embarkation, but by 4.30 p.m. the last man and horse and the last piece of impedimenta were on board. The District Commandant personally superintended the operation. He was accompanied by the Chaplain-General, the Most Rev. Dr. Riley, Archbishop of Perth, whose kindly and encouraging words gave great heart to those setting out on so serious a task. In a letter to the Commanding Officer he had written—"Will you tell your officers and men how proud I have been of their conduct in camp and how we all trust the honour and reputation of W.A. in their hands with the utmost confidence. Good-bye to you all, a safe journey, valiant work, and a speedy return crowned with victory."

About 5.30 p.m. the transport left the quay and moved towards Gage Roads. Although the evening meal had been arranged for on the troop decks, very few attended. Nearly all desired to wave a last good-bye to those they were leaving behind and to catch a parting glimpse of the land they might never see again. Gage Roads was reached and darkness coming down shut out the last view of Australia. Here final matters in connection with the records and pay of the troops were arranged, the embarkation and pay staffs left the ship, the engine bells rang, and the long voyage began.

The transport was the s.s. "Ascanius," known officially as the "A 11," a steel twin-screw vessel of the Blue Funnel Line, built in 1910, and with a registered tonnage of 10,048. She had a length and breadth of 493 feet and 60 feet, respectively, and was fitted with three decks. The two lower decks were divided into areas and a certain number of tables and forms were placed in each area. Each table accommodated a mess of a number varying from 12 to 22 men. Before leaving Blackboy Hill the troops had been divided into messes corresponding to the ship's equivalent space. Consequently, on arriving at the top of the gangway when embarking, each party was met by a guide and taken direct to its quarters. Hammocks, blankets, and eating utensils were issued forthwith and they were shown where to stack their rifles and kits. Also, instruction was given as to the measures necessary to prevent fire or an outbreak of disease. Later on, when the decks were cleared, boat stations were pointed out, boats' crews detailed, and collision-fire measures practised. The promenade and boat decks were kept free for recreation and instructional work. The after well-deck held the horse shelters and an auxiliary kitchen. Under the fo'c'sle head was the main kitchen. Situated on the poop deck was a small isolation hospital. A separate mess and quarters received the warrant officers and sergeants; whilst the officers were allotted what had once been the accommodation for passengers.

The ship had commenced its journey at Brisbane, and on arrival at Fremantle already carried the two Queensland companies of the 26th Battalion (Majors F. M. O'Donnell and P. Currie), the 17th Company A.A.S.C. (Captain A. E. Harte), and a portion of the 7th Field Ambulance (Lt.-Col. R. B. Huxtable, V.D.). At the W.A. port the Brigade Commander and the Staff-Captain embarked. Altogether, with the western unit, some 1,750 of all ranks were now leaving Australia.

Here it may not be out of place to mention that certain statistics concerning the 28th Battalion, collected during the voyage, showed that approximately 50 per cent. of the officers and other ranks were Australian born. The other moiety was composed almost wholly of natives of the British Isles. A Russian, a Maltese, a Scandinavian or two, and a few others, were the only exceptions. The average age was in the vicinity of 24 years and only 143 married men could be counted. The recruiting area had been extensive and those enlisted included the professional and business man, the artisan, clerk, shop assistant, and labourer from the metropolis; the shearer, drover, and pearler from the northwest and far north; the farmer from the eastern and south-western districts; the timber worker; and the miner and prospector from the goldfields. In all some 150 civil occupations were represented, the principal ones being as follows:—Labourers 199, farmers and farm hands 109, miners and prospectors 70, timber workers 64,

THE FAREWELL AT FREMANTLE.
9th June, 1915.
Photos. lent by Mr. E. L. Mitchell, Perth.

clerks 60, carpenters and joiners 27, horse drivers 18, pearlers 17, grocers 16, engineers 13, and butchers 13.

For the first two or three days of the voyage the rather choppy sea and consequent motion of the boat caused some sickness. This prevented close supervision and the adoption of strict routine at the outset and laid much extra work and worry on those who had good sea legs. However, about the third day out very few were absent from meals, the ship was becoming known, and it was found possible to put into execution plans for training, exercise, and amusement. The deck space was so used that each unit had definite periods and places on it. Sufficient room to work all the troops at the one time was not available, but by the methods adopted every man got at least three hours' active training daily. The utmost use had to be made of the opportunities afforded. For the purposes of training, the time spent at Blackboy Hill had been all too short. So much still remained to be taught and to be learned; also, the period for acquiring knowledge that would be allowed at the other end could only be conjectured—in any event it was likely to be of short duration. Stress, therefore, was laid, firstly, on keeping the physical exercises going and, secondly, on continuing the instruction in musketry, and getting the soldier more and more used to the rifle as his main weapon of offence and defence. Theoretical instruction was given on half a hundred subjects ranging from the hygiene of the person to the rôle supposed to be played by the cavalry and artillery in a general action. All ranks were quick at assimilating knowledge. Perhaps the best results were obtained during the informal talks which took place between officers and men in the "sit easy" periods. The specialists were given opportunities for paying greater attention to their own peculiar work, and in this, in particular, the signallers made great strides. Machine gunners had facilities for practice at floating targets, which targets were also used for revolver firing.

The Warrant and Non-Commissioned Officers had longer hours. After parades were dismissed they were often required to attend lectures dealing with the functions of subordinate leaders. Officers, as a rule, had a very full day. The personal attention demanded from them in respect to all matters affecting the welfare of their platoons or companies, the supervision of the duties necessary for the effective working of the ship's services and routine, and the study of the subjects for the following day's instruction, left them little leisure. Their own education was not neglected. Twice daily lectures were given in the saloon—usually in the presence of the Brigadier. Lecturers were detailed in turn and the subjects were varied. On the whole the lectures were good. A

THE 28th: A RECORD OF WAR SERVICE, 1915-19. 19

few fell short of what was required, but usually the discussion which followed such effort made up for any defect in the lecture itself. Occasional flashes of unconscious humour often saved the indifferent performer from boring his audience.

Duties absorbed a platoon or more daily. Guards had to be found to provide sentries to give the alarm in case of fire, accident, or collision. Police were detailed to see that the orders designed to prevent outbreaks of fire or disease were observed. Sweepers and swabbers cleaned down the decks twice in every 24 hours. Stable picquets looked after the horse deck. Mess orderlies saw to the drawing of rations, serving of meals, and cleansing of mess utensils. On entering the tropics the ship's captain asked for volunteers for work in the coal bunkers. His crew was hard pressed. These volunteers were forthcoming and for their services received extra pay.

Within a few hours of leaving Fremantle no less than seven stowaways were found. The first discovered was a small lad, dressed in the uniform of the military cadets, who said his age was 17 years. He gave his name and address as Herbert Hamilton, of Midland Junction, and, when brought before the C.O., manfully expressed his desire to serve in the army. By means of the wireless telegraph his parents were communicated with and their consent to his enlistment obtained. As the Battalion was already at full strength, Hamilton was taken on the roll of the Queensland infantry. For a time the Brigadier took him under his personal care, but after Gallipoli he joined his unit and did good service with it throughout the remainder of the war. The balance of the stowaways were men from Blackboy Camp. One or two had been discharged from service there and merely wanted to "get away." They were given work in the ship. The others were anxious to serve and, after examination, were also taken on by the 26th Battalion. In addition to stowaways four men had been taken on board who belonged to the 27th Battalion and had failed to re-embark on the departure of the "Geelong" from Fremantle.

After the first few days the routine of the ship went very smoothly. Eight N.C.Os., appointed Troop Deck Sergeants, were responsible for the cleanliness and order of their respective quarters. Satisfactory results were thus obtained. Competition in regard to the best kept mess was keen. Utensils were polished like silver and arranged in designs that often displayed much originality on the part of the mess orderlies. "A" Company gained especial credit in this respect.

Discipline remained good, the only offences being minor ones. The food provided was, now and then, a cause for complaint. In the first place the scale laid down by the Imperial authorities was inadequate to satisfy the appetites of a meat-eating race like the Australians. Secondly, the method of cooking showed lack of knowledge on the part of the ship's staff and was not economical. Add to these two factors the want of experience on the part of the mess orderlies in equally dividing up the food supplied them—then the occurrence of the complaints can be easily understood.

The living quarters in the ship were well ventilated—additional draughts of air being ensured by the free use of wind-sails and chutes. This, and the regular exercise daily, together with the anticipation of the life and work ahead, kept all ranks in good health and spirits. Measles and influenza appeared a few days after the commencement of the voyage and claimed 40 or 50 victims, but no serious results ensued. One bugler contracted pneumonia, but was well on the way towards convalescence before Suez was reached. A single mental case came under notice, necessitating the placing of the subject under close observation until he could be handed over to the care of the authorities at the port of disembarkation. All ranks were inoculated against smallpox and typhoid. Many of them developed "arms" and temperatures as a result and were decidedly unwell for a few days.

In the tropics 50 per cent. of the troops were provided with deck accommodation for sleeping purposes. The heat when nearing Aden, and during the passage of the Red Sea, was intense, but all ranks bore it well. As far as was possible the dress was adapted to the climatic conditions—special precautions being taken to guard against sunstroke. Unfortunately, one of the ship's crew succumbed. He was buried at sea, the ship laying-to whilst the burial service was read by the chaplain. A collection afterwards taken up on behalf of the widow was generously contributed to and realised over £50.

One chaplain only had been allotted to the troops on the transport. This was the Rev. J. H. Neild, of the Methodist denomination. He conducted service twice daily on Sundays and spent many hours on the decks at other times. He was particularly earnest in his endeavours to help, and his efforts were universally appreciated. Very great regret was expressed by all who had come in contact with him when, shortly after reaching Egypt, his health became so impaired as to necessitate his return to Australia.

On so crowded a transport it was difficult to arrange satisfactorily for amusements. However, the best possible was done under the circumstances. Sports meetings were held once or twice a week. In most of the competitions the Western Australians showed up well. The keenest interest was displayed in the inter-unit tug-of-war, the

H.M's AUSTRALIAN TRANSPORT A11 ("ASCANIUS.")

Photo. lent by Mr. E. L. Mitchell, Perth.

final of which was won, after an exciting struggle, by the team from "D" Company. In boxing, the honours went to the Queenslanders of the 17th A.A.S.C., who produced several very good performers of medium and heavy weights. Much laughter was engendered when, after the tea hour, the tyros donned the gloves with one another. Several concerts were arranged and held on or near the well-decks. Perhaps the most popular singer was the youthful stowaway. The regimental band, conducted by Sergt. W. T. Hocking, assisted at these functions. Endeavours had been made to form this before leaving Blackboy Hill, but time permitted of little being done beyond collecting a certain number of instruments. Once on the ship all men who could play were invited to attend practice. Thus a nucleus was formed. By the time that Suez was reached good progress had been made and the band was in a promising condition. In Egypt, however, and later in France, bands were not encouraged—having to be more or less shelved. In 1917 their true value began to be understood, and every facility was given to form and maintain such organisations.

For the individual of certain tastes other diversions existed beyond attendance at concerts and athletic competitions. Card games were played—"bridge" being the first favourite, but "poker" also having a large following. Gambling was forbidden by the regulations. Nevertheless, the usual veteran of other wars was found on board who was prepared to initiate all who were tempted into *some* of the mysteries of "banker" or "crown and anchor." This individual, however, met discouragement from the ship's police who, whenever opportunity offered, seized and confiscated his plant. "Two-up" and "House" were not then so popular as they became a few months later.

For mascots, the friends of the Battalion had sent on board two or three of the ring-necked parakeets, generally known as "Twenty-eights." These were made pets of during the voyage, but had either died or escaped before its end.

An Australian Imperial Force Canteen was established on board. This supplied pipes, tobacco, cigarettes, sweets, non-alcoholic drinks, and a variety of other odds and ends, which could be purchased. The ship was "dry"—that is, no spirits, wines, or beer were supposed to be available to other than the ship's crew. This arrangement was in accordance with the policy of the Australian Government and obtained on all sea transports. Whilst the usual stimulant was thus missed by many who were accustomed to it, on the whole the system in force did more good than harm and was a considerable aid to the preservation of order and comfort. So far as could be observed, the rule was strictly adhered to on the "Ascanius"; nevertheless, the Commanding Officer, during his morning inspections of the ship, was more than once heard to comment on the absorbent capacity of the crew, as evidenced by the number of empty ale and stout bottles cleared from their quarters.

In all that was done for the comfort and welfare of the troops, great assistance was rendered by the Master of the ship and his officers. Perhaps the Chief Officer was more concerned in protecting the interests of his owners than of giving much latitude to the men who were in transit. At times in early morn, and again late at night, his voice could be heard in altercation with some unfortunate Australian, who had surreptitiously made his bed in a forbidden area, or had violated some other rule of the ship. He and his myrmidons were suspected of undue zeal in impounding and placing in the ship's store any hammock, blanket, or mess utensil, whose owner had momentarily left them unguarded on deck or in some other open space. Later on, the articles so impounded were shown as shortages in the ship's stores returned by the troops and had to be paid for from the Battalion's funds. That Chief Officer was not popular, but he was a good manager of his crew and kept the ship in excellent condition.

The Master, Captain F. Chrimes, was a Lancashire man, of rather striking personality and appearance. Some writer, who had travelled on the ship as a passenger, has already portrayed him in one of his published books. Captain Chrimes admired the men and, although in his official and daily inspections he assumed an air almost of indifference to what he saw, he was really closely observant and suggested much—and did more—to make the conditions of life on board less uncomfortable. In quiet hours he chatted deferentially with the Brigadier, played chess with the doctors, or gently "pulled the legs" of the young officers. Of stories, he had a fund. These ranged from stirring personal experiences with lions in the East African jungles to a pathetic incident connected with the death of his family's favourite cat. As a mark of affection, the corpse of this cat was buried in the garden at the foot of an old grape vine. In the first subsequent crop of fruit—so the Captain related—each grape appeared with a slight coat of fur!

On the whole the voyage was pleasant enough and almost without unusual incident, bar an accident or two to individuals. Perfect good feeling existed amongst the different units during the whole of the journey. Many friendships were made, and these early associations proved of great value later on during the stress of work in the field. For the first few days out wireless communication was kept up with the s.s. "Geelong." The equator was crossed on about the twelfth day but, at the expressed wish of the Brigadier, King Neptune held no court.

Early on the 24th June the African coast, just south of Ras-Jard-Hafun, was sighted. Near here was observed the first ship seen since leaving Australia. A few dhows were visible close in shore, and in the bay sharks and rays could be discerned in motion. For a few hours attention was centred on this first glimpse of a foreign land. "The doctor has left off vaccinating us to go and admire the scenery," said one man in a letter home. The foreshore, cliffs, and mountains of Somaliland were searched with glasses for signs of habitations. So desolate, however, appeared the country, and so few the signs of life, that, as a diversion, the men cheered whenever an occasional school of porpoises or a solitary albatross came more closely under view. Cape Guardafui was passed soon after lunch, and the following evening the ship stopped her engines for half an hour in order to exchange messages with Aden, which was dimly visible through the thick bluish haze of stifling heat.

The 26th June witnessed the entrance to the Red Sea. The Master for the previous few days had seemed apprehensive in regard to possible enemy action. Consequently certain additional sentries had been posted and the machine guns mounted in positions that would give them effective arcs of fire. From now on the African coast was hugged, but little scenery was evident after passing Perim Island. Away to the north-east a momentary glimpse was obtained of Jebel Musa (Mt. Sinai). About this time the Southern Cross disappeared below the horizon.

The destination of the transport was still unknown, notwithstanding that gossip had mentioned Suez, Port Said, Alexandria, and even England. Nevertheless, preparations had to be made either for disembarkation at the first-named port or for the passage through the Canal. These were put in hand at once. About this time arose the first crop of rumours, or "furphies," which ever afterwards seemed to be an inseparable feature of military life. Perhaps one of the most extraordinary was to the effect that news had come on board of great anxiety existing in Western Australia over a supposed disaster to the ship and its living freight. As no such news *had* come on board the source of the rumour could not be traced. Subsequently, in letters received from the homeland, it was ascertained that such a rumour was actually current there coincident with its first being mentioned on the transport. Possibly its origin may be remotely connected with the fact that, simultaneously with the arrival of the "Ascanius" in the Gulf of Suez, a sister ship struck a mine at the entrance to the Bitter Lakes and had to be beached. The hull was visible to passengers on the Suez-Cairo railway.

On the evening of June 29th the lights of Suez came into view. Shortly before midnight the transport dropped anchor some distance from the town. Next morning a rather unattractive panorama was

Signaller H. H. Holmes. TWO VERY YOUNG SOLDIERS. Bugler A. J. Shipway.
Killed in action in France, August, 1916.

unveiled to view. On the west were the bare heights of Jebel Attaka; to the north Suez lay with its rambling and squalid-looking houses; to the north-east was Port Tewfik, and beyond that—running down east and south-east—were the desert sands of Sinai. The waters of the Gulf were calm, but every revolution of the screws stirred up filth and polluted the air. Some distance away lay another ship obviously also carrying troops. Greetings were exchanged at long range. Eventually it was learned that the transport was the "Ballarat" with a load of invalids for Australia. Amongst them evidently dwelt a pessimist, for in reply to the new arrivals' stentorian and unanimous "NO!" to the question "Are we downhearted?" a disconsolate voice sounded across the water, "Well, you ———— soon will be."

As rather exaggerated accounts had been received in Australia as to the dangers of communicating with the native inhabitants of Egypt, special precautions were taken to prevent bumboat men from coming on board or too closely approaching the sides. Two boats' crews patrolled round about and sentries armed with loaded rifles stood at the tops of the gangways. This resulted in an amusing incident when a dhow, manned by a very fat Arab fisherman and a small native boy, came too close to the troopship. No heed being taken of signals to keep further away, the sentry on duty was instructed to fire a rifle shot across the bow of the small craft. This proved most effective, and everyone roared with laughter when the stout fisherman hastily dived below the gunwale out of sight and forced the terrified small boy to take the helm and steer away out of danger. In spite of this, however, preliminary bargaining went on with other boats' crews and first impressions were gained of the ways and manners of the gentle Egyptian. All that day the ship lay at anchor and little communication took place with the shore. Nevertheless it was learned from the port authorities, that as soon as another ship, then at the wharf, had cleared, the troops were to disembark and journey by train to a camp near Cairo. In preparation a small advance party of three officers and 40 other ranks was put ashore with instructions to proceed to the named area in order to get the camp in readiness for the troops.

At 7 a.m. on the 2nd July the "Ascanius" moved in and berthed. Here the voices of Egypt were heard in concert. A motley crowd of natives was grouped about—evidently watched and herded by dapper little policemen, armed with canes which they seemed to delight in using with or without provocation. In one place a small gang of labourers, to the music of its own voices, was building a ramp. In another, seemingly fierce argument was going on as to the moving of a heavy gangway into position. Still more men and boys were gazing up at the ship and calling loudly for "bakshish."

"Bakshish" was forthcoming first of all in the shape of copper coins, later on in scraps of food, and again in raw potatoes. All these were wildly scrambled for, and even the party operating the gangway forsook duty in the pursuit of gain. The aim with the potatoes became rather accurate, and after the head serang had been temporarily incapacitated by a direct hit in the region of the belt, the fusilade had to be stopped in order that the work of disembarkation might proceed.

Getting the troops off the ship was a matter of comparative ease, but the landing of sick, issue of rations, handing over of ship's stores, and the unloading of horses, wagons, and over 1,250,000 rounds of ammunition, entailed much organisation and a great deal of hard labour. Notwithstanding this, the O.C. Troops was able to leave the ship before 5 p.m., having left behind a small party to finally adjust matters with the ship and disembarkation authorities. This rear party rejoined the unit three days later.

As the Battalion commenced to disembark the transport "Geelong" came to anchor off the town.

CHAPTER III.

FIRST STAY IN EGYPT.

Four trains, running at intervals of two hours, were used to convey the troops from the ship's side to the neighbourhood of Cairo. For part of the journey the railway ran parallel with and in sight of the Canal. Near Ismailia it turned west and led across the northern part of the Arabian Desert (once the Land of Goshen) to Zagazig, where it took another turn, to the south-west, and entered the capital. Though almost entirely desert, the country was not without interest to the new arrivals. Sand was not unknown in Western Australia, but had never been seen over such tremendous tracts and giving off such colours which, probably due to atmospheric influences, had very distinctive beauty. Here and there the oases, and the irrigation areas, were marked by palm trees or by crops of a vivid green hue. There was also seen much that at once directed attention to the fact that the land was one famed in biblical history. The costumes of the natives; the flat-roofed mud-coloured dwellings; the old fashioned wells, the hooded and veiled women bearing pitchers on their heads, the humble donkey, and the more dignified camel, instantly carried minds back to the pictures that were popular in childhood's days.

By midnight the last of the troops, detrained at a military siding near by, had reached the camp and taken shelter for the time being in a number of open-sided wooden huts.

The camp site, called Abbasia—after the adjacent quarter of Cairo, was in the desert just north of the Suez Road and about five miles from the centre of the city. The ground here was quite flat, and had been extensively used at different times for military reviews. It was also near the scene of a battle in 1517, when the Turkish conqueror, the Sultan Selim, overthrew the Egyptians. A second battle took place here in 1800, on which occasion General Kleber with 10,000 French defeated six times that number of Turks. On the west side were situated the cavalry and infantry barracks, at that time occupied by the 2nd Mounted Division (Yeomanry). To the north lay the quarters and hospital of the Egyptian Army units doing guard and escort duty for the new Sultan. North-east, a little over a mile away, the new city of Heliopolis, with its splendid buildings, was in full view. In other directions only the desert was to be seen, marked here and there with low hills—the highest being Jebel Ahmar, an outpost of the Moqattam Range.

The first day in the new camp was one of discomfort and worry. No brigade or divisional staffs were present to assist and advise as to the new conditions. The source of supplies had to be ascertained, kitchens constructed, baggage sorted, and the lines, which were indescribably dirty, cleaned up. All ranks were tired with the previous day's long hours and badly needed a hot meal which, at first, could not be satisfactorily supplied. A few men strayed away to Heliopolis, where they found members of the 5th and 6th Brigades, whose local knowledge they availed themselves of in their search for creature comforts. Fortunately other friends were near in the 13th Light Horse Regiment, which was temporarily occupying part of Abbasia Camp. The members assisted greatly in the settling down process and, in consequence, by the night of the third day tents were pitched, cooking arranged for, and the comfort of the individual much improved. Very shortly after, further advantages were provided in the shape of a regimental institute where fruit, groceries, and liquor could be procured. This scheme was subsequently extended in the direction of establishing a restaurant, a fruit and ice cream tent, a newsvendor's stall, and a barber's shop. This institute was valuable for several reasons. It afforded a means of supplementing the indifferent ration; prevented the infliction of exorbitant prices; guaranteed fair quality; reduced straying; ensured the profits coming back to the battalion; and did away with the necessity for admitting to the lines the clamorous and often filthy multitude of hawkers. After this no Egyptian or foreigner was permitted to approach the tents without a pass. Most of the local vendors had methods peculiarly their own. The agents for the "Egyptian Times" or "Egyptian Gazette" described their sheets in language which suggested guilelessness and earlier association with the 1st Australian Division. The orange, chocolate, and "eggs-a-cook" (small hard-boiled eggs) sellers seemed to possess the faculty of rising from the earth or dropping from the blue, for whenever bodies of troops, exercising in the desert, halted for rest, some half-dozen of these people—not previously in view—would suddenly appear, and, dragging their wares from somewhere between their not over clean garments and less clean skin, would offer them to the soldiers at "two fer a arf" (piastre).

Of course news of the progress of our troops on the Gallipoli Peninsula was eagerly sought. At first information was difficult to obtain. The only sources from which it could be gathered were the wounded and sick in the neighbouring No. 1 Australian General Hospital housed at the Heliopolis Palace Hotel, and the adjoining Luna Park. These men related their own experiences and impressions. Their auditors were able to appreciate the stupendous task of the landing parties and the heroism with which they had held on to the ground gained under devastating enemy fire and the ravages of disease. Of the relative positions of the opposing forces little of a definite nature was known, nor could anything be ascertained as to the plans for the future. The fact that so many troops were collecting in Egypt did, however, point to probable further developments, and gave the Battalion great hopes of being allowed to participate. The achievements of the Western Australian units already at the front had been proved more than worthy of emulation, and the 28th was determined not to be found lacking.

The situation in Egypt at this time was not without cause for anxiety. Some months earlier the Khedive Abbas Hilmi, an intriguer against Great Britain, had been replaced by Prince Kamil Hussein, who was proclaimed Sultan under a British protectorate. Sir Arthur Henry McMahon was High Commissioner, but the country was virtually under martial law administered by the G.O.C. in Egypt—Lieut.-General Sir John Maxwell. There was more than a little unrest amongst the civil population caused by the efforts of the Turkish and German propagandists. On the eastern frontier precautions had to be taken to meet a repetition of the raid of February made by Djemal Pasha on the Suez Canal. Towards the west the attitude of the Senussi, a great religious sheik, indicated pretentions to temporal power which must inevitably bring about a conflict. To meet this situation there were a few brigades of the Indian Army on the Canal,* whilst for the remainder dependence seemed to be placed on the units and reinforcements passing through to the Dardanelles. Maxwell made the most of these, and greatly impressed the populace by displays of force. These displays consisted of marching brigades of Yeomanry and Australians through the city and thickly populated suburbs. The 28th Battalion frequently took part—the marches mostly being carried out at night and forming part of the training in march discipline. The natives looked on sullenly, but there was little in the way of openly hostile display.

The organisation of the forces in Egypt brought the Australians under the supreme command of Sir John Maxwell, but they, and the New Zealanders, were grouped under the immediate command of Major-General J. Spens and known as the Australian and New Zealand Training Depot. For self-contained organised units this arrangement was fairly satisfactory, but with regard to reinforcement drafts their management was the subject of much adverse criticism. Discipline was very weak and actual training not,

---

* These troops were commanded by Major-General Sir Alexander Wilson, K.C.B., who was Military Commandant in W.A., 1895-98.

ABBASIA CAMP.
"D" Company marching in. Jebel Ahmar in the background.
Photo. by Sergt. Arundel.

THE ADJUTANT AND "TIM."

apparently, a primary consideration. These defects continued for many months. They were not due to the men themselves, but to the absence of a policy in regard to the command and administration of training battalions generally. In later years the Australians managed these things for themselves, and with such good results that the British Service found it profitable to copy some of their methods.

General Spens visited the Battalion's camp early in the morning following its arrival. He questioned the Commanding Officer as to the unit, and after being assured that the material was excellent, though far from being perfectly trained, contented himself by saying "Ah well, give 'em plenty of shootin'."

On the 5th July the Battalion was drawn up to receive Sir John Maxwell. Sir John arrived with a considerable staff, including young Prince Leopold of Battenberg. The General closely inspected the unit, both he and his staff commenting most favourably on what they described as a "magnificent regiment." Sir John afterwards made a short address, referring to the work of the first four brigades and the hopes for the future. Doubtless having in mind the recent disturbances in Cairo, he also pointed out that Egypt was now a British Protectorate and that the Egyptians were, equally with the Australians, British subjects. He expressed a wish, therefore, that there would be no "knockin' 'em about."

At the date of the 28th's arrival in Egypt, one or two battalions of the 5th Brigade, and the whole of the 6th Brigade, were already in Aerodrome Camp, just without and on the north-east side of Heliopolis. The 4th Light Horse Brigade, minus the 13th Regiment, was also camped near by. The complement from the "Ascanius" was the nucleus of the 7th Brigade. The 27th Battalion, after landing, went first to Aerodrome Camp, but moved to Abbasia within a fortnight. The 25th Battalion, the second half of the 26th Battalion, and the remainder of the 5th Brigade troops did not arrive until about a month later. About the same time, Sergt. Faulkner and his drivers reported to their unit (8th August). They had been detained at Blackboy Hill a month after the departure of the "Ascanius," finally embarking on the "Boonah" on the 12th July. Observing instructions received, their horses had been left behind in Western Australia and fresh teams had now to be drawn from the local Remount Depôt, in which there existed a surplus.

From the foregoing it will be seen that August had arrived before the 7th Brigade and its staff was actually mobilised and complete.* In the meantime the 4th Light Horse Brigade had, for the most part, been broken up in order to provide reinforcements for the three horseless brigades then fighting on Gallipoli. The 13th Light Horse moved to its own camp but retained its entity, and as such afterwards served through the war.

After reaching Abbasia the all-important consideration was training. This was pressed on vigorously. At the commencement the routine provided for reveille at 4.30 a.m. and parades to be held from 6 to 9 a.m. and 4.30 to 7 p.m. Indoor (i.e., in huts) instruction was carried out between 10.30 a.m. and 1 p.m. These hours were fixed in order to meet climatic conditions, but they rendered satisfactory arrangements for meals difficult. Three hours' work on an empty stomach in the early morning did not induce enthusiasm or vigour in practising attack formations and movements. Nor was the long interval between 1 o'clock dinner and 7 o'clock tea conducive to contentment with other work of an exhausting nature. A little was done to meet the situation by providing an early morning cup of coffee and biscuit, but the poor quality of the rations and the limited regimental funds prevented an entirely effective solution. Nevertheless the discomforts were submitted to cheerfully and the presence of the other battalions of the Brigade gradually gave rise to a spirit of emulation, resulting in keenness and genuine progress.

The training was continued on from the stage reached at Blackboy Camp and practical application was given to the principles inculcated in some of the lectures of the voyage over. Bayonet fighting was assiduously practised and knowledge obtained of recent changes born of the experience of the war. Early in August a musketry course was fired by the whole unit. Attention was then given to the more advanced forms of exercise in attack and defence, combined with the construction and use of earthworks. Here began that intimate knowledge of the shovel and pick which, during the war, was acquired by every infantryman. All fighting soldiers loathed these implements, but, at the same time, recognised their utility and appreciated the protection they made it possible to provide. Occasionally the Brigadier assembled the four battalions and, after a little close-order work, would lead them on a five to ten mile night march. Apart from the purpose already referred to, these night marches had great value as steadying influences. Battalions vied with each other in displaying good form. To see them marching to attention with no sound audible but the tramp of thousands of feet,

---

* Composition of 7th Australian Infantry Brigade—
Headquarters. 28th Battalion.
25th Battalion. 2nd Signal Company (No. 3 Section).
26th Battalion. Brigade Train (No. 17 Coy., A.A.S.C.).
27th Battalion. 7th Field Ambulance.
Strength:—149 officers, 4,403 other ranks, 520 horses, 8 machine guns, 52 bicycles, 7 carts, and 94 wagons.

or, again to hear un'ts. when "at ease," singing some stirring song with 800 full-throated voices as one, was indeed inspiring to the bystander.

Now and then night work took the form of occupying and entrenching a position, or of moving over unknown desert guided only by compass. There were times when the dust nearly choked one, or when the lights and shadows made it impossible to ascertain whether one was likely to fall down a slope or stumble on to the side of a hill. Notwithstanding these difficulties, the 28th never once lost its way or failed to reach its objective to time. On one occasion a move was made for some miles along the Suez Road and a bivouac, protected by outposts, established in the Wadi-esh-Shem. The remainder of the Brigade represented a hostile force based on Cairo. During the night an attempt was made to penetrate the 28th outpost line. The attempt was unsuccessful. Early the following morning the West Australians advanced westwards in attack formation and succeeded in driving one of the opposing units off a line of hills commanding the road to Cairo. This was the most elaborate set-piece during the training period and, whilst the execution was defective in several respects, the general form shown placed the "Growers" an easy first in the Brigade in point of efficiency. Nor had the specialists been neglected. In addition to the original Machine Gun Section, a first reserve section was trained and a commencement made with the second. These gunners acquired a highly technical knowledge and were subsequently utilised for the examination and repair of the armament of the other sections of the Brigade. The formation of trained reserves for the Signallers was also undertaken and due attention paid to other requirements.

All training was supervised by the Brigadier and his Staff, but the latter had not that experience likely to be of assistance either to its chief or to commanding officers. General Spens lent one or two officers and non-commissioned officers who had served in the first campaign in France and whose experience should have been of value to the new troops. The N.C.Os., genuine "Contemptibles," were really useful and of a fine stamp—able to impress the young Australian and communicate many useful lessons. On the other hand, the officers were not, apparently, selected with any regard to their capacity as instructors but merely for the sake of giving them something to do. They lectured frequently in a didactic manner—playing fast and loose with the training manuals, and advocating experiments for which they could give no sound reason. When pressed on these matters it seemed to them sufficient to say that they "thought they were good ideas." This engendered much vexation amongst the Australian officers, more especially as the Brigadier very often did not see his way clear to withstand the

BRIG.-GENERAL JAMES BURSTON, V.D.
Who commanded the 7th Brigade in 1915.
Photo. lent by Mrs. Burston.

LIEUT.-COLONEL C. R. DAVIES, O.B.E., SECOND-IN-COMMAND, 1915-16.

innovations. The immediate result was to humbug officers and men and negative many of the sound lessons already taught.

A further drawback in training was the large number of men which had to be supplied for duties outside the Brigade. At times these amounted to over 200 on the one day and comprised town picquets, guards on hospitals, etc. The absence of these men broke up platoons and also disrupted the continuity of instruction. There was no way out, but it was thought that the "dizzy limit" had been reached when a request was received for church orderlies, billiard markers and barmen—all for a British formation. The Brigadier ventured a protest, but for his pains was treated to a severe official snub.

One factor, however, which was a distinct aid to acquiring a knowledge of warfare, was a School of Instruction held at Zeitun and commanded by a distinguished officer of the Guards. A considerable number of the junior officers and N.C.Os. attended, together with a proportion of the machine gunners and signallers. Each course lasted three weeks. At the examination held at the termination of the course the 28th men did exceedingly well—the officers averaging 89 per cent. of marks and the N.C.Os. 92 per cent., in their respective classes. The Commandant of the School subsequently despatched the following note to Colonel Collett— "The results of the four classes attending this School from your Battalion, viz., officers, N.C.Os., signallers and machine gunners, are most satisfactory. I would especially draw your attention to the roll of gunners; there is not a second class gunner among the whole section, which is most gratifying to myself and the instructors." A feature of this School was an officer of its staff who was not favourably disposed towards Dominion troops. He was known to commence one of his lectures somehow like this— "Discipline is a subject of which the Australians know nothing." It is understood that subsequent events, together with an interview with Sir John Maxwell, caused him, if not to change his view, at least to modify his tone.

An important development, which had a beneficial effect on the unit, was the constitution, early in August, of the 2nd Australian Division. The three new brigades of infantry which had recently arrived in Egypt led General Birdwood, with the approval of the Australian Government, to group them in a major formation. The command he allotted to Major-General J. G. Legge, C.M.G., who had succeeded the late Sir William Bridges with the 1st Division. By the 4th August General Legge had arrived at Heliopolis, where he established his headquarters, and on that date the troops passed from the immediate control of General Spens.

The divisional commander brought with him a staff of experienced officers, and these immediately set about the higher organisation of the brigades and the formation of the divisional troops. The 13th Light Horse became the divisional mounted force, but the signallers and engineers had to be completed by the transfer of suitable men from the infantry. Many good men were in this way lost to the Battalion.

Mention has already been made of the poor quality of the rations in Egypt. The system provided for a daily issue, by the Army Service Corps, of meat and bread; in addition there was an allowance of 8½d. per man for the purpose of purchasing groceries and extras. On paper the scheme looked excellent but in practice was execrable. In the first place the A.S.C. procured their supplies from the local Supply Depôt. Although the meat was passable, the bread—heavy, sodden, and often mildewy—was a source of daily and indignant protest. Complaint after complaint was lodged with the Supply people but improvement was almost despaired of, especially after verbal intimation had been received through semi-official channels that if the West Australians wanted better bread they would have to pay for it. Eventually, however, a change took place and the article became more palatable. The groceries were purchased from the Army canteens, which at this time were farmed out to contractors. Here the trouble was in the rising price of staple articles, the want of variety, and the scarcity of supplies. Tea and coffee were ample, but the sugar ration was hardly sufficient for these let alone any surplus being available for puddings, etc. Of the side-lines, such as tinned fish, rice, prunes, oatmeal, etc., what there was of these did not go far to appease the appetites of men used to better fare and having now to undergo hard training. The 8½d. could not work miracles, and try as they would—and did—those responsible for the welfare of the men found themselves hard pressed in ensuring that their charges were even decently fed. Nor was the procuring of suitable and adequate rations the only trouble. Cooking them also presented many difficulties. Travelling kitchens had not then been supplied to the new units, and the only cooking vessels available were the camp kettles or dixies. Consequently such food as had to be cooked could only be boiled or stewed, and even then the results were not always satisfactory. The cooks themselves were untrained and often had to be changed. They lacked the knowledge and experience necessary to secure the best results and avoid waste. They were also handicapped for want of proper fuel and plant. The fuel was wood. What kind of wood it was, or where it came from, nobody knew. It had the appearance and endurance of that stray log which sometimes arrives in loads from Australian woodyards and which the self-respecting householder absolutely declines to tackle except in the last extremity. It played havoc with the temper of the cooks' fatigues and also with their tools.

Clothing was an important factor. The heavy woollen material of the Australian uniforms was unsuitable in a climate where rain was almost unknown and where the daily temperature averaged over 90deg. in the shade during the whole time of the Battalion's stay. Furthermore, a number of hats had been lost overboard during the voyage from Fremantle. There were no present means of replacing these; meanwhile men were in daily danger of heat stroke. It was decided, therefore, to clothe all the troops in khaki cotton shorts (trousers reaching only to the knees), linen shirts, and pith helmets. These they wore with the ordinary underclothing and with boots and puttees. This issue was completed within ten days of arrival. It added considerably to the comfort of the individual and the dress in itself was not unattractive. One individual of French extraction refused for some unknown reason to wear the shorts. He was proof against persuasion and eventually had to be removed from the Battalion and given an opportunity for fuller reflection.

Perhaps it was inevitable that the drastic change from the Australian to the Egyptian climate, soil, and conditions of life, should adversely affect the health of the individual. At any rate such turned out to be the case, and for the first ten days after arrival at Abbasia there were some 130 to 150 men out of action each day. The principal causes were an acute form of diarrhœa and tonsilitis. Amongst others were severe colds, septic hands, knees, and feet, ophthalmia, and two or three slight cases of heat stroke. Measles did not re-appear after the landing at Suez, although the camp was placed in quarantine for 14 days and visits to the neighbouring towns were forbidden. After the tenth day the number of cases reporting to the medical officer began to decrease and by the 20th July had dropped to 50, about which figure it remained during the following few weeks. One death occurred—that of Lance-Corporal J. K. Quick, of "B" Company, who succumbed to pneumonia on the 14th August whilst a patient in No. 1 Australian General Hospital.

To assist in the preservation of health everyone was encouraged to lie down during the heat of the day, to keep the hair of the head cut short, make frequent use of the shower baths, and consume no liquor, except such as could be obtained within the camp. Undoubtedly the root cause of many of the ailments was the pollution of the desert soil. One had only to observe the habits of the natives to become aware that the earth of Cairo and its environs was saturated with the filth of ages. This was stirred up by the feet of the infantrymen in training and by the horses going to exercise or water. Horses were numerous about this time. The brigades of Light Horse on

CAPTAIN J. J. S. SCOULER.
Signalling Officer, 1915-16.

MAJOR J. KENNY, A.A.M.C.
The Regimental Medical Officer.

Gallipoli had left their mounts behind. These, augmented in August by the 2nd Mounted Division, totalled nearly 10,000, and were cared for in a large Remount Depôt established not far from Abbasia Camp. The dust caused by them was at times almost intolerable and the subject of frequent protests by those who soldiered on foot.

The method of dealing with the sick was as follows: A "sick parade" was held daily at the medical officer's tent at 5.30 a.m. and again at 2.30 p.m. All men feeling unwell attended this parade, were examined, and were prescribed for according to their condition. If their symptoms were those of a complaint likely to lay them up, or render them unfit for duty for several days, they would be "evacuated" to a neighbouring hospital and detained there for treatment. Once a man was evacuated he ceased, for all practical purposes, to be a member of the Battalion and came under the control of the medical administration. If he was quickly cured of his complaint he was sent back to his unit. If, on the other hand, his recovery was retarded, he remained for some time in hospital, or in a convalescent depôt, and, perhaps, finally returned to Australia either for a change or discharge.

Through sickness, transfers, and one or two other causes, the wastage in the Battalion was considerable. This was partly replaced on the 17th August by a first draft from the reinforcements camped at Zeitun. Lieut. J. Quilty brought over 84 and 54, respectively, from the 1st and 2nd Reinforcements. These were also first class men and were quickly absorbed into the companies.

Factors which affect the conduct and character of a soldier on active service are numerous and all weighty. Amongst them may be mentioned his treatment as regards work, food, pay, recreation and amusement, and mails from home. The first two of these have already been referred to and, after reflection, it cannot reasonably be said that whilst in Egypt he received too much of either. Pay very early became a vexed question. Letters from relatives indicated that the distribution of allotment money and separation allowance was being very imperfectly carried out—resulting in much hardship and consequent anxiety. Although this was eventually straightened out, it unsettled many men and bred a spirit of discontent very difficult to allay and eradicate. The pay of the troops themselves was drastically affected by the issue, in mid-August, of an order limiting the drawing to two-fifths of the daily rate. The exact reasons for this restriction were not given, but it is believed that those responsible desired, firstly, to remove the distinction which existed between the British and Australian rates and, secondly, to encourage thrift and retain for the soldier on his discharge a sum, beyond his deferred pay, which could be spent more wisely in Australia and not go to fill the pockets of the Egyptians. To many this restriction was a genuine hardship, whilst others circumvented it by drawing on their private funds by means of the cable service. This was extensively done, and those who had the wherewithal established a system for regularly receiving remittances from the home land. Payments were made in the local currency—the Egyptian pound of 100 piastres being equal to £1 0s. 6¼d. The piastre (sometimes termed "disaster") was worth about 2½d. There was a smaller coin—a millieme—equal to one-tenth of a piastre. English and Australian sovereigns were at first plentiful, but an attempt was made to restrict their circulation, as it was believed that the natives were hoarding them.

Mails arrived from Australia every week or ten days, and were heartily welcomed. Those who received newspapers handed them round for others to read. The Australian proved himself an inveterate letter writer and found much to describe to his relatives and friends. The signallers were rather noted for the amount of work they gave the officer who had to sight their correspondence. They seemed to devote much time to writing and to have a large circle of lady friends. As a rule, the soldier observed the censor's injunctions, and, in doing so, made the work of his officer light. Occasionally a transgression came under notice. In such cases, the letter was either returned to the writer or the offending part struck out. In one instance, the soldier had drawn attention to the harrowing conditions under which he said he was living—working from dawn to dark, with little or no food, and without pay. Questioned as to his reason for this action, he confessed that he was short of money and had intended to so play on the feelings of his friends as to prompt them to send him financial aid.

Censoring letters was a valuable education for an officer. It gave him a deep personal knowledge of the men he commanded and was to lead. It also enabled him to realise that in most situations there were points of view other than his own. He was the better for the knowledge. There were many letters to read. Most had a grave earnest tone running through them. Some were pathetic. Others were humorous and, again, others cleverly descriptive of the passing life and scenes. The trend of thought of some soldiers will be illustrated by the following:—In 1916, whilst assisting to hold the trenches in front of Messines, a member of the Battalion wrote a lengthy and comprehensive criticism of a recent book dealing with the Darwinian theory. About the same time, and from the same place, another member—a brave and sincere man, but a little pharisaical—violated the censorship requirements by criticising the army system generally and his own comrades in particular. His company commander adopted the unusual but effective punishment of reading the letter aloud in the presence of the writer and the fellow members of his platoon. A story is told of a padre of the 5th Brigade who, whilst censoring, discovered that one man had declared his undying devotion to two different girls, and to each had repudiated any allegiance to the other. The censor was so indignant over this act of treachery that he transposed the envelopes of the two letters before sealing them down.

Of amusements there was no lack. These will be referred to later on. On the whole, therefore, the soldier had little to complain of in the treatment he received, nor did he give the Commanding Officer any cause for anxiety as regards his conduct. Breaches of minor regulations were common enough, but in most cases the offences were venial and such as were likely to be committed by any recruit. Only two cases were remanded for trial by court-martial. Nor were the evils resulting from excessive drinking conspicuously present. Precautions, however, had to be taken to prevent any lowering of the standard which the Battalion was working towards, and in this respect examples had to be made in a few cases where the individual held rank, and in other cases where sickness appeared to be simulated.

One little incident seems to be worth mentioning. A soldier, who had been freely sampling a Reading brew of beer, encountered a certain warrant officer. An exchange of compliments took place, during which the private referred disparagingly to his superior's figure and parentage. On the next day he appeared at "orderly room" and was awarded a brief period of enforced retirement. Declining to walk to the place of detention he was placed on a stretcher, but the stretcher bearers were so inexperienced then that after a journey of about 200 yards he elected to march. On his release, the offender, very contrite and desiring to make the *amende honourable*, approached the warrant officer and explained that the statement previously made in regard to his *figure* was entirely without foundation.

Some rioting had occurred a few months previously in Cairo, and overseas soldiers were said to have been concerned in it. A further outbreak was reported during the last week of July, followed on the next evening by a disturbance in Heliopolis. Whatever were the causes of the first two outbreaks, the third was directly traceable to the fact that Cairo was suddenly placed out of bounds when leave men were waiting for trams at the Heliopolis terminus with a view to securing passage to the city. The military police, in attempting to deal with the situation, behaved rather tactlessly, and incurred the resentment of the men, who indulged in some stone-throwing and roughly handled a few individuals. Charges of wholesale looting were laid against the troops, but a court of inquiry, of which the commanding officer was a member, found on close investigation that £50 would cover the whole of the damage done. The claims submitted by the native shopkeepers totalled up to some £3,000. During the early months of the A.I.F's. stay in Egypt, the Military Police, a newly constituted force, incurred the dislike of the bulk of the troops. This dislike engendered an antipathy which endured until the end of the war. In the first instance there appears to have been some reason for it. The police were not selected with sufficient care, and included a number of men whose actions, to say the least, were shady. On several occasions decent and well-behaved members of the Battalion were received from the police cells, bereft of their money, much bruised and battered, and accompanied by a charge sheet accusing them of crimes which one moment's consideration would show they could not have committed. Strong representations on these matters had no immediate effect, but ultimately the Provost Corps was purged of the bad element and became a body of experienced men of great value in the prevention or detection of crime and the regulation of military traffic.

So far as could be learned, the men of the 28th had no part in either of the disturbances. In fact, so uniformly high had been their standard of behaviour that it had come under the notice of Sir John Maxwell, who sent and asked the Battalion to supply picquets for duty in the disturbed area. This action rather raised the resentment of some units and created a certain amount of ill-feeling. So acute did this become that on one occasion the Battalion of its own volition was on the point of "standing to" with entrenching tool handles to repel a threatened raid. However, common sense prevailed and good feeling with the men of the Eastern States was soon re-established, but not before the title "J——'s Own" had been conferred upon the Western Australians.

With the complete mobilisation of the Brigade the number of chaplains in the camp was brought up to four. Services were held in the huts every Sunday morning, attendance at which was compulsory. Dean Brennan identified himself with his flock. The Rev. J. H. Neild, so long as his health endured, was assiduous in his desire to help all who sought his aid. The Presbyterian chaplain, the Rev. W. J. Stevens, had served in the ranks in the South African War. He was very earnest and direct in his addresses.

He inclined towards mysticism, and spoke much of the "Angel of Mons." Otherwise he knew men well and was later noted for his activities during the Brigade's stay on Gallipoli. The Anglican chaplain was inclined to dogma. Very early he gave an address, "Why I believe in the Church of England." As no one was interested in the subject he rated his audience for its inattention, and thereafter ceased to exercise any influence amongst its members. In France he recovered some ground and did good work, amongst other things, in the organisation of institutes and coffee stalls behind the lines.

CHAPTER IV.

FIRST STAY IN EGYPT.

(continued.)

As has already been stated, the Battalion was quarantined for 14 days after its arrival at Abbasia. To find amusement during that period was a problem. At first the immediate environment produced some distraction. The hawkers and their cries, the arguments between contractors and labourers, the labour gangs at work, the habits of the crowds of scavenging kites, the Yeomanry exercising in the desert, the Egyptian Army recruits drilling in front of their barracks in time to drums beating at 140 a minute, and the circus-like performance of the Arab grooms taking remounts to and from water, all helped to pass an idle hour or two. Occasionally there was a visit from a little party of juvenile acrobats, who gave exhibitions of their prowess in return for "bakshish." One visitor was a youth of about 12—an extraordinary caricature, suffering from ophthalmia and dressed in various ragged and dirty portions of uniform. He laid claim to the name of "Saghen Mechenzi" and had an uncanny knowledge of the rifle, which he handled like a guardsman, and defied all attempts to confound him. Another and more welcome visitor was a youth of French extraction, who sold very fine picture postcards at a reasonable rate and would also undertake commissions for purchases in the city. Victor displayed unexpected traits of honesty and on being questioned thereon replied—"My father is French, he is honest, therefore I am honest." Nothing more could be said.

To relieve the monotony of the period during which no leave could be granted, it was decided to arrange a route march through the city as far as the Citadel walls, halt there for rest and return in the cool of the evening. During the afternoon of Sunday, the 11th July, the Battalion in drill order, and without rifles, set out led by a guide and preceded by Victor mounted importantly on a white donkey. According to the map the total distance to be covered was about ten miles, but owing to detours necessary in order to avoid the narrow streets the Battalion actually traversed some 14 or 15 miles. The heat was considerable, and a number of men fell out on account of the sickness which was very prevalent at this time. However, there was much to be seen. Palaces and hovels, magnificent hotels and humble coffee houses. Strange people and stranger costumes. Weird sights, sounds, and smells. Some streets no wider than our back lanes, teeming with people, filth, and squalor, and every window, doorway, or hole in the wall with something in it for sale. Veiled women and shuttered upper windows in the better class residential quarter hinted romance to those who had read the adventures of the Khalif. A wedding procession, and, again, a funeral procession were passed. The effect of the first was unusual, and the music that accompanied it had a mournful touch not noticeable in the second. The native police along the route were most attentive and cleared the way on every occasion. The traffic was considerable—mostly pedestrian, but with electric tramcars, donkeys, and horse gharris in large numbers. After one or two rests on the way, the Battalion at length came to a halt on an open space under the massive west wall of the Citadel. This place was to become better known later on, but on this occasion curiosity and interest were subordinated to the desire for cool drinks and rest. About an hour later the return march was commenced and camp reached some time after dark.

On the 17th July the quarantine restrictions were removed. A system was instituted whereby 25 per cent. were able to leave camp after evening parade on week days, 12 noon on Saturdays, and 8 a.m. on Sundays. Leave was usually commenced by tours within the city and visits to the Mouski for the purpose of purchasing gifts for the people at home. Here western methods were copied by some of the shopkeepers, and a sign which read—

SUCCOUR SALE, DRAPERIE HIGH LIFE

suggested that bargains might be hoped for. Gharri drives were popular but some men, with humane feeling, were averse to being hauled by a beast almost too poor and degraded to be longer termed a horse and one which, in our own land, would have received the attention of the S.P.C.A. The drivers of these vehicles cleared their way through the pedestrian traffic by cries such as "Ya meenuk" (To the right), "She maluk" (To the left), or "Owar riglak" (Mind your legs), repeated incessantly.

Donkey rides seemed to provide a certain amount of amusement. The beasts were hardy, and it was no uncommon sight to see two or three Australians trying the speed of their mounts down one of the main streets—enthusiastically encouraged by the donkeys' owners. Occasionally donkey and rider were facing in opposite directions. When tired, the soldier could go for rest to the Club established in the open air of the Esbekieh Gardens by the Australian Red Cross Society and Y.M.C.A. Here, comfortable seats, meals, and music could be obtained. O'her laces were picture theatres, and the "Kursaal" and "Casino" where varie y entertainments were given nightly—mostly by French artists. Some very good turns were to be seen at the Kursaal, the popular favourite being a soprano, Mimi Pinson, who could bring the house down by her rendering of "Two Eyes of Grey." At the Casino the audience sat about at tables and consumed cool drinks whilst listening to or watching the performers on the stage. The feminine element predominated here, and there was an air of friendliness about their open glances and conversation at first somewhat bewildering to the unsophisticated. The officers, in their peregrinations made free use of the large hotels—such as "Shepheard's" or the "Continental," and the various clubs such as the Italian and Ghezirah Sporting

THE WALL OF THE CITADEL.
From which the Mameluke leaped. The twin minarets are those of the Mehemet Ali Mosque.

Photo. by Sergt. Arundel.

Clubs. Shepheard's Hotel had been placed out of bounds to all but officers. Various reasons for this step were suggested. What, however, is believed to have had a good deal to do with it is the fact that during dinner on one occasion a rather stout and pompous senior general, sitting at table with his wife and daughters, was very affectionately greeted, embraced, and kissed by an hilarious youth from the southern seas.

At the commencement of all tours guides were offering freely, and were often required. They were of two kinds. The genuine type was usually a graduate of one of the educational institutions, and would arrange and conduct, more or less satisfactorily, any expedition—were it to visit the Cairo Museum, the Pyramids and

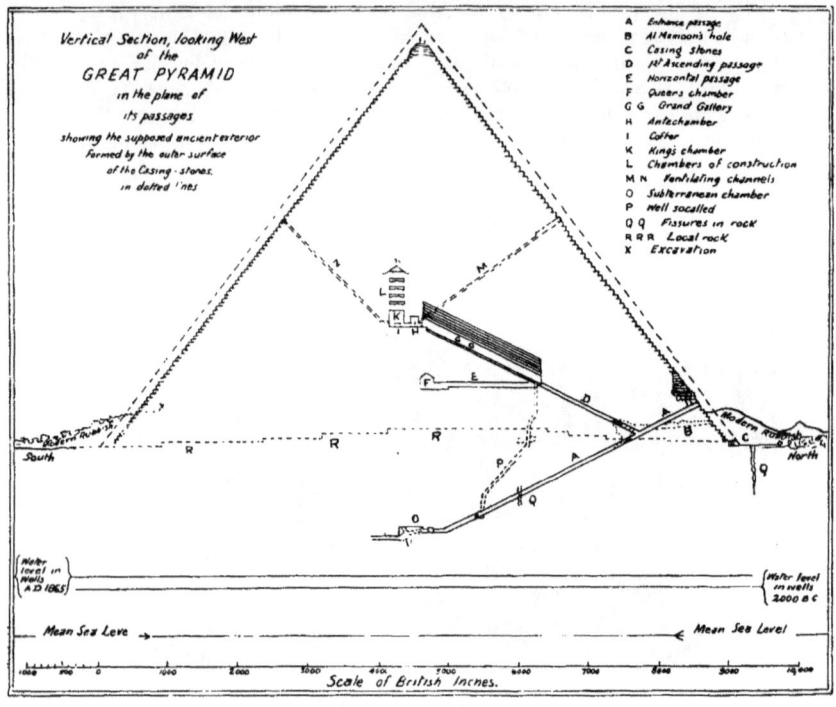

THE GREAT PYRAMID.

From the plan by C. Piazzi Smyth.

other monuments, or to go duck shooting near Alexandria or gazelle hunting in the Fayum. The other type of guide hailed from somewhere at the back of the bazaars; he was loudly importunate, proclaimed himself as named Macpherson, Abdullah, or Johnson, and stated that he was "dinkum." The possibilities with him seemed extensive. Anyone who employed this kind of person, and expected to have a kind of Arabian Nights entertainment, returned richer by his experience but, usually, unless he was very very careful, with the sensations of having just emerged from a garbage pit.

The Australian's interest in Egypt was immense. He had no marked admiration for the existing inhabitants, but his reading had given him an insatiable longing to know more of the ancients and their great works. He let no opportunity, therefore, escape him of viewing and studying the monuments which had withstood the ravages of time for so many centuries. Various expeditions were arranged by bands of friends who, after engaging a dragoman, would often pool their resources in order that the day might be as pleasant as it was instructive. As a rule the first expedition was to the great Pyramids at Gizeh—distant glimpses of which can be obtained from points not far from Abbasia. Situated about eight miles from Cairo, the route to this objective lies through the city, across the Nile bridge, and along the delightful causeway said to have been built by the Khedive Ismail for use by the Empress Eugenie during her visit on the occasion of the opening of the Suez Canal. On arrival at the village, camels and donkeys are used to traverse the stretch of heavy sand which intervenes between the road and the plateau upon which the Pyramids stand.

The Pyramids are three in number, but vary in size. The largest is that of Cheops, the second that of Chephren, and the smallest that of Menkaura. The tomb of Cheops attracts all visitors and, once having been "done," any curiosity in regard to the remainder is, as a rule, entirely lacking. There are two ways of "doing" it. One is to climb up the exterior to the summit, and the other to go inside and visit the King's and Queen's chambers. No ordinary individual has the strength to achieve both in the one day. The visit to the top gives the better result in a magnificent view of Cairo, the Nile, and the surrounding desert, but gaining this involves a climb to a height of 451 feet by means of the several courses of stone, each course being about three feet high; nor is the descent very much easier. To inspect the interior it is necessary to first ascend about 30 feet to the entrance. Here, on the occasion of the Western Australians' visit, were met the guides or caretakers attached to the place. Bedlam instantly broke out. All wanted a job or "bakshish." Some grabbed the soldiers' sticks, others their boots and leggings. After much remonstrance, and an occasional hard knock or kick to some too enthusiastic native, the party, in its stockinged feet, eventually passed within the entrance. The passage was narrow, low, steep, and extremely slippery. With an Arab to each hand—as a precaution against a nasty fall—the soldier, breathing a muggy atmosphere, sweating at every pore, and filled with repulsion at the close proximity of his yelling conductors, made a crab-like and painful progress through darkness over the 220 feet of distance to the King's Chamber. This apartment, viewed by candlelight or a flare now and then from a piece of magnesium wire, does not present, beyond some carvings on the walls, anything of great interest.

After a brief rest the party retraced some of its steps and visited the Queen's Chamber, situated lower down. Here it was necessary to have another breather, and at this stage some Arab evinced a desire to foretell the fortune of anyone who would listen to him and, of course, produce the necessary monetary encouragement. Finally the open air was regained, perspiration ceased to pour, and with luck it was possible to recover those portions of clothing left behind when entering. Now thoughts were directed to the Pyramids Hotel at Mena—noticed earlier in the day—where, under the shade of trees, tables were set and lunch could be obtained, together with much good and cool English ale. Sometimes the parties had enough energy left to first pay a call on the Sphinx, which is situated about 300 yards distant from the great tomb. Very few thoroughly explored this relic of the ancients, but its great antiquity, alleged by some authorities to date long prior to the creation as fixed by the Christian calendar, and the riddle associated with it, demanded that everyone should at least go and gaze on its face for a little while. Here it was customary to submit to the camera man. Many photographs were thus secured which, when posted, were of great interest to the friends at home.

The next place of interest was the site of the City of Memphis—the ancient capital of Egypt—and its necropolis at Sakkara. Memphis was reached either by train or donkey ride from Cairo, or by a ride of about two hours across from the Pyramids at Gizeh. Of the city itself nothing is left to mark its ancient magnificence except the two giant statues of Rameses II. However, the country between there and Gizeh is one vast cemetery containing the tombs of the notables. The most conspicuous of these is the Step Pyramid—the oldest of such and the resting-place of the body of King Teheser. Less conspicuous, but more interesting to the new-comers, were the Apis Tombs, which contain the sarcophagi of 24 of the Sacred Bulls. These sarcophagi, complete with lids, are of an immense size—each weighing some 65 tons. Near by are the tombs of Ptah-hetep and Ti, in which the rich and well-preserved mural decorations give a very full representation of the life and habits of the inhabitants of the city in their time. Other interesting remains, some Greek and some Roman, were also to be seen, but by this time the average Australian had had enough for one day, and turned to the means of getting back to the more congenial surroundings of the modern city or camp.

Having seen so many of the tombs, parties took an especial interest in the Cairo Museum, wherein they inspected wonderful

VIEW OF CAIRO FROM THE CITADEL WALLS.
The Sultan Hassan and Khedivial Mosques in the foreground.
Photo. by Sergt. Arundel.

THE MOQATTAM HILLS.
Showing the quarries and the Causeway leading to the summit.
Photo. by Sergt. Arundel.

statuary; mummies of men, women, cats, dogs, monkeys, and crocodiles; also coffins and other relics going back in origin, some of them, to a period nearly 4,000 B.C. The jewellery, said at one time to have been worn by Queen Cleopatra, attracted much attention, as did also specimens of boomerangs—a weapon which almost every Australian had thought was peculiar to his own country.

Time did not permit of visits up the Nile to the ruins at Luxor, Thebes, Philae, and Karnak, so the programme of viewing ancient remains had to be somewhat restricted. Consequently little was now left to do except to visit Mataria (about four miles north of the camp), view the Tree and Well associated with the Flight out of Egypt, and then proceed to the obelisk near by, which marks the site of the old Heliopolis—the City of the Sun.

Other and more modern buildings and structures, connected with the early Christians and the Saracens, are plentiful in Cairo, and to these the visitors now turned. Chief amongst them is the Citadel, the erection of which Saladin began in A.D. 1166. From its walls a fine view of the city and its environs can be obtained. To the south the Aqueduct built by the Saracens comes under observation; and near by, on the east side, the Moqattam Hills—scarred by quarries and surmounted by a fort from which Napoleon silenced the guns of the Citadel. Within Saladin's walls are to be seen Joseph's Well—some 300 feet deep; the costly mosque of Mehemet Ali with its dome and twin minarets; two or three smaller and older mosques; and, on the wall, the hoof print of the escaping Mameluke's horse.

Opposite to the main entrance to the Citadel, and without the walls, are two mosques of unusual size. One, the mosque of the Sultan Hassan—noted amongst other things for its wonderful arches, doors inlaid with gold, and a cannon ball still sticking in the wall facing the hills which bear Napoleon's fort; the other containing the tombs of the Khedivial family and distinguished by the richness of the decorations and inlay of sandalwood, ebony, silver, and ivory.

Mosques and shrines in Cairo number nearly 500. There is plenty to see in this respect, but after a few of the principal ones, including the Blue Mosque of Ibrahim Agha, had been inspected, and similar calls paid on some of the old Coptic churches, interest waned and the soldier, looking for a change, sometimes turned to the Roman and Arab remains in Old Cairo and Fustat, or else visited the Tombs of the Khalifs and Mamelukes on the edge of the desert. Here he was, perhaps, successful in obtaining genuine souvenirs of the "Dead City."

Apart from short trips on the Nile, per steam dahabiyehs, two other excursions must be mentioned. One was to the Island of Roda

CAIRO AND ENVIRONS

to view the spot where the infant Moses is alleged to have been found by the Pharoah's daughter; and the other by tram or gharri along the Mena Road to the Zoological Gardens. This institution is said to have been one of the many extravagances of the Khedive Ismail. The visitors greatly admired the grounds and also the fine collection of the larger African animals.

Driving back in the evening from the Gardens, the soldier was able to see Cairo taking the air under the shade of the lebbok trees and observe the wealthy and official classes in their carriages and motors. He was not slow to notice the arrogant air of the Egyptian male aristocracy, accompanied as they often were by rather fleshy ladies of foreign origin. Nor did he fail to feel impressed by the neat and wholesome appearance of the few British ladies who took exercise on this highway.

With the exception of two days at the beginning of August, when Cairo was placed out of bounds owing to the rioting, and the 12th to 14th August, when the Festival of Bairam was being observed, sight-seeing went on at leave periods during the whole of the Battalion's stay in Egypt.

On the 16th August the Battalion, when carrying out a night operation in the desert, was recalled to camp and ordered to proceed the following morning to garrison the Citadel. At 7.30 a.m. on the 17th August the 28th, leaving the transport behind under a small guard, commenced the march to its new home which, after a trying time in the heat, was reached in due course and quarters found in the various blocks of barracks. These quarters, it was discovered, were alive with vermin, necessitating the whole Battalion being set to work for several hours in an attempt to clean the place. Iron bedsteads and palliasses were available for the use of the troops, but as the palliasses also showed signs of life very few were used. After Gallipoli was reached an account for 40 of these iron bedsteads, which the unit, it was inferred, had taken with it or disposed of in some other unlawful manner, was received from the British authorities. Needless to say it has not yet been paid.

The C.O. was, for the time being, the Commandant of the fortress which was the home of the ordnance stores and reserve of ammunition of the Army of Occupation. Besides the British and Egyptian staffs to work these, there were other troops within the walls. These included details of the 2nd Mounted Division, recently embarked for the Peninsula; British and Indian General Hospitals (both full); a hospital for convalescents; a detention barracks; and about 40 Turkish Officers under guard as prisoners of war. Amongst these prisoners was a major, a nephew of the Senussi, who had been visiting Constantinople at the outbreak of war and found himself immediately requisitioned for a tour through Arabia for the purpose of promoting a holy war against the English. Himself an Arab, who had always looked upon Great Britain with friendly eyes, he undertook the mission rather unwillingly. In course of time he joined Djemal Pasha's army approaching the Canal and was finally captured by its defenders.

Owing to the large numbers of men required for special duties, all training, except that for the section, platooon, and company, had to cease. What little was done was carried out in the barrack yards or else, in the early morning, on the top of the adjacent Moqattam Hills, which was reached by a kind of causeway running up through the quarries. The duties consisted of providing guards and sentries for the various gates of the Citadel; guards on some of the hospitals and detention barracks; and patrols which had the unpleasant duty of traversing the highways of the city for the purpose of preserving order and looking after the interests of the army and the men on leave.

Existing orders did not permit any civilian to enter the gates of the Citadel unless provided with an official pass. The enforcement of this order caused some dismay amongst the women from the neighbouring houses who had been in the habit of visiting the Citadel stables for the purpose of obtaining material for the manufacture of fuel, which was a scarce commodity with them. The ladies' method of explaining their mission was clear, if not delicate, and brought a blush to the faces of the sentries on the Moqattam Gate.

The Warrant and Non-commissioned Officers had a good mess, which was presided over by the Regimental Sergeant-Major. The Officers joined and took over control of the Garrison Officers' Mess —very well and cheaply run. Here many pleasant acquaintances were made and a good deal learned in regard to the organisation and working of the British units.

Short leave was still granted liberally to those desiring it, but numbers found sufficient attraction in or near the Citadel to pass away many hours. The views from the walls, or from the tops of the old towers, the mosques, the well and its echo, the remains of Saladin's palace, the Church of England chapel (established in the bathroom of a former Sultan's harem), where service was frequently held, all received much attention. Occasional trips by souvenir hunters were made to the adjacent "Dead City." These were sometimes fruitful, for in one barrack room an ancient skull was observed reposing on a shelf above an inmate's bed.

Now and then concerts were given for the benefit of the hospital patients, and an invitation for members of the Battalion to attend was received.

On Sunday, 29th August, a visit was received from a party of Western Australians who were friends and relatives of some mem-

THE CITADEL.

As seen from the Mogattam Hills. Cairo and the Nile in the distance.

Photo. by Sergt. Arundel.

bers of the 28th, and were making a short stay in Egypt. The party included the Rev. E. M. Collick, Archdeacon of Kalgoorlie; Mrs. Campbell Wilson; Mrs. and Miss Montgomery; and Mrs Makeham.

About the middle of August news of the heavy fighting, which had been going on at the Dardanelles, began to dribble through. It was gathered that the results had not been entirely such as could have been hoped for, and that the casualties—particularly of the 10th Light Horse, the 11th and 16th Battalions—had been heavy. Information was also received of a disaster to the Yeomanry on the 21st August.

Hospital trains began to arrive and discharge large numbers of wounded into the hospitals. From the less seriously injured some idea of the last advance was obtained, and it seemed evident that the 2nd Australian Division would soon be called upon to play its part. In the third week of the month the 5th Brigade marched off *en route* to the front, and was followed a few days later by the 6th Brigade.

These indications caused some stir in the Battalion and, although definite orders had not been received, preparations for another move were commenced.

On the 24th August were issued the colour patches which were to be worn sewn on to the upper part of each sleeve of the jacket. In the case of the 2nd Division the patch was diamond in shape. The 7th Brigade colour was a light blue and the Battalion colour white. The "28th" therefore wore a blue and white diamond, and by this badge was ever afterwards distinguished.

About this time a slight change was made in the Battalion Staff. W.O. J. Gettingby was promoted to be Quartermaster and Hon. Lieutenant. His position as R.S.M. was filled by C.S.M. P. T. C. Bell.

On the 28th August orders were received that the Battalion would be relieved on the following Monday and march out to camp. On the 30th August the 5th Australian Training Battalion, commanded by Major J. S. Lazarus, took over the garrison duties and the 28th, after being photographed in mass formation, moved by way of the desert road, through the Tombs of the Khalifs and Abbasia, to Aerodrome Camp, recently vacated by the 5th Brigade. Only tents were available here, and the camp was very dusty. As the tenancy was likely to be of a few days duration only, these inconveniences were submitted to with a good grace.

Wheeled transport and riding horses could not, at that stage, be either safely or profitably used on Gallipoli, so to the bitter disappointment of Lieut. Graham and his section, the Divisional Commander ordered that they be left behind—later on to be grouped with the rest of the Divisional Train, exercised, and held in readiness against being required.

On the 1st September a message from Brigade Headquarters directed that the Battalion would proceed "overseas" on the 3rd September. All surplus stores were at once got rid of, and spare baggage collected to be handed over to the care of the Australian Base. The Regimental Orderly-room Clerk, Staff Sergeant S. S. Thompson, was detailed and departed for duty at the Australian Headquarters in Egypt, where he would be responsible for the proper keeping of Battalion records.

The 2nd September witnessed the departure for Alexandria of a small advance party, under Lieut. H. E. C. Ruddock, charged with the duty of making all necessary arrangements for the reception of the troops when arriving at the wharf. Tents were struck that afternoon and a bivouac formed for the night.

After the evening meal on the following day the Battalion fell in, and a check of the *personnel* was made. Previously a number of sick, and the few men in detention, had been struck off the strength and shown as transferred to the Training Depôt. It was now found that three or four men were missing. As time did not permit of a search being made, a report was sent to the A.P.M., and the additional names were also removed from the roll.

Late that night the move commenced to Qubba station, where the train was boarded. Each man was bearing a heavy burden. All ranks were fitted with web equipment, carrying in their packs great coats and a few necessaries and personal belongings, and bearing a blanket, waterproof sheet, three days' rations of biscuits and preserved meat, together with an emergency ration in a sealed tin, and (for those with rifles) 200 rounds of ammunition. Officers carried revolvers, field glasses, prismatic compass, and various other extras. They were also allowed to place their valises on the train but, according to rumour, it was doubtful if they would ever reach them on Gallipoli.

The entrainment was expeditiously carried out and, with the usual amount of discomfort, the journey to the quay at Alexandria was completed by daylight on the 4th September. Here Lieut. Ruddock was waiting and, after some delay, the Battalion embarked on the transport in a similar manner, minus the sympathetic crowd, to that witnessed at Fremantle.

CHAPTER V.

GALLIPOLI.

At this stage it is necessary, in order that the future environment may be fully understood, to give some account of the Gallipoli Peninsula and of the events of the 25th April, 1915, and later.

The Peninsula forms the European side to the Straits of the Dardanelles and is about 53 miles in length. On the north-western side it is washed by the waters of the Gulf of Xeros and on the western side by the Aegean Sea. Near its northern end, at Bulair, it is only two and a half miles across. At Savla Burnu* it broadens out to about 12 miles, but narrows again between Gaba Tepe† and Maidos to a bare four miles. Gaba Tepe is about eight miles south of Suvla Burnu and Helles Burnu—the southern end of the Peninsula—13 miles further. Cliffs of marl or sand, rising very abruptly and varying in height from 100 to 300 feet, mark the greater length of the shore. These are broken here and there by the gullies which bring away from the interior the waters of the heavy autumn and winter rains. From Gaba Tepe northwards to Suvla Bay there is an almost uninterrupted stretch of beach from which, opposite the latter feature, a somewhat marshy plain runs back to the foothills of Tekke Tepe.

Groups of hills are marked features of the interior, the most prominent being known as Sari Bair‡ which rises to a height of 971 feet at Koja Chemin Tepe and is the one most familiar to the Australians. These hills possess very steep—even precipitous—slopes which are much excoriated by wind, rain, and frost, and broken into an amazing tangle of gullies and hollows. Firs and stunted oaks, brushwood, oleanders or rhododendrons, and other shrubs are thick wherever they can hold, and form no inconsiderable obstacle —two to four feet high—to anyone's passage.

Before the war a very small part of the land was under cultivation. A few miniature olive and currant orchards, attempts at vineyards, and trifling patches of beans and grain, represented the sole efforts at tillage. There were no railways, and the few roads in existence were in poor condition. In or near what afterwards became the British zone, the only communities were those grouped around the fortifications near Helles and the villages of Krithia, Kurija Dere,

---

* Burnu=cape.   † Tepe=hill.   ‡ Bair=spur.

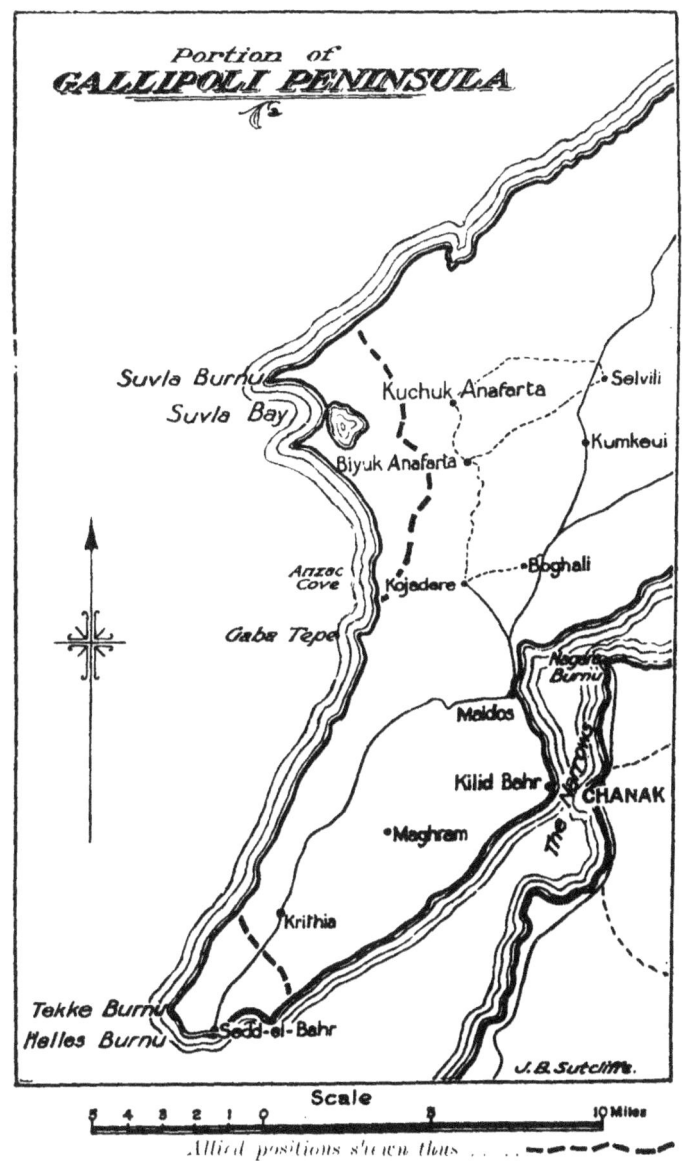

SHOWING ALLIED LINES AT THE TIME OF THE EVACUATION.
Map by Australian War Museum.

Biyuk Anafarta, and Anafarta Sagir. On the side nearer Asia, Maidos, Galata, and Gallipoli boasted the status of towns. Between these last-named points and into the Sea of Marmara the communication and trade were mostly carried on by means of boats.

The Gallipoli Peninsula formed part of Thrace of the ancients. Through it Xerxes, the Persian king, after crossing the Dardanelles, attacked the Greeks with an army and followers estimated at over 2,000,000. This was about 480 B.C. It also lay in the route of Alexander the Great in his march on Egypt and India commenced in 334 B.C. Later on it was overrun by the Gauls, recovered by the Greeks, occupied by the Romans in the 2nd century A.D., passed into the possession of the Venetians 1,000 years later, and was finally held by the Turks as a result of their invasion of Europe in 1356. In 1807 a British naval squadron forced the passage of the Straits but suffered considerable damage, when returning, from large stone shot fired from the guns of the forts. Again, in 1853, the British and French fleets sailed into the Sea of Marmara in support of the Turks who were on the verge of war with Russia. At Bulair, in March and April, 1854, the British troops on the way to the Crimea landed, and, in conjunction with their allies, constructed across the neck of the Peninsula the fortifications known as the Bulair Lines.

Following the outbreak of the great European War, Turkey, on the 31st October, 1914, definitely threw in her lot with Germany. In order to deal with the Ottoman, and at the same time restore communication with Russia through the Black Sea route, the French and British Governments decided to force the Straits. A bombardment was opened on the 3rd November, 1914, but lasted for a few minutes only. On the 19th February following, and succeeding days, a heavy bombardment was carried out and small craft were engaged in mine-sweeping up towards the Narrows. Again, on the 18th March, the attack was renewed—some ships penetrating the Strait eight or ten miles—but the Turks loosed some large mines which floated down and sunk three of the battleships. Now it became obvious that the aid of land forces must be sought in order to deal with the enemy defences. That task was committed to an army already assembling in Egypt and on Lemnos Island. This army was under the command of General Sir Ian Hamilton and was composed of a French Division, the 29th British Division, the Royal Naval Division, and the Australian and New Zealand Army Corps; the last-named formation being commanded by Major-General Sir William Birdwood.

Very early in the morning of the 25th April, 1915, the attack was commenced. The French troops landed at Kum Kale—on the

THE 28th: A RECORD OF WAR SERVICE, 1915-19.

Asiatic side of the Strait; the 29th Division, and part of the R.N. Division, at five places at the southern end of the Peninsula; the Anzac Corps at a cove about 3,000 yards north of Gaba Tepe; whilst the major portion of the R.N. Division was sent under convoy to make a feint in the Gulf of Xeros near to the Bulair Lines.

The Australian attack was led by the 3rd Brigade (including the 11th Battalion). After a week's heroic fighting (in which the 16th Battalion took a prominent part) under conditions never before experienced in warfare, and the loss of 9,000 killed, wounded, and missing, a position was made good which extended in an arc from the foot of Walker's Ridge, on the north, up to Russell's Top, across the head of Monash Gully, to MacLaurin's Hill, continuing to Bolton's Ridge and reseeting the beach about 2,000 yards north of Gaba Tepe. The base of this arc measured about 2,700 yards and the enclosed area did not exceed three-quarters of a square mile.

During the next three months the Corps was reinforced by various drafts, and four brigades of Light Horse dismounted. Attempts were made from time to time to improve and extend the Australian position, but little progress was made. At the same time the Turks were by no means idle for, apart from fortifying their positions, they frequently attacked in endeavours to drive us off their soil. The heaviest assault was on the 18th May when 30,000 fresh troops were flung at the 1st Division and the New Zealanders. So effectually were they repulsed that the Turks begged for an armistice for the purpose of collecting and burying the dead.

Sir Ian Hamilton, who had been strengthened by several new divisions, planned a fresh attack for early in August. On the 6th of that month the 1st (N.S.W.) Brigade stormed Lone Pine. On the following morning attacks were made from Steel's Post, Quinn's Post, Pope's Hill, and Russell's Top, but all of these were unfruitful and caused heavy losses. The main attack in the Anzac sector was, however, delivered from the left. This commenced on the night of the 6th August and swept up the Sazli Beit and Chailak Deres,* over Big Table Top, Bauchop Hill, and Rhododendron Spur, to a position—afterwards called "The Apex"—within 400 yards of the summit of Chunuk Bair.† A portion of the force detailed for this advance moved up the Aghyl Dere and endeavoured to take Koja Chemin Tepe from the west side but, after many casualties, had to entrench on some of the under-features (Cheshire Ridge-Warwick Castle).

---

* Dere.—Valley with stream.   † Portion of Sari Bair group of hills.

During the progress of this fighting the IX. Corps made a fresh landing at Suvla Bay (6th-7th August). The combat was heavy and eventually a junction was effected with the Australian left, but not one of the real objectives was gained.

The operations were continued until the 29th August, on which date the 10th Light Horse, sent north to reinforce there, stormed Hill 60. This was the last Australian attack on the Peninsula. Henceforth attention was given solely to holding and strengthening the positions gained. The 2nd Australian Division took no part in any of these operations, but one of its battalions—the 18th—arrived in time to join in the fighting for the hill feature just mentioned.

The net result of the August fighting gave to the Anzac and IX. Corps a continuous line of about 12 miles. This ran from the Brighton Beach to the Gulf of Xeros. Behind this the depth did not average more than $1\frac{1}{4}$ miles but the Anzac area was enlarged from 300 acres to 8 square miles. This gain cost the Australasians 18,000 casualties. The exhausted troops remaining were gradually relieved by the 2nd Division pending the further development of the British plans.

* * * * * *

To return to the record of the events with which the 28th Battalion was concerned after leaving Alexandria.

The knowledge gained during the voyage of the "Ascanius" enabled the troops to settle quickly in their new quarters. In addition to the W.A. Battalion there were on board two companies and the headquarters of the 27th Battalion. The transport, the "Ivernia,"* was a comfortable ship of 14,000 tons register belonging to the Cunard Line. The captain and officers at first displayed a rather cool and curt manner towards their new passengers but in the course of a day or two visibly thawed. The captain afterwards, in explanation, stated that from information he had received in regard to the Australians he had expected to find in them an absence of discipline and a tendency to "smash things." He was now agreeably surprised to discover them so tractable and well-behaved—comparing them in a most favourable manner with other contingents he had carried.

Routine was quickly instituted. Special precautions had to be taken in regard to enemy sub-marines which at this time had become

---

* The "Ivernia" on the 1st January, 1917, when in the Mediterranean, was torpedoed and sunk by an enemy submarine; 153 lives were lost. Dr. Riley, Archbishop of Perth, was a passenger.

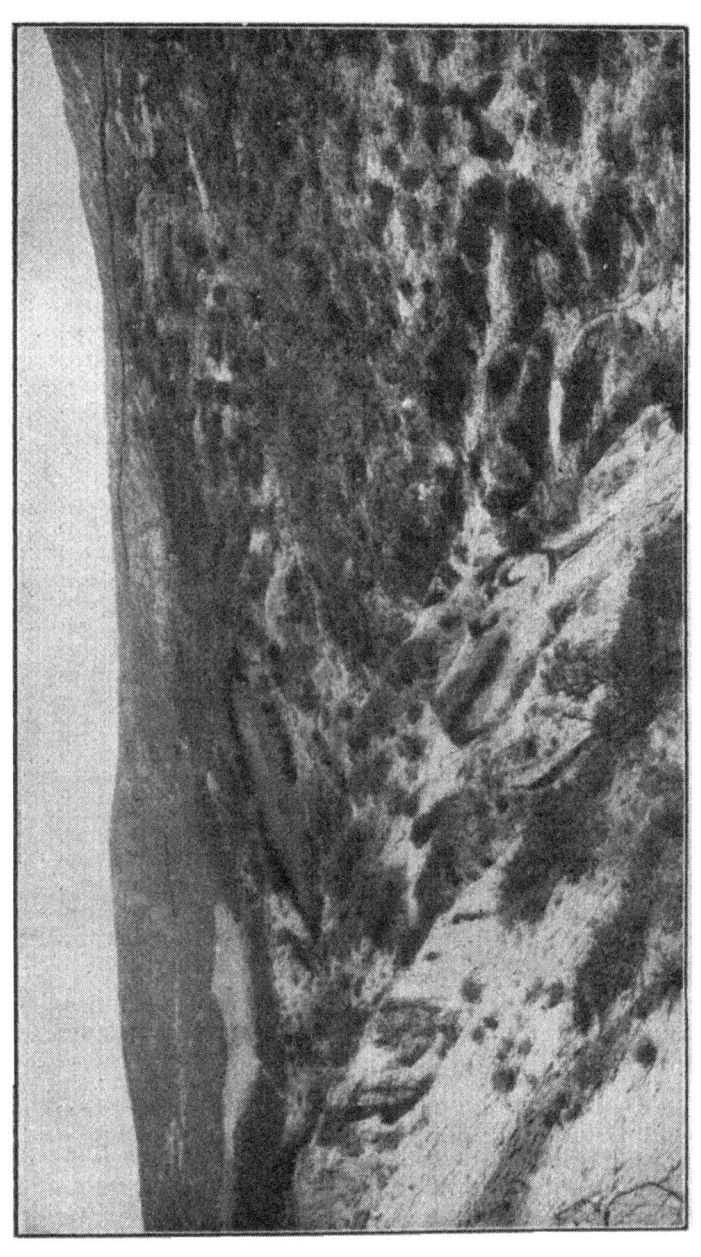

CHUNUK BAIR.
Taken from Table Top—looking East. Corner of Rhododendron Spur at top of right side.
Official Photo, No. G. 1830c. *Copyright by Australian War Museum.*

very active and had lately torpedoed the "Southland" conveying the Brigadier and portion of the 6th Brigade as well as the G.O.C. and Staff of the 2nd Australian Division. News of this occurrence had reached the Battalion just prior to embarkation and naturally excited great interest. However, the voyage proved uneventful, the weather good, and the colours of the sea and evening skies a never failing attraction.

Heading towards Crete, the transport skirted its western coast and thence wended its way through the Grecian Archipelago. Arriving off Mudros Bay, Lemnos Island, on the evening of the 8th September, it was found that a boom was across the entrance and the harbour closed for the night. Nothing remained to be done but to stand on and off during the hours of darkness. To cast anchor would have rendered the ship an easy prey to the underwater craft. The sight of the "Southland" on a neighbouring beach lent point to this possibility.

Shortly after sunrise the appearance of a British destroyer coming from the direction of the Bay indicated that the entrance was now open. Threading its way between numbers of British and French men-of-war and other vessels the transport came to rest something less than a mile from the shore.

Anchored in the vicinity was the R.M.S. "Aragon," now used as quarters for the Inspector-General of the Line of Communications and his staff. From this source orders were received to disembark the Battalion on the following day. The arrangements necessary were few, consequently there was little to do and most of the afternoon was spent in bathing at the ship's side or in writing letters. Word had gone forth that the last mail before reaching Gallipoli would close that night. So numerous were the missives that it was found necessary to make every available officer a censor for the time being in order that delay might be avoided. The writings, as usual, were apropos of the occasion but it was found that one man, anticipating events, had informed his mother that he was writing his few words "by the light of the bursting shells."

Disembarkation was to commence at 2 p.m. on the 10th September but the movement proved to be merely a transhipment to the Weymouth-Channel Islands packet boat "Sarnia" which arrived, after a delay of one and a-half hours, and tied up alongside the transport. Coincident with this there appeared several staff officers delegated to "assist." The Senior Naval Transport Officer, a captain in the Royal Navy, endeavoured to make up the 90 minutes lost by urging speed in the move from one ship to the other. When the futility of expecting fully equipped men to move quickly over the solitary 15-inch plank laid down as a gangway was pointed out to him, he showed signs of irritability and threatened an adverse report on the handling of the troops. On being informed that it was his privilege to make such a report he left the ship. However, he was later observed in altercation with the skipper of the smaller vessel and eventually a second gangway was rigged. When this move was commenced there was room on the main deck for two companies only. The other two were kept clear and their officers took refuge on the boat deck. There they were found, reclining in chairs, by another staff officer duly be-tabbed, trousered, brogued, and carrying a cane. He seemed to be amazed at the indifference of the Australians to their impending move and burst out "I say, you fellows, do you know that you've got to be off this —— ship in half an hour?" Being greeted with roars of laughter he disappeared down the companionway calling plaintively, "Where's the Colonel? Where's the Colonel?"

Within ten minutes of the time originally allowed, the Battalion had passed over to the "Sarnia." As she sheered off loud cheers were given for the captain of the "Ivernia" and groans for one of his officers whom the men considered had been, on the voyage, over niggardly with the rations. The packet boat, her decks rather tightly packed with troops, moved down the Bay between the lines of the warships, whose crews cheered and cheered again those now leaving for the front. Darkness was falling as the transport entered the open sea and steamed at 17 knots in the direction of Anzac—60 miles away to the north-east.

Some two hours elapsed and then star shells, bursting over Achi Baba, near the Southern end of the Peninsula, gave the new-comers a first glimpse of the "real war." Later on the guns could be heard and shell explosions witnessed on the plain of Helles where the VIII. Corps and the French had been for the previous five months. Keen were the watchers on the deck of the "Sarnia" and keener still they became as the rugged mass of Sari Bair loomed out of the sea. It was then known that the end of the journey was at hand.

Nearing the Peninsula at this point—opposite Williams' Pier—resembled somewhat an approach to Mt. Eliza on a dark night by boat from Perth Water. Lights shone out from dugouts constructed in the steep slopes, moving lights were discerned on the beach beneath, and the crest line was in darkness except when now and then illuminated by the flash of a bomb, shell, or gun. The simile could be pursued no further, for to those who had not yet been in action the noise going on seemed to indicate that some fierce fighting must be in progress. The dull but powerful thud of exploding hand bombs, the sharper crashing explosion of shell, the report of a discharging gun and the roar of its projectile, echoed and re-echoed, in its flight along one of the numerous ravines, induced belief that very little time must elapse before the 28th would be "in it." It turned out otherwise, however, and subsequent experience showed that these signs and sounds were the mere accompaniment of a "quiet night."

WILLIAMS' PIER.
Where the 28th landed. Stores in the foreground. The vessel on the left was sunk to act as a breakwater and afterwards used as a reservoir for drinking water. Trawlers in the distance.
Photo. lent by Mr. T. Pritchard.

The "Sarnia" stopped her engines when about a mile from the shore. Almost at once one or two flat craft, black in colour and without funnel or rigging, were observed approaching. As they drew alongside a staff officer came up the transport's gangway and delivered the orders for landing the troops. The disembarkation commenced at once—the officers and men filing down the gangway on to the waiting barges. These barges had been given the name of "beetles." They were constructed of bullet-proof iron plates, were propelled by motor engines set astern, could attain a racing speed of five knots, and were designed to carry 50 horses or 500 men with stores, ammunition and water. Built for the Suvla landing, the "beetles" had fully proved their usefulness, but certainly they lacked every element of comfort.

During the disembarkation it was noted that a destroyer had moved in on the right and was directing her searchlight on Gaba Tepe and vicinity. This prevented any observation of the landing process from the direction of the Turkish lines in that quarter. Occasionally she fired her guns and generally gave the impression of intense watchfulness.

By midnight everybody was free of the ship, and the Battalion, leaving Williams' Pier and guided by a staff officer, stumbled along the beach in a northerly direction for a little over a mile to the shelter of Waterfall Gully—a small hollow in the western side of Bauchop's Hill. Two platoons of "A" Company, under Captain Montgomery, had been left on the beach for fatigue duty there. They did not rejoin the unit until the 25th September.

Fatigued with the long day, and overburdened with the load of equipment, rest was the first essential. An attempt was made to form a bivouac, but so small was the space available, and so rough the ground, that the idea had to be abandoned. The men were told to lie down where they were—amongst disused trenches, numerous latrine pits, and close to the remains of the 5th Connaught Rangers (88th) who had been decimated in the fighting of the previous month.

During the night two companies of the 27th Battalion, under Major Jeffrey, were landed. Within 24 hours the Brigadier and staff and the remaining units of the brigade were also disembarked and sheltered in various features near the beach. For the time being the brigade formed part of the New Zealand and Australian Division which normally consisted of the N.Z. Mounted Rifle Brigade and the N.Z. and 4th Australian Infantry Brigades, together with certain artillery, engineers, and other troops. The division was commanded by Major-General Sir A. J. Godley, K.C.M.G.

At dawn of the 11th September, those of the 28th who were still sleeping were rudely awakened by guns firing close at hand. A destroyer had moved in to within a few cable lengths of the shore and was viciously shooting over the heads of the infantry at some target which the enemy on Sari Bair afforded.

During the next few hours contact was gained with the 16th Battalion in reserve in Hay Valley near by. The new arrivals were heartily welcomed by the exhausted remains of that famous unit whose adjutant was, on this morning, shot through the chest whilst on his way to visit the 28th. Nor did the inhabitants of Waterfall Gully escape the hostile bullet, for before noon two members (Private F. T. Mitchell was the first) were hit when they left the shelter of the valley to proceed to a well (kuyu) on the adjacent beach. These were the earliest casualties as a result of the enemy's fire.

Orders having been received to relieve the 4th Australian Infantry Brigade, astride the Aghyl Dere, a party moved up and, after the C.O. had conferred with Colonel Monash, reconnoitred the advanced positions. Later in the day these orders were cancelled, and the 28th was directed to take over the "Apex" salient from the Otago Battalion, N.Z. Infantry. At 7 o'clock that evening Waterfall Gully was evacuated and the Battalion moved up the Chailak Dere to the ravines between Bauchop's Hill, Little Table Top, and Rose Hill. There the night was spent and next evening, the "Apex" position having been reconnoitred, "C" and "D" Companies moved to the front line and relieved the New Zealanders. "A" and "B" Companies took up a position in reserve some 300 yards in rear, near the head of the Chailak Dere. One platoon of "A" Company and the Machine Gun Section were posted on Canterbury Slope—a position in support of the 3rd Light Horse Brigade and on the left flank of Rhododendron Spur.

The position the Battalion was now responsible for was the neck or junction of the Rhododendron Spur with the Sari Bair feature. On the right was the Sazli Beit Dere, and on the left the southern arm of the Aghyl Dere. Behind was the ravine of the Chailak. The trenches ran along in a pothook shape from Rhododendron Spur down to the Cheshire Ridge, on the north side. Opposite to the centre was the actual summit, which was called the "Pinnacle," and was held by the Turks. Here they had erected a block house, which stood about 50 yards from our own trench. The enemy earthworks lined the opposite sides of the gullies at a range varying from 100 to 250 yards from our position—the right of which could be enfiladed from the blockhouse

To hold this salient was of vital importance. Its loss would have severed the Australian line, turned the flank of the Cheshire Ridge, and exposed to enfilade fire most of the ground gained to the northward during the August fighting. A strong garrison and special vigilance were both necessary. To this post of honour the Western Australian portion of the 7th Infantry Brigade was allotted by reason of the high standard of efficiency it had attained during the training period.

The remainder of the 7th Brigade was disposed as follows:— 25th and 27th Battalions on Cheshire Ridge, the left of the former resting on the Aghyl Dere, and the right of the 27th joining up with the 28th, near Apex. The 26th Battalion was held in Divisional Reserve, at Taylor's Hollow, and supplied working parties for engineering and beach duties. One company of the 27th was available

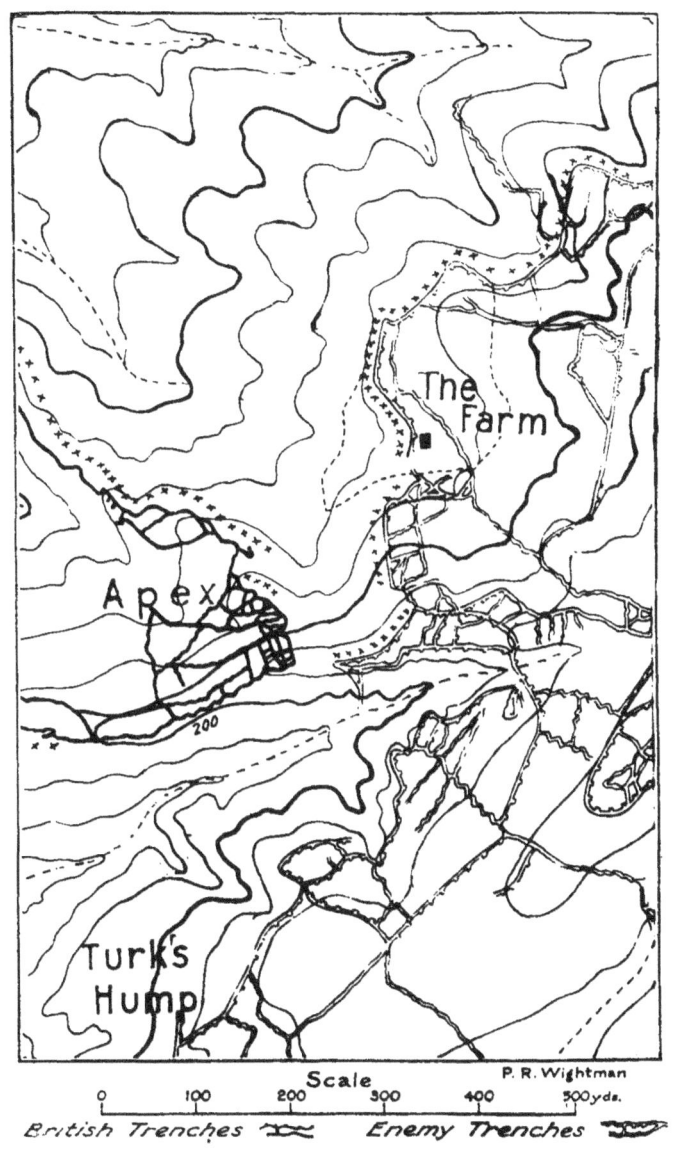

THE TRENCHES AT "THE APEX."
Map by Australian War Museum.

as a reserve in the hands of the Brigadier, who was located about half-a-mile from the front line, at the Western foot of Table Top.

For tactical purposes, the "Apex" position was divided into four posts—numbered from the right. "C" Company took Nos. 1 and 2 and was afterwards relieved by "B" Company. "D" Company took Nos. 3 and 4 and later handed over to "A" Company. Nos. 3 and 4 Posts were the closer to the enemy and, consequently, of greater importance. Each post was further divided into a certain number of Groups—each under a Non-commissioned Officer. Three machine guns were mounted in the parapet. After the first week, Lieut. Shaw took these over and also mounted additional guns in secret emplacements, which were constructed by digging through the escarp and tunnelling forward and upward.

The trenches were at least six feet deep and excavated in a kind of conglomerate, which needed very little revetting and was a good bullet or splinter stopper. A ledge or firestep ran along the inside of the trench. Upon this the garrison stood if an attack was to be repelled. The instructions for the posts required that men in them were to be always in a state of readiness, *i.e.*, rifle loaded, bayonet fixed, and equipment worn. One man in each group acted as sentry. He usually sat on a bag full of earth, placed on the firestep, and by means of a periscope, watched for any movement of the enemy. In the wall of the trench little excavations held boxes of reserve ammunition and hand-bombs of various sorts.

The trenches having been commenced only a few weeks earlier, were in a very incomplete state and required much labour and development. Especially was this so in connection with the main communication trenches. Support trenches had also to be constructed and excavations made to establish a direct covered way to the Light Horse, on the southern face of the Rhododendron Spur. These works were undertaken by men from the supports and Battalion reserve. Many hard, long, weary hours were put in with the pick and shovel and the sandbag—which last was the only means of carrying away the spoil.

The defence at first was without any properly arranged plan for support from the artillery or flanking units. Before the brigade left the sector, however, the New Zealand Field Artillery Brigade, a British 6-inch Howitzer Battery, and a 4.7-inch Battery, all had their lines laid down for fire to cover the front. An Indian Mountain Battery also lay in a nook in the Chailak Dere—ready for any emergency. In addition, no less than 31 machine guns—in front and on the flanks—could be brought to bear on the threatened point. To assist in the machine gun work, and advise on local conditions, the Battalion was fortunate in having attached to it for a time Captain

THE 28th: A RECORD OF WAR SERVICE, 1915-19.

Rose, a British Service officer of the Division, and that gallant soldier, Lieut Percy Black, D.C.M.,* 16th Battalion.

As part of the defence arrangements, telephone communication was maintained with brigade headquarters. The aerial wires were, however, much exposed to hostile artillery fire and frequently cut.

THE APEX.

The exterior viewed from the South side. Our trench was where the figure is standing. The nob shown at the right centre is the Pinnacle, and marks the enemy trench. The horizon between was No-man's Land. In the background are the trenches on the southern shoulder of Chunuk Bair.

Official Photo. No. G. 1909.   *Copyright by Australian War Museum.*

To repair them Lieut. Scouler and his linemen, under Corporal Curran, made many journeys across the exposed portion of the slopes of the ravines. Flag signalling was unnecessary, but a lamp was mounted and sighted so that in case of a sudden attack after dark support could be immediately summoned.

---

* Afterwards Major P. Black, D.S.O., D.C.M., C. de G. Killed at Bullecourt, 11th April, 1917.

Beyond the actual trenches there was little cover for the garrison. A few excavations in the earth—designated "dugouts"—roofed with waterproof sheets, afforded moderate protection against the weather, but none against shrapnel, splinter, or bomb. The C.O. was the possessor of quarters boasting a covering of two sheets of corrugated iron which had a thin layer of earth on top. This, however, demonstrated its degree of usefulness by falling in upon its occupant. Later on excavations were made in the walls of the communication trenches—each to afford a "comfortable" sleeping place for two or more men.

To assist the newcomers it had been arranged to leave in the trenches a few officers and men of the New Zealanders. Major W. W. Alderman was attached as Staff Officer to the Commanding Officer. A N.Z. Field Company of Engineers had charge of the works in the area, and for the first week the N.Z. Infantry manned the machine guns. The help thus rendered was invaluable to the inexperienced, and a strong feeling of mutual regard sprang up between the members of the two Dominions. The majority of the New Zealanders thus remaining were Maoris—a body of men of fine physique, who had demonstrated their capacity to endure and also proved their worth as keen and sterling fighters. The Maoris had their own chaplain and medical officer. The latter (Dr. M. P. Buck) later commanded the N.Z. Pioneer Battalion.

The attitude of the opposing armies at this time was not altogether passive. A war of attrition was carried on continuously. This took the form of daily bombardments by the artillery of positions and areas behind the trenches; also the raking of parapets of opposing trenches, and No Man's Land, by machine gun fire at night. Sniping with the rifle had become a fine art, and authenticated cases, wherein a Turk had been knocked over, were mentioned in Orders. One Light Horseman, it was recorded in Corps Orders, had over 200 of the enemy to his credit. This sniping was done from carefully concealed positions (possies), from steel loopholes built into the parapet, or by means of the periscope rifle which latter enabled the user to fire over the sandbags without any exposure of his own body.

Sniping with field guns was also indulged in. In this the enemy had the advantage by reason of being on higher ground and able to overlook most of the Australian sector. Working parties, parties in movement, and individuals who came under observation, were usually treated to a dose of shrapnel fired with excellent aim and timing from 77 millimeter guns of high velocity. The projectile from this gun was usually designated a "whizz-bang" on account of the short space of time which elapsed between the first sound of its approach and that of the explosion of the shell. By some grim humourist it was said that if one could hear the shell coming there was no danger to be feared, but if, on the other hand, the sound was not audible, then there was no need to worry. The burial parties would do all that was necessary.

In fighting between trench and trench, considerable use was made, besides the rifle, of bombs or grenades. These were of varied types, with either concussion or missile effect, and some were thrown by hand whilst others were propelled from mortars or catapults. The Mills grenade had just made its appearance, and was regarded as a special reserve of power in case of an enemy attack. The numbers of these available were small but other types were more plentiful and included the jam tin, cricket ball, time and friction, match head, and hair brush. Some were ignited by mechanical action and others by match or portfire. Portfires were made by wrapping a piece of khaki drill tightly around a thin strip of pine wood. One of these when once lit would burn for hours.

Of Trench Mortars the Apex position possessed two—one a 3.7 inch and the other, smaller, a Garland Howitzer. These threw light bombs a short distance. Their effect was quite local and, except in case of a direct hit on a person, hardly more than moral. One of these mortars was located on either flank of the position. Private F. Congdon was placed in charge of that on the right and Private J. B. Deering that on the left. These soldiers soon learned to use their weapons so effectively that the Turk was discovered, early one morning, to have placed a protective wire-netting screen in front of and over the Blockhouse.

Later on the Battalion made the acquaintance of the Catapult. This machine resembled a large "shanghai" fixed to timber, one end of which rested on the parapet whilst the other—in the trench—was packed in a manner to give the required elevation. A cricket ball or jam tin bomb was placed in the pouch and the rubbers were then strained by means of a crank handle winding up a wire attached to the pouch with a trip hook. When the required tension was obtained one man lit the fuse and retired to cover. The other, the expert, allowing the fuse to burn for a certain time—to suit the range, pulled the string which released the trip. If all went well the bomb sailed over towards the Turk. Sometimes, however, the trip would fail, or the rubbers foul. Then the bomb would make a very short flight and might not even clear the home trench. In consequence of these possibilities, the local area was never overcrowded with inquisitive people and the experts became expert also at taking cover.

In some parts of the line bombing was carried on from "bombing bays." These bays were small earthworks constructed, usually, in

AT THE APEX.
Using the Periscope Rifle.
Photo. lent by Mrs. H. Simm.

"THE FARM."
Taken from No. 4 Post at the Apex.
Photo. lent by Mrs. H. Simm.

advance but connected with the main trench. Two men were placed in occupation of each. One man was an experienced thrower and the other, as the Turk had the unpleasant habit of retaliating, held a half-filled sandbag which he dropped upon any enemy bomb which happened to land within the bay. With low power grenades this method was effective but failed when applied to such as were invented by Mills.

Two other types of weapons may be mentioned here. One used by us and the other by the enemy. The first was a Japanese mortar which fired a 50lb. bomb having a good range and a large bursting charge. This had been used by our ally during the Russo-Japanese War. The Battalion made its acquaintance when the move to Russell's Top took place, in December, but unfortunately the ammunition was too scarce to permit of any lasting benefit being derived, although the few rounds that were fired proved their destructive effect on the opposing trenches. The Turkish weapon was known as the "broomstick bomb" and was also propelled from a mortar. It consisted of a 4-inch cartridge case filled with a high explosive and also containing metal such as boiler punchings, nails, etc. (in one case gramophone needles were discovered), and provided with a percussion cap. It was fitted to a stick about two inches thick and five feet long. Its descent into our lines or support area was almost vertical—hence no cover then available was proof against it. Its effect was very destructive and its toll of life heavy. A sentry usually watched for and gave warning of the approach of one of these missiles, and the scene which followed his stentorian "Look out!" was somewhat animated. Hairbreadth escapes from destruction were numerous. Two of these will bear relation.

A batman, preparing an evening meal, was interrupted by the arrival of a bomb which had glanced off some obstacle and now came to a halt across the cooking fire. The batman hurriedly evacuated his position but, fortunately, the uninvited guest did not explode and was carefully removed out of harm's way by the adjutant. The very next morning a second missile came to rest on the waterproof sheet furnishing cover for this same man. This was more than he could bear— "it was over the odds"—and he complained. Some difficulty was experienced in restoring to him the correct viewpoint in regard to such occurrences.

The second incident was an experience of Lieut. G. A. F. Smith, who, whilst sitting in a newly constructed "safe" dugout, and enjoying a meal, was startled by a sudden clatter and almost blinded by an upheaval of earth and dust. Clearing his eyes he discovered the ruined remains of his repast, and, lying between his legs, an unexploded broomstick bomb that had glanced off the opposite wall of the communication trench and slid into the excavation

Somebody in the Battalion tacked a story on to this occurrence. It was said that this officer's batman, having observed the arrival of the bomb, approached the dugout and, peering cautiously into it, was greeted with "Hallo! What shall I do with this?" His reply was: "If you will wait until I get around the corner, you can do as you ——— well like with it."

CHAPTER VI.

GALLIPOLI

(continued).

The first night (12th-13th Sept.) in the trenches was not without serious mishap. Lieut. F. E. Jensen, who had seen service in the South African War, and was one of the most promising of the junior officers, was shot through the face when standing on the firestep instructing one of his platoon. He died a few hours later.

The hours of darkness were punctuated by short bursts of machine gun fire and occasional rifle shots at movement, or suspected movement, on the other side. Now and then one of our guns would send a shell over towards the Turks. Subsequent experience showed that at night time the enemy rarely replied to these, as he feared that the flashes from his artillery would disclose his positions and thus afford an opportunity to the watching Navy with its heavier weapons.

Every soldier in the front trenches was alert. Post commanders moved about supervising, and the attached New Zealanders imparted useful information in regard to trench warfare methods, such as how to outwit the wily Turk; the essential discipline; and precautions to ensure safety to the individual. Opportunity of gaining an acquaintance with No-Man's Land was afforded through the necessity of examining and repairing the protective wire entanglements, which were thrown out in front and consisted of a few strands of barbed wire and French wire very imperfectly secured. Now and then senior officers passed down the forward trench intent on seeing that the general plan of defence was being adhered to.

Dawn brought increased activity. At that hour—the then accepted hour for an attack—every man in the Battalion was awake and stood at his post fully armed and equipped. This state of readiness was referred to in "orders" as the "Stand To," and was observed morning and evening. Thus the soldier remained until some 30 minutes later, when the order "Stand Down" was passed along. On such occasions the absence of fuss and noise in movement, it is generally agreed, is an indication that a unit is well disciplined. One of our battalions momentarily went astray in this respect, and its men in the front trenches, early one morning, were treated to an unexpected touch of humour on the part of the enemy, from whose locality a voice, in more or less perfect English, was heard calling "Stand to, —th Baitalion!"

To the 28th the "Stand Down" brought some relaxation, both mental and physical, as the rising of the sun restored sight to the sentries and imparted increased confidence to the whole. Light revealed rather a marked change in the appearance of individuals.

IN THE FRONT LINE AT THE APEX.
Photo. lent by Mr. A. J. Shipway.

The chill of the night air had impelled many to put on their greatcoats. Some had even donned their Balaclava caps, which, showing only the eyes, nose, and mouth of the wearer, and surmounted by a hat or cap, gave a grotesque effect. Clothing smeared with earth, eyes bloodshot for want of sleep, and scrubby chins disclosed the need and benefit of, amongst other things, a wash. Water for this was, however, not available except in small quantities, and the man was lucky who secured one that day. The next best thing was a meal, and this consisted of army biscuit and tinned meat (bully beef) washed down by a small quantity of tea, which the Quartermaster had sent up hot but which reached those who needed it in a lukewarm condition.

Following that was the cleaning up of the trenches. This consisted of collecting all scraps of food, empty tins, bits of paper, etc., and removing from the floor the debris that had fallen from the walls, or parapet and parados, during the previous 24 hours. Then came attention to rifle and bayonet, which were to be kept free of obstruction and rust. The reserve ammunition and bombs, some of which were open to the air, had also to be wiped free of verdigris and dust so that they would not jam or clog when required for use. This daily cleaning up had become almost a fetish in the army, but it undoubtedly engendered habits of orderliness—thereby

EXCAVATING A "BIVVY" IN THE SUPPORT TRENCHES. THE APEX.
Photo. lent by Mrs. H. Simm.

promoting efficiency, and also had a material effect on the health of the individual by keeping down the flies, which would swarm around any tins or other receptacles which had contained food, or any of the food itself.

This day brought the Battalion for the first time under direct artillery fire. It was the enemy's custom to indulge in a "hate" morning and afternoon. This would take the form of a bombardment of from 20 to 80 rounds of 77 millimeter shrapnel and high explosive shells. Large calibre guns were not directed on the Apex whilst the Battalion was stationed there. With the high explosive projectiles was used a percussion fuse, and these were intended more for the demolition of works than man killing. Actually they did little damage and, except on one occasion when a direct hit was secured in a machine gun emplacement, no one was injured. Shrapnel was used in a different manner, and was far more dangerous. The fuse was for time, and the range and fuse were so harmonised that the shell burst in the air, short of and above the target, thus allowing the bullets it contained to sweep forward and downward, spreading out fan-like as they progressed. Many of the small missiles thus entered the trenches, but by keeping close to the forward wall of the excavations immunity from damage was generally secured to the individual. Occasionally the Turk threw in a few rounds from a mountain gun which he had secreted somewhere on the slope of Sari Bair. These simply whizzed through the air and buried themselves in the earth without doing any damage to either man or trench.

The 28th stood its baptism of fire well, and was more curious than alarmed at the noise, smoke, and earth upheavals caused by the enemy's action. Some of the men early disclosed the possession of the "souvenir" habit by collecting specimens of the shrapnel pellets. Unfortunately that portion of the Battalion in reserve, not being under any cover except a slight fold in the ground, sustained a few casualties by wounds.

Early in the morning the Brigadier paid a visit to the lines and was indefatigable in his zeal for the safety of the position and the welfare of his command. Throughout the short period of his stay on the Peninsula his characteristics in this respect were most marked and, for a man of his advanced years, the wonders he achieved in hill climbing, and the risks he ran from enemy snipers, were a subject of frequent comment.

About noon the Battalion made the acquaintance of Sir William Birdwood, who went through the trenches accompanied by Sir Alexander Godley and a staff officer. His attractive personality, unassuming manner, and his kindly and tactful inquiries, instantly earned the regard of the newcomers. A particular incident which occurred that morning may serve to illustrate his general attitude. He came to a Western Australian and a New Zealander standing together. To the W.A. man he said, "Are you 28th?" Receiving an affirmative answer the General placed a hand on the man's shoulder and remarked, "We are very glad you've come. You know what your comrades of the 1st Division have done, and we know that, when the time arrives, you will do the same." Then placing the other hand on the Maori's shoulder, he concluded, "And you can show him how to do it, can't you?"

Of a different disposition, the Divisional Commander contented himself, during his first visit, with merely observing and asking a question here and there. His subsequent visits were frequent and seldom welcomed by the rank and file, who found him awe-inspiring and hypercritical. He was, however, known to unbend and show generous appreciation of honest effort and good work. On rare occasions he unexpectedly revealed the possession of a sense of humour.

Other visitors came on this first day. From the 10th Light Horse, which was located near the Sazli Beit Dere; from the 11th and 12th Battalions, holding the line far down on the right; from the 16th Battalion, awaiting embarkation for Lemnos Island, where they were to have a well-earned rest; and from the 8th Battery, also with the 1st Division. These came to see relatives and friends in order to exchange news of home and of pals who had gone under or been wounded. With the advent of the 2nd Division began a system of transfer of individuals of one unit to another whereby an elder brother, say, in the 11th Battalion, could apply for permission for a younger brother who had arrived in the, say, 28th Battalion, to join him. If the younger brother was agreeable to the change, approval for the transfer was seldom withheld.

When the line was "quiet" the men were enabled to examine the enemy's positions with the aid of periscopes. No signs of movement could be discerned, but the long lines of trenches rising tier above tier on the opposite hillsides indicated how difficult would be the task should a further advance be ordered. The observers on Nos. 2 and 3 Posts mostly concentrated their attention on the ground in the vicinity of the Pinnacle. From there a sniper was taking shots at any object which appeared above our parapets or at a loophole. Very rapid and accurate as he was, it was soon found that a certain amount of skill was required to camouflage and look through a periscope without having one's eyes destroyed with broken glass. A small Union Jack, mounted on a stick less than half an inch in diameter, was cut down at the sniper's first attempt.

In No-man's Land, in front of the two posts mentioned, could be seen the remains of a trench dug by the New Zealanders in their August advance. This they had been compelled to abandon together with their dead comrades who lay about, still unburied, rapidly decomposing in the sun which yet retained the strength of summer.

Picks, shovels, rifles and equipment also littered the landscape. Within our own area there were likewise grim reminders of the fight. Here and there a limb protruded through the wall of a newly cut trench, whilst in other places a piece of biscuit box, or a rifle stuck into the earth muzzle down, both bearing a name written in indelible pencil, indicated the last resting place of some fallen comrade.

From No. 4 Post the observer could look down on "The Farm." This was a spot on the side of Chunuk Bair at the head of the Aghyl Dere, and had formerly been cultivated. Now the Turk had commenced to entrench across it, and was apparently working on it under cover of darkness. Beyond, to the north, running up over the ridge (Kiretch Tepe Sirt) which bordered the Gulf of Xeros, could be seen the whole of the line held by the 54th Division and IX. Corps. The principal features were Hill 60 (Kaijak Aghala). W Hills (Ismail Oglu Tepe), the village of Anafarta Sagir, Chocolate Hill, the salt lake near Suvla Bay, and the bay itself with the hill Lala Baba on its southern side.

The support of the Royal Navy was further manifested by the presence in the Bay, behind the IX. Corps, of a cruiser and some smaller craft. From one of these a sausage-shaped balloon occasionally ascended some few hundred feet and afforded observation of the enemy's rear lines. A glance down the ravine of the Chailak, between Bauchop's Hill and Table Top, revealed H.M.S. "Grafton," a second class cruiser, anchored about two miles from the shore, whose 9.2 and 6-inch guns supplied a powerful backing to the weak artillery of the Anzac Corps.

September 14th did not pass without loss. That morning witnessed the deaths of Sergt. F. W. Ball and two other members as the result of shrapnel fire. Later in the day another member succumbed to wounds. Snipers also levied their toll of those moving about where the reserve was situated. In consequence of this a move was made to a more sheltered quarter and the unsafe dugouts were evacuated. On the 16th there were two further fatal casualties.

During the next two days the men became more accustomed to their life and surroundings. Those in the front trench had by far the easier time. Those in support had to handle the pick and shovel in the works for the improvement of the position. Digging was hard. The conglomerate-like composition of the soil resisted the shovels and turned the points of the picks. Recourse was had to the Navy, who supplied a small forge for the sharpening of the latter. Thus to other noises was added that of the hammer on anvil. The reserves were utilised by the Brigade and Division for

VIEW FROM BABY 700.

Showing Sivla Bay, the Salt Lake, the Plain, and the distant hills bordering the Gulf of Xeros. The mouth of the Chailak Dere is opposite to the hulk on the beach.

Official Photo. No. G. 1898. *Copyright by Australian War Museum.*

works in rear of the position. The demands of the Engineers seemed never ending and were often in excess of the number of men available. This caused considerable confusion and irritation followed by requests from the Division for explanations as to labour not being forthcoming. These requests had usually to be met by lengthy and involved "returns" which very few people understood and which served no useful purpose except to temporarily alleviate the strain. As a rule the exasperating situation was restored next day. Nor was the necessity for the work at first apparent to the men. They thought they came to fight with the bullet and bayonet only. But enlightenment came and one experienced miner voiced it, after a solid week on excavating, when he said "I have just discovered I have been a blanky soldier all my life."

Long hours of hard work usually induce sound sleep at night, but with the platoons in support this happy condition was difficult to achieve. A few had "bivies" excavated in the walls of the trenches, but most men had only the floor of the trench upon which to lie. Here, clothed in their overcoats and wrapped in their single blankets, they slumbered—only to be rudely awakened now and then by the pressure on some part of their anatomy of the feet of a passenger to or from the front line. On dark nights careless senior officers when going their rounds were treated to loud and homely descriptions of themselves which in daylight and cold blood would scarcely even have been whispered to a comrade. In the front trench, where the garrison was relieved by the supports every 24 hours, sleep was, theoretically, not to be thought of. However, the normal man felt that at some time during the 24 hours it was good to close his tired eyes—if only for a few minutes. After all, a seat on a sandbag, and a good solid wall against which to rest one's back, did give a little comfort. The officer in making his tour of inspection would ask a question here and there and occasionally mount the firestep and talk with the sentry. Usually the noise of his approach was sufficient to ensure alertness on his entering a bay that was manned, but, now and then, stertorous breathing and the attitude of the sentry, as revealed by his silhouette against the light of the moon or stars, would indicate that the flesh had momentarily vanquished the spirit. The touch of a hand was sufficient to restore wakefulness. Apropos of this, a senior officer, rather irritable at the moment, once touched an apparently sleeping sentry on the knee, at the same time asking the question "Look here! Are you asleep?" He was rather confounded at receiving the undoubtedly truthful answer "No, Sir."

At 4.30 p.m. on the 18th September, the Turks suddenly commenced a heavy bombardment of the position and back areas. Shrapnel and high explosive were supported by rifle and machine-gun fire at a rapid rate. A glance in the direction of Suvla revealed a sight resembling an exhibition of gigantic chrysanthemums—the white smoke of bursting shrapnel, before dissipating, closely resembling that flower in form. Here and there columns of black smoke and earth would suddenly spring into existence indicating the arrival and explosion of large calibre shells. Everything pointed to some important move on the part of the enemy. Orders were instantly given for the garrison to "stand to" and the reserves to move up in close support. These orders were obeyed with alacrity. All ranks were eager and the answer to the oft-repeated question, "What are we here for?" seemed to be at hand. Rifles and revolvers were loaded, grenades served out, and the New Zealanders manned their machine guns. Within a minute or two of the opening of the bombardment our own guns commenced to reply on the enemy trenches. For a time the noise was deafening—a regular babel of sounds through which, in spite of the crashing of shells, could be distinguished the tapping of machine guns and the swishing of bullets in flight. However, the enemy stuck to cover. Whether or not he intended to make a demonstration only is not clear, but information received later from Suvla showed that a few officers had jumped on to the parapet and waved their swords in the apparent vain attempt to lead their men, who, whilst shouting loudly, were reluctant to leave the safety of the earthworks. In half an hour the firing died down, and normal conditions were resumed. The Battalion had suffered no casualties and had demonstrated its steadiness under sustained fire.

On Sunday, 19th September, a party consisting of one officer from each battalion of the Brigade made a tour of inspection of the Lone Pine position and the trenches running down to Chatham's Post on the extreme right. Additional parties went on the 21st and 23rd. These tours were arranged for instructional purposes, and were valuable aids to acquiring a knowledge of trench warfare methods. Further, they gave the participants many ideas on the use that could be made of ground and of the wonders performed by the troops who made the original landing on 25th April.

At dusk the Maoris assembled just below the Apex. Divine service was conducted by their own chaplain in the Maori tongue, but in accordance with the Church of England liturgy and with the orthodox intoning. The scene was an impressive one, and will not easily be forgotten by those who witnessed it. Other gatherings for worship were held when circumstances permitted, but, as a rule, senior officers objected to their men gathering in numbers when so few spots in the limited area behind the lines were not exposed to shell fire. Chaplains, therefore, had to visit the individual members of their flocks wherever they could find them. This meant much hill climbing and the running of considerable risk from gun and rifle fire. Many a padre acquired great merit by his unselfishness and disregard of danger. Should casualties have occurred during the day, small knots of people might be seen at night down near the beach, or on some other exposed slope, reverently interring a comrade who had fallen. Here the padres performed the last offices for the dead.

Early in the morning of the 20th occurred one of those incidents which have often been narrated but seldom authenticated. Private G. J. Owen, whilst standing on the firestep observing, felt a blow on the chest. On an examination of his clothing it was found that a bullet had penetrated his greatcoat and jacket, and also a wallet in his jacket pocket, and finally spent itself in the centre of a small Bible that he was in the habit of carrying with him. Owen was quite uninjured and has, since his return to Australia, published his own story.

This day the Pinnacle was heavily shelled by our 6-inch howitzers in an attempt to demolish the Blockhouse and a small redoubt behind it. Both works were looked upon as serious obstacles to possible future operations locally.

"C" Company having been in the line for seven days, was relieved by "B" Company and moved into a reserve position. The following evening "A" Company similarly relieved "D" Company.

On the 21st September two enemy shells accounted for five of the Western Australians. This day Sir Ian Hamilton visited the Brigade, but as the climb was steep, and the sun hot, he did not ascend to the Apex. In his "Gallipoli Diary" he thus records his impressions—"saw the new Australian Division—very fine fellows. Bullets were on the whistle and 'the boys' were as keen and happy as any real schoolboys. Memories of the Khyber, Chitral and Tirah can hardly yield samples of a country so tangled and broken. Where the Turks begin and we end is a puzzler, and if you do happen to take a wrong turning, it leads to Paradise. Met various Australian friends—a full blown Lord Mayor—many other leading citizens, both of Melbourne and Sydney."

The next day brought trouble for the Battalion, the enemy's shrapnel killing three and wounding 10 or 11. Sergt. J. Hodgson was also fatally shot through the chest by a bullet, which entered the trench through a crevice near a loophole. Most of these casualties were suffered by "D" Company in reserve, and as the whole of the upper part of the Dere now seemed to be searched by the Turkish fire, the reserve company was moved lower down to ground in the vicinity of that occupied by the 27th Battalion. During the first days, a good deal of this fire was attracted by the men, in disregard of repeated orders, foolishly exposing themselves on the open spaces. At that time they had little knowledge of distances, of the searching effect of shrapnel and machine gun fire, or of the powers of observation possessed by the enemy. Moving about in their blue cardigans—their khaki jackets being discarded when not in the trenches—they afforded an easily distinguishable mark for the hostile gunner. Later on wisdom, born of experience, preserved many lives or limbs. Before leaving Egypt, the Brigadier had said, in a manner that caused his audience some grim amusement, "No one doubts your bravery, but you should not take unnecessary risks. If you do, you may only get wounded and thus become a heavy expense to the Government."

About this period, the Corps Commander directed the commencement of tunnelling operations at the Apex. It was intended to drive under the enemy's works and, when the time was ripe, blow them and their occupants into the air. As the 28th had many miners in its ranks, it was asked to supply the labour which would be applied under the direction of the Engineers. Lance-Sergeant E. A. Arundel, who had been a mine manager on the Goldfields, was placed in charge of the party. The work was carried on for many weeks before the party was relieved. Eventually, a mine was blown here on the night of the final evacuation by the Australians.

The 22nd September also saw the return of Lieut. Davey's platoon from Canterbury Slope, it having been replaced by one from the 25th Battalion.

Next day the Battalion was interested in the arrival of the first specimen of the "broomstick" bomb. No casualties resulted. Some activity developed on the left of the IX. Corps front, where an artillery duel continued for some time. The warships in the Bay joined in but eventually the gunfire died down. Outbursts of firing would frequently occur at night in the neighbourhood of Hill 60 and beyond. These could be heard and witnessed from the Apex and it was generally understood that the British were endeavouring to improve their ground or positions by sapping forward. Occasionally a naval searchlight would illuminate the area. At other times flares, made of oakum soaked in petrol and secured to wooden contrivances, would be thrown out into No-Man's Land—there, for a time, to burn merrily. Pistol flares were then only just making their appearance and very few had been issued.

4.40 a.m. of the 24th September witnessed the Battalion in a state of expectancy. Brigade headquarters had sent warning that an attack might be expected. Beyond, however, several bombs falling harmlessly near the bivouacs nothing happened. At 8 o'clock that night a demonstration was made by the troops on the right. These consisted of the 1st and 2nd Australian Divisions. The 3rd Light Horse Brigade joined in and for half an hour a very brisk fire from guns, rifles, and machine guns was kept up. These demonstrations were made for the twofold object of harassing the enemy and compelling him to disclose his dispositions. They seldom achieved the latter.

After "C" and "D" Companies were relieved an attempt was made to gain further knowledge of No-Man's Land and the enemy's works and movements at night. Patrolling was the only means available and as the distance between the opposing trenches was, at this point, so small the undertaking was extremely hazardous and needed the exercise of great caution. Lieut. A. H. Davey took out the first patrol which, going out from No. 4 Post, crawled amongst the dead and *débris* towards the Pinnacle. It returned 30 or 40 minutes later without having been observed and without information of any special value. On its return journey it collected the identity discs from some of the unburied bodies. Subsequent patrols had little better luck. The enemy seemed, on his part, to be quite content to stick to his cover and to run no risk by appearing on the open ground. Our patrols, however, also did other work. They salvaged a considerable quantity of rifles, tools, and equipment. These articles were collected and sent down to the base on the beach. Turkish rifles were almost as valuable as our own, as the same pattern was in use by the Belgians, and any captured or recovered were intended for their use. A later Corps Order commented favourably on the work done by the 28th in this respect. As patrols could not move in any force without attracting unwelcome attention, three or four men, including an officer, were sufficient for the purpose in view. Rifles being inconvenient to carry when crawling, the party was usually armed only with revolvers and a couple of Mills grenades. Further patrolling was done each night down a long sap connecting the left of No. 4 Post with the 27th Battalion on Cheshire Ridge. Also from the right of No. 1 Post in order to keep in touch with the Light Horse on Rhododendron Spur pending the completion of the communication trench.

In such broken ground it was not impossible for a man to lose contact with the other members of a patrol. It is on record that one individual, having lost his way, was observed approaching our trench. Seeing a head and shoulders suddenly appear through the bushes in front of him, the sentry was about to fire, but, being restrained by an officer, challenged instead and exclaimed in a voice full of intent, "Speak! Who are you?" The stray, whose position between the two lines was not an enviable one, replied hurriedly, "Private William M——, of Subiaco, Western Australia." "Come in, you ruddy fool," rejoined the disappointed sentry. But M——'s luck was still out, for, in endeavouring to respond to the invitation, he got foul of the wire entanglements and crashed heavily to the ground. There he lay for some time until eventually he was dragged in by his comrades.

In country of the nature mentioned the most careful arrangements and fullest exchange of information between neighbouring units, when the sending out of patrols was contemplated, was of vital importance. Through the neglect of these measures collisions, resulting in casualties, occurred on two occasions between patrols and the men in the front line trenches.

On the 25th September Captain Montgomery's party rejoined from the Beach.

On this day, and on the 27th, the Turk showered quite a considerable number of the broomstick bombs into the position. A few casualties resulted. Our artillery were telephoned and retaliated with 6-inch howitzer and 18-pounder shells. The arrival and powerful burst of the former missiles were received with cheers by the harassed garrison, and the enemy soon desisted. There was a strong back blast from our heavier projectiles and a few men, some distance down the Dere, were struck by splinters. As there was some uncertainty as to the exact daily error of our guns, it was, on occasions, necessary to thin the front line garrisons in order to guard against a shell falling short. One man, engaged cleaning up the trench which led down to the 27th Battalion, was buried to the neck as a result of a naval shell landing a few feet behind him and driving in the wall of the excavation. Fortunately he was able to call out and was quickly released.

The 26th and 27th were days selected for inter-company reliefs. "C" and "D" Companies went back into the line.

As it was believed that the morale of the enemy had been lowered considerably by the heavy losses he had sustained, attempts were made to induce him to desert. One of the means adopted was propaganda literature—in Turkish and Arabic—which was attached to "dud" grenades and propelled into the enemy area. It is not known whether this method had any success, but the infantry sent along a story—told at the expense of another arm of the service— that one man did come in and surrendered himself to the commanding officer's cook, whom he had to awaken.

Enemy espionage was suspected and a native barber, who used to wander around the support and reserve areas, came under surveillance. He disappeared, and his ultimate fate is unknown, but rumour had it that the Light Horse had "given him a start over the parapet."

CHAPTER VII.

GALLIPOLI (continued).

Up to this time poison gas had been unknown in the Dardanelles campaign, although all ranks were supplied with a small respirator which covered the nose and mouth and was secured with tapes that tied behind the head. It was understood that the British had, in reserve, effective means of retaliation should the Turk resort to it. However, on the 28th September, the enemy, who had been rather aggressive all day with shrapnel, bomb, and rifle fire, in the afternoon loosed a broomstick bomb, which burst in the air above the Apex and emitted a whitish vapour. This vapour drifted down into the trenches and had a decided lachrymatory effect on those with whom it came into contact. It passed off in a few minutes, and no further bombs of that nature arrived. The incident was important enough to warrant a report being made to Divisional Headquarters. As a similar occurrence at Hill 60 was noted within a few days, some attention was given to anti-gas measures. The result was the issue of certain instructions and a new respirator (P.H.) which, made of cloth and provided with goggles, was worn over the head and gave the wearer the appearance of either a partly equipped diver or member of the Spanish Inquisition. This article was to be carried on the person at all times.

The 29th September saw more activity on the part of the enemy, whose shrapnel fire seemed to increase in accuracy daily. Our own artillery, through lack of commanding positions for observation purposes, and also through scarcity of ammunition, was not able to reply effectively. At times a message would come from Brigade or Division to say that such and such a battery intended, at a given hour, to fire on such and such a target. The necessary preparations were made but the infantryman was inclined to be derisive when, at the appointed hour, the gunners would loose a few rounds only and then remain silent until the next day. Occasionally the infantry selected targets for the artillery—such as enemy working parties, enemy troops on the move, or occupied gun pits. One afternoon a platoon of the enemy was reported near the road leading into Anafarta Sagir. The gunners were telephoned, but their longer stay on the Peninsula had given them a better local knowledge, and they were able to point out that the target was the tombstones and shadows of a small cemetery.

It was the practice of the Brigadier to make a daily tour of the front line. The Divisional Commander came once or twice a week, and General Birdwood—sometimes accompanied by Brig.-General C. B. B. White—paid occasional visits. At times Brig.-

MAJOR J. A. CAMPBELL WILSON.
Commander of "A" Company.

General H. G. Chauvel, who commanded the 1st Light Horse Brigade, acted for the G.O.C., the N.Z. and A Division. This day Sir Alexander Godley especially inspected the improvements that had been made to the position and expressed his approval with the work done. The cutting of new trenches, the deepening and widening of the old ones, and the repair and adjustment of the parapets and parados, had entailed much hard work. Here and there, where it was possible for the enemy to fire into the trench with rifle or machine gun, overhead traverses had been constructed. These consisted of filled sandbags supported—for want of timber—

on old rifles or tools, the ends of which rested on the two sides of the excavation. The main communication trench had also received attention, and it was now possible to move up the Dere without forsaking cover.

CAPTAIN J. GETTINGBY.
The Quartermaster.

As has already been mentioned, the General's visits did not meet the popular taste. However, on one occasion he created some amusement when he pointed out, from No. 4 Post, the distant village of Anafarta Sagir. To an officer, who had once been Lord Mayor of Melbourne, he said—"That, when the advance is made, will be one of our objectives and, if the 7th Brigade captures it, you will have the opportunity of becoming the first Lord Mayor of Anafarta." His idea of duty was exemplified in his reply to the soldier in charge of a trench mortar which was situated in a bay adjacent to a communication trench. The dialogue was as follows:—

> General: "What would you do if an enemy bomb landed in this bay?"
> Soldier: (indicating C.T.): "I would get for my life round that corner."
> General: "You would do nothing of the kind! You would stay here and send two bombs back."

To a young officer, to whom he had pointed out certain things to be done, and who had replied "I will do my best," he said petulantly "Don't do your best, do *it*." The majority of the members of his staff were mortally afraid of him and frequently "let the infantry down," when in the presence of the General, by suddenly reversing a previously expressed opinion on some tactical arrangement or in connection with the works.

The last day of the month was marked during the evening by the arrival of a fog, which seemed to come over Sari Bair from the Asiatic side. It poured down into the valleys—for a time quite obscuring the country to the west and north. The enemy became very restless and shortly opened a heavy rifle and machine fire somewhere to our right. This, combined with a fire which suddenly sprang up in front of the Apex, gave occasion for extra watchfulness, and the reserve companies were ordered to be in readiness to move. By 9 p.m. the fog had cleared and all was quiet again. The fire was believed to have originated through a bullet striking the ammunition in the equipment of one of those who still lay out in front of the trenches. Sometimes the clothing would catch fire and then the body, which for nearly two months had been lying out in the open, would burn for hours. Once an exploding shell blew a corpse right into the front trench. Then it had to be taken away and buried as decently as circumstances would permit.

On the 1st October, during the early morning, a member of the N.Z. Engineers was killed whilst at work on the wire entanglements.

The usual amount of shelling occurred on this and the following two days. On the third the whole of the N.Z. *personnel* was withdrawn and moved off for a rest and refit at Lemnos Island. The Battalion was sorry to part company with those who had been of such great assistance to them and with whom many friendships had been formed.

A broomstick bomb during this morning provided an example of the scriptural warning that "the one shall be taken and the other left." Many of these bombs landed near the junction of three communication trenches. A notice had been put up: "Do not loiter here." Despite this the Pioneer Sergeant and two other men selected the spot for a rest and were sitting down—the Sergeant between the other two. A bomb was seen to rise from the opposite trenches. Unfortunately the sentry's warning was of little avail, the missile descending and exploding just in front of the reclining trio. From the cloud of black smoke emerged the Sergeant quite uninjured. His two companions were not so fortunate.

The fourth day of the month was one of alarms. At 9 a.m. "Jacko"—as the Turk was called—suddenly opened a heavy fire with all weapons. This was continued for some time and preparations were made to receive an attack. Nothing eventuated at the time, and after a while normal conditions were resumed. Late in the day Brigade Headquarters reported a considerable body of the enemy moving south from Anafarta, and ordered a state of readiness. The reserves stood by all night, but again the enemy failed to show himself and the tired troops returned to the bivouacs after daylight on the 5th.

Companies continued to relieve each other every six or seven days, but on the 4th October it was decided to relieve the whole Battalion. One company of the 25th Battalion arrived this day and took over from "B" Company, which proceeded to the lower portion of the Cheshire Ridge. On the following day the relief was completed. However, the Machine Gun Section, a mining party of 20 men, a trench mortar party, and a certain nucleus for each post, were left in the line to carry on the works and assist the Queenslanders. A platoon of "C" Company, under Lieut. R. C. Phillips, was sent to Canterbury Slope, and Major Welch's company was directed to remain in its old position as brigade reserve.

The 24 days in the crowded narrow limits of the Apex had considerably reduced the strength of the Battalion. By the end of September, 13 had been killed, 9 died of wounds, 46 were wounded, and 35 evacuated sick. The dead had been buried in the little cemeteries which had been arranged on one side of the Chailak Dere or down near the sea beach. For these the Battalion Pioneers made neat little wooden crosses which were placed to mark the head of each grave. The wounded were first attended to by the stretcher-bearers, who made use of the "first field dressing"—an antiseptic bandage which every man carried in a special pocket on the inside of the skirt of his jacket. More than one of the stretcher-bearers lost his life, or was sorely wounded, when bravely setting about this duty. The wounded were then taken to the Regimental Aid Post, where the Medical Officer patched them up temporarily. Afterwards they were conveyed in stretchers, or walked, to the nearest forward dressing station of the Army Medical Corps, and thence passed to a Casualty Clearing Station, where they remained until embarked on a hospital ship which took them to either Lemnos, Alexandria. or Malta.

As sickness accounted for more than one-third of the casualties in this short space of time, it may be as well to touch on the factors which affected the health of the individual. The climate in September, and early October, was similar to November weather in Western Australia. Thereafter it became cooler, with occasional falls of rain, up to the end of the eleventh month. This latter date marked the downward limit of the thermometer, and the subsequent weather was almost spring-like until the evacuation. On the whole the climate was not disagreeable to the man from the Antipodes, and even when he did find it a little too warm for comfort he met the situation by discarding his jacket and shirt and moving about with a sleeveless undervest as the sole covering for the upper part of his body. Occasionally he was seen garbed only in hat, shorts, and boots.

Another reason for being rid of every unnecessary garment was the prevalence of vermin. Whence they came nobody knew; but within a few days of landing on the soil very few men had escaped their attention. No effective arrangements for dealing with the pest were practicable, and the scarcity of water, with the consequent difficulty of securing changes of clothing, made the discomfort all the greater. A fortunate few argued amongst themselves as to whether the services to the Empire of a certain insect powder manufacturer had ever been adequately recognised. The soldier's relative who sent a cutting from the "West Australian's" agricultural column headed "The Vermin Board. Position of the Squatters" showed both an appreciation of the condition of the soldiery and the phase of strategy which the campaign had reached. And here may be retold the story of the exasperated man who interrupted a conversation by exclaiming, "The Kaiser! I wish he had *two* withered hands and my shirt!"

But the worst enemy was the fly. This fattened and multiplied on the filth which marked the ground the Turk had occupied, and on the unburied victims of the battle who tainted to nausea the atmosphere breathed by the garrisons in the elevated positions. Whatever precautions against them it was possible to take were adopted, but the scarcity of sheet iron and timber, and the restricted space, rendered these of little avail. The water supply was not materially affected, as most of this was Nile water, properly filtered, and brought to the shore in tank barges by the Navy. But the flies, in such numbers and with such enterprise as had never before been witnessed by the most travelled bushman, could not be kept out of the food. Diarrhœa and dysentery quickly affected the Australians. Little effective relief was at hand. Castor-oil alleviated it tem-

SERGEANT C. R. FIELD.
The First N.C.O. to gain a Commission in the Field. Afterwards Captain and Adjutant of 2nd Machine Gun Battalion. Twice mentioned in Despatches.

porarily, and this was consumed in such quantities that, one war correspondent has said, it threatened to become the Australians' national drink! Typhoid, and what was described as paratyphoid, fevers followed these maladies. Later came jaundice in epidemic form. In addition, rheumatism, pneumonia, and heavy colds, made their levy.

So great were the losses from these causes, that in August the Anzac Corps was evacuating 500 men a day. Early in October the IX. Corps' return showed over 700 for one day. Also, about this latter date, in spite of the presence of comparatively fresh troops, the N.Z. and A Division was being reduced at the rate of 60 per diem—not more than 15 per cent. of which were battle casualties.

Nor were the troops in a condition to successfully cope with the inroads of disease. "Worn out with hardship and incessant shell fire, from which even when in reserve they were never free," * ill-sustained by a monotonous diet of food—in part of doubtful quality, and always short of sleep and of supplies of water necessary to rest the body and keep it clean; their vitality and powers

REGIMENTAL QUARTERMASTER-SERGEANT R. G. SEXTY.
Afterwards Captain and Transport Officer.   Mentioned in Despatches.

of resistance to disease were considerably reduced, and they fell an easy prey to the virulent and prolific germs.

The army ration consisted of meat, bread, vegetables, and groceries. Meat included tinned and fresh meat and bacon. Bread

* Gallipoli Diary.

included ordinary bread, biscuits, and flour. The groceries were tea, sugar, jam (or cheese), pepper and salt, with such alternatives and additions as tinned milk, rice, prunes, curry powder, and raisins—which last were rarely available. The 28th's experience was that, when supplies were available and the weather permitted of them being landed, Argentine chilled beef and baker's bread left little room for complaint. However, the two factors mentioned did not always coincide and the Battalion, for days on end, had to be content with substitutes. The tinned meat ("dog" or "bully beef") was also from Argentine, and had already been dealt with for "extract" besides being extremely salt in flavour. The only way to make it palatable was to fry it up with bacon fat and chopped onions, or boil it again and add rice and curry powder when procurable. Nevinson [*] says that when the Anzac men threw over tins of meat to the Turks in exchange for packets of cigarettes it was a cheap gift, and the enemy returned the messages, "Bully beef non, envoyez milk." Now and again one came across a treasure in the form of a stray tin of a Canadian brand, or of "Maconochie" (a very substantial and nourishing stew), but looked in vain for the well-known Australian and New Zealand products.

The bacon, mostly very fat, was known as "lance-corporal bacon," i.e., with only one thin streak of lean running through it. This was issued ad nauseam. One man expressed his feelings when he said that he would never be able to look a pig in the face again.

There are no biscuits like the army issue. To those whose dentition was not perfect the masticating of them was tedious and painful. Some men made graters out of biscuit tin lids and grated the article to a powder, afterwards making a kind of porridge with it. Others discarded them as food and carved them into frames for photographs, or cigarette pictures, or contrived other mementos of a disagreeable period. Fresh vegetables were rarely seen. Now and again an enterprising individual would return from the beach with a cabbage, or a few potatoes, which he had purchased from one of the Navy or looted from some unsuspecting person who had them in charge. So far as can be remembered, not one single issue of potatoes was made to the Battalion during the whole of its stay on the Peninsula. Onions, however, were plentiful and of first-rate quality. Other substitutes were preserved or desiccated vegetables, which were found quite unpalatable and quickly refused by the Quartermaster.

Of the groceries, the issues of tea and sugar were insufficient for the occasion. The Australian tea-drinking habit (amongst others) had not then spread through the army. The Canadian

---

[*] H. W. Nevinson. The Dardanelles Campaign.

THE 28th: A RECORD OF WAR SERVICE, 1915-19.

cheese was excellent, but the jam lacked in all three essentials—quantity, quality, and variety. Bairnsfather has placed on record the soldier's feeling in this regard.

Certain other articles of importance were issued weekly. These included lime juice, rum, and tobacco. Rum was a new experience to many, but its value as a stimulant for tired troops was soon appreciated—even by the teetotallers. The virtues of rum and condensed milk were extolled. The precious liquid was contained in earthenware jars bearing on the outside the letters "S.R.D." The popular interpretation of this legend was "Seldom Reaches Destination," from the belief that, small as the authorised issue was, it was either reduced in quantity, withheld, or weakened with water by those through whose hands it passed between the supply depôt and the people for whom it was intended. Instances were not lacking which gave foundation for this belief, and an incident is well remembered in which a member of one formation regaled himself for two nights on his company's share and finished up the carouse by giving the "alarm." He left for Australia shortly afterwards. The Battalion made the acquaintance of tobacco and cigarettes of many brands and as many qualities. In some cases the name on the package was the only indication of its supposed contents. Some of the issues were at the cost of the Government and others as a result of gifts by soldiers' aid societies in Australia and England.

It has already been said that water was scarce. A few wells existed, but were quite unequal to the demands made upon them. It was therefore necessary to carry the water for some distance. Two-gallon petrol tins were used for this purpose by special fatigue parties. Larger quantities were carried in "fantassies"—10-gallon tanks borne in pairs on mules—and delivered to the Quartermaster, who was responsible for the distribution of all supplies and stores. Not always was it possible to secure sufficient for ablution purposes, and at one time—during November—the issue was restricted to quarter gallon per diem per man for all purposes. At the Apex, whilst water was scarce, small parties from the reserve companies were taken in turn to the beach and allowed to bathe. A certain amount of risk was attached to this proceeding, as the enemy shelled the locality whenever a target offered. Fortunately the parties escaped without casualty.

The cooking of food was first carried on by individuals. The mess tin could be used as either saucepan or kettle, and its lid as a frying pan or drinking vessel. With the aid of the entrenching implement, which each man carried, a little excavation would be made in some convenient place and a fire built of any available fuel. As a support for the tin when laid on the embers any number of stones was available. On some of these heat had a peculiar effect, and the unwary one was sometimes startled by a loud report and the sight of his meal being hoist in the air. Usually two or more men combined in the cooking process, but the preparation of food by the individual was found to be wasteful and injurious to health in that it attracted many flies and lacked thoroughness. The company system was therefore reverted to, and the dixies brought into use in kitchens constructed outside the trenches. The dixies were then taken forward and the meal served out in equal shares according to the numbers to be provided for. The change at first was not popular, but its beneficial effects became apparent later, and the system was not again departed from except for very brief periods when extraordinary conditions existed.

Fuel was by no means plentiful, and anything at all that would burn was carefully collected. Under cover of darkness individuals would forage on the exposed slopes and return with arms full of twigs and brushwood. In the back areas fatigue parties were at work daily collecting firewood which was brought to a depôt for issue to units. These parties worked under brigade orders and a number of 28th men were, on one occasion, sent up an exposed slope accompanied by a white donkey. The animal, so easily distinguishable against the background of dark verdure, soon attracted the enemy's artillery fire and some casualties resulted. The Regimental Medical Officer and two or three stretcher-bearers very gallantly ascended the hill and attended the wounded despite the continuance of the Turkish shrapnel.

Supply and transport on the Peninsula was no easy problem. Supplies in bulk were landed on the beach from barges when the weather permitted. There, near the two piers, a reserve of at least seven days was stored and supply staffs lived between walls constructed of boxes of biscuit and tinned meat. These walls were lined with sides of bacon resting on a plinth of filled rum jars and certain medical comforts intended for the sick or wounded. In the neighbourhood huge piles of all manner of articles abounded, and sandwiched in between them one would occasionally discover a howitzer, which would come into action intermittently. From these depôts the Army Service Corps attached to Divisions drew what was required or available and transported it to their own areas. There it was again divided up, according to the actual number of men present with each battalion, and the Quartermasters took delivery.

The means of transport consisted of carts, mules, and donkeys. Few horses were kept at Anzac. The only ones the 28th saw belonged to the 6-inch howitzer battery, and were stabled up on a hillside the face of which had been cut away so as to afford safe cover. One other horse seen was used by a despatch rider who almost daily went somewhere towards the left of our line and as frequently was the target for snipers. The carts were two-wheeled, with mule draught, and could only be used at night, when they conveyed supplies to the 54th Division which lay at the northern end of the Anzac Corps areas. These carts had made a well defined track, and their passage was easily marked by the creaking and groaning sounds they gave forth. Yet they were seldom, if ever, shelled by the enemy. They were driven by Maltese or natives of India who, during the daylight hours, camped in some of the crevices in the cliffs near the shore. As carts could not ascend the ravines, mules were used for carriage to the forward positions. They were sure-footed and capable of carrying a substantial load. Shell-fire had not much effect on them, but occasionally they became fitful and, despite the lurid exhortations of their drivers, would discard their loads at most inconvenient places. They were awkward creatures to meet in a sap. One might attempt to pass them on the side where there appeared to be the more room, only to find that, when nearly through, the mule would lurch over and pin you to the wall of the trench with the corner of an ammunition box or water tank.

Each battalion had the use of a certain number of small-sized donkeys. A few men had to be detailed to look after these and drive them—being responsible to the Quartermaster, who was known, sometimes, as "the O.C. Dunks." The donkeys carried loads suitable to their strength and were found to be most useful animals in the areas near the front line. Sometimes they got shot. A story is told of one of the 28th drivers who was rather attached to his pair of animals. One day in the Dere a shell killed one of his donkeys and the concussion from the explosion knocked the other one over. With a little persuasion he got up again, but the driver, in explaining the loss, said that he had had one beast killed and that the other had *fainted*.

CHAPTER VIII.

GALLIPOLI (continued).

Lower Cheshire Ridge, the Battalion's new position, was in part a razor-edged feature which faced the steep north-west slope of Sari Bair. In between the two, and diagonally across the front, ran the Aghyl Dere which passed through the trench line at the 28th's northern boundary. Here a high breastwork had been constructed which carried a firestep and at the same time allowed room for the passage of water underneath. This breastwork, and the line for some distance beyond, was manned alternately by the 5th Norfolks and 10th Londons, both of whom belonged to the 162nd Brigade, 54th Division, and were Kitchener Army men. Both battalions were much reduced in strength and contained many men whom disease had rendered really unfit for work other than that of the lightest nature. However, they hung on with the Tommy's well known stoicism.

The 28th line was very varied. Commencing from the left of the 27th Battalion, it ran through a hilltop to a place where an L-shaped cutting had to be made to secure any footing at all. Thence about a dozen steps, cut in a face, took one to a lower level which ran along towards the Dere and terminated in a series of firing bays opening out from tunnels which had been excavated by the 4th Brigade and further improved by the 25th Battalion. Portions of three companies were detailed to hold the line, "B" Company being on the right and "A" Company junctioning with the British. Immediately behind the line was a deep hollow which sheltered the supports and provided space for the kitchens and headquarters of the Battalion. Little Table Top and Rose Hill formed the western side of this hollow, and across their summits had been constructed a reserve line with machine guns in position.

The nearest enemy trenches were some 600 yards distant. The intervening space was mostly covered with scrub, but in the breaks and on the bare patches could be seen the bodies of many of those who had taken part in the ill-fated attempt of Baldwin's Brigade to storm Chunuk Bair on the 10th August. Boxes, tins of biscuits, coils of wire, and various portions of equipment were scattered broadcast about the valley.

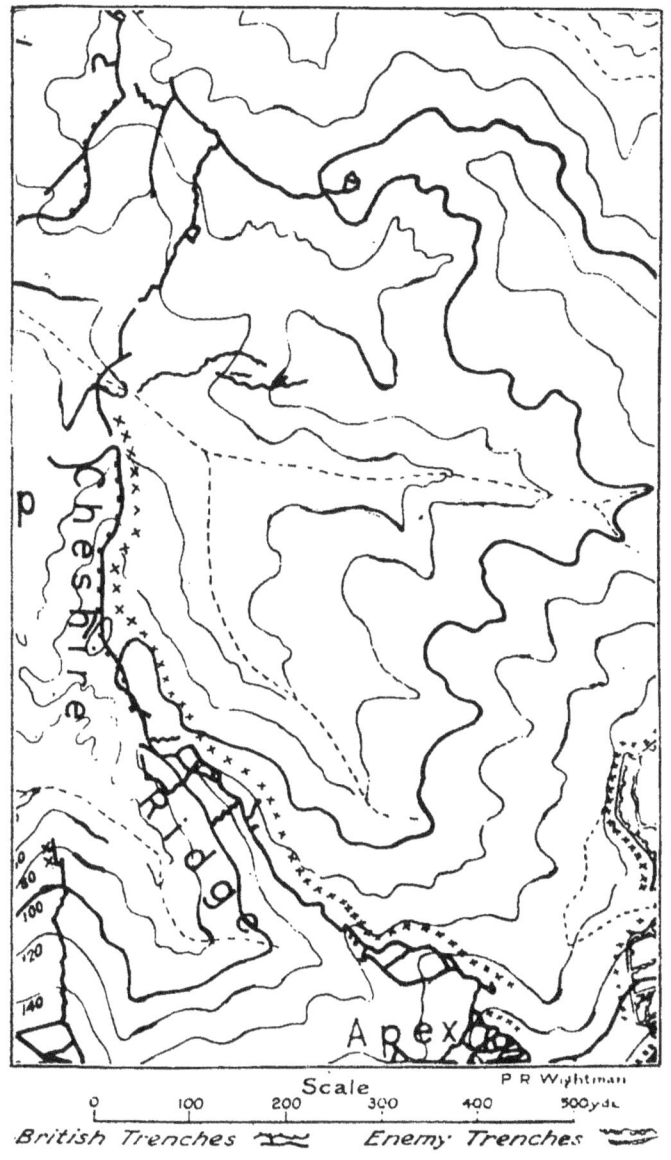

THE FRONT LINE ON CHESHIRE RIDGE.
Map by Australian War Museum.

Life at Lower Cheshire Ridge was peaceful as compared with that at the Apex. A daily dose of shrapnel was sent along from the direction of Abdel Rahman Bair, to the north-east, but this seldom did any harm. On the evening of the 7th October a machine gun fire demonstration was made by our divisions on either flank without any apparent effect. At 7 p.m. on the following day the wind rose and was soon followed by drenching rain which lasted most of the night. About an hour after it commenced the Turks opened a heavy rifle and machine gun fire against the Light Horse Brigade and Walker's Ridge. This continued for some time but there was no further development. Owing to the weather the Battalion spent a very miserable night.

About this period, a method of recording time that was novel to most of the Australians was brought into vogue by the adoption of the French system. This at first led to some little confusion, but was considered essential in order to ensure proper co-ordination in the efforts of the Allies. Later on, it came naturally to all. The difficulty of easily recognising the figures "0015" as representing 12.15 a.m., "1430" as 2.30 p.m., and "2245" as 10.45 p.m., may be quite understood.

Apart from holding this part of the line, the officers and men were principally engaged, during their stay here, in improving the accommodation for the supports and providing for their protection in the winter. A detachment of New Zealand Engineers was attached to the Battalion to advise. However, little progress could be made owing to the scarcity of timber and iron and the nature of the soil, which, in this quarter, was composed of the scourings of the hills and had no stability. Difficulty was also encountered with the plans of the Commanding Royal Engineer of the Division, which were frequently changed, in order to conform to the varying moods of the Divisional Commander. In consequence, much labour was expended, but little real progress made for some time. Defensive works included the deepening of the front line trench, which was carried down to a depth of ten feet—in some places—without any material increase in width. This was the policy of the day and was based on securing immunity from shrapnel fire. Had the enemy used heavy shells, with delayed action fuses, these same trenches would have proved veritable death traps for their garrisons. Near the junction of "C" and "A" Companies' sectors, two tunnels were driven in the direction of the enemy's lines. From the heads of these, it was intended to construct a lateral underground trench, which would join up with the forward works of the neighbouring battalion on the left. The trench was to be completed almost entirely underground, and then finally the crust of earth would be broken through in one night and the enemy at dawn would discover a finished work having a command of the whole of that portion of the Dere as well as the ravine running down from the north. The Battalion did not stay in this sector long enough to witness the completion of its labours and the work was afterwards carried on by the 4th Brigade.

The scarcity, which has been referred to, of timber and iron was exemplified in another manner when a change in garrisons took place. Units marching in and out of a position would take their precious bits of wood and sheet iron with them and their transport was personally supervised by an officer. This, in the case of a company or battalion being relieved, sometimes led to the partial dismantlement of works. As a result stringent orders on the subject were issued. These were not always regarded as they should have been. Once, during the gales, a barge laden with timber was wrecked, and her load distributed along the beach, at the foot of Chailak Dere. Within a few hours—whilst the Engineers were thinking of organising salvage parties—the whole of the spoils had disappeared into the valleys and up the slopes of the Light Horse and Infantry positions.

The prominence given to sniping has been referred to earlier. To counter the Turks' efforts in this direction, the Brigadier organised a body of men composed of expert rifle shots, chosen from each battalion. This was placed under the command of Captain H. B. Menz, of the 28th Battalion, who had Lieut. W. P. Devonshire, 27th Battalion, to assist him. These snipers were equipped with powerful telescopes and were disposed in carefully chosen positions in the line—or beyond or behind it. Their usefulness, aided as they were by other men from the companies, was soon demonstrated. In a few days not a Turk dare expose himself within 600 or 700 yards distance of our lines, and scarcely ever was a hostile rifle loosed during daylight hours. After dark, Jacko would take courage and pot in the direction of our trenches. The snipers were also of use to the English, who were being harassed on the other side of the Dere. The tactful offer of the loan of two or three Australians in a few days removed the cause of their trouble. The Turks occasionally resorted to ruses, but these were quickly negatived by the Australians, who showed themselves no mean masters of craft. Nearly across to the opposite side of the valley were revealed, by the telescope, the shoulders and black face of a dummy sharpshooter located behind a bush. Some distance up the valley, to the north, a piece of iron piping protruded from cover in imitation of a gun. Dummy loopholes abounded. On the slope of Chunuk Bair, a communication trench wound down. At a certain hour of the afternoon a man coming down this trench would, at one turn under observation, be preceded by his shadow. Our snipers watched for this shadow and made deadly practice at the substance. After a few days, the enemy ceased to move in that quarter whilst light lasted.

Captain Menz was also supplied with a Hotchkiss quick-firing gun which discharged a 3lb. solid shot. This was placed in a carefully chosen nook in one of the hollows and camouflaged with green bushes. In the charge of Corporal C. T. Ballingall, an ex-citizen force gunner, this weapon was a powerful and effective means of knocking out sniper posts whenever they were located.

THE CHAILAK DERE.
Looking towards the sea from Table Top. The razor-back leads to Old No. 3 Post.
Official photo. No. G. 1829. Copyright by Australian War Museum.

A system of patrolling the bed of the ravine, and of the lower slopes beyond, was carried out. Platoon commanders usually took charge of small parties of men which debouched from "A" or "C" Companies' lines and cautiously explored No-Man's Land. Competition in this work became keen at times. One young officer—small of stature—claimed to have pinned a white handkerchief on a tree close to the enemy's wire. Another officer—the reverse in figure— averred that he got through the wire and dropped his cigarette butt right on top of a sleeping enemy sentry. Daylight revealed the white patch on the tree, but nobody seemed anxious to investigate too closely the tale of the cigarette.

VIEW OF THE AGHYL DERE.
Looking North-West.   Cheshire Ridge position on the left.   In the foreground are reminders of the August fighting.
Official Photo. No. G. 2002.   Copyright by Australian War Museum.

About this time occurred one of the Mohammedan festivals. High authority considered that this fact might engender an offensive spirit in the opposing force. Patrols, therefore, were instructed to be especially vigilant. Nothing important was discovered. One patrol did report that it had heard some musical instrument being played in the enemy's area, the sound of voices, and the barking of a dog. The officer who compiled the daily intelligence report wrote: "sounds of jollification were heard issuing from the enemy trenches." This phrase seemed to tickle the official ear, and was repeated by all reporters, and appeared finally in Sir Ian Hamilton's summary.

Patrols also performed a good deal of salvage work and brought in a considerable quantity of material from between the opposing lines. Several identity discs were likewise collected and forwarded on for the information of the records section of the Army.

On the evening of the 11th October a welcome addition was made to the strength of the Battalion by the arrival of portion of the 2nd and 3rd Reinforcements under Captain E. A. Coleman and Lieut. A. M. Hope. These were distributed the following day amongst the four companies, and Captain Coleman took over command of "B" Company. As was the case with the later drafts, these new-comers proved themselves to be excellent fellows.

The death of Lieut. F. E. Jensen had created a vacancy in the commissioned ranks which was filled by the promotion of Sergeant C. R. Field—a trainee under the Australian Universal Military Service scheme. Casualties amongst the non-commissioned officers were replaced by the appointment and promotion of men who showed themselves possessed of the necessary qualifications. In a few instances promotion was declined by the individual. Various reasons were given for this step. Some individuals lacked ambition, others were reluctant to accept responsibility, and again others preferred to retain the close company of the friends of their section—promotion resulting in a mild form of aloofness and isolation, a condition which the exercise of authority rendered almost inevitable.

About this time the first Battalion Bombing Squad was formed. This was a result of some lessons from the campaign on the Western Front, where experienced bomb-throwers, properly organised, had proved of great value in offensive and defensive operations. This squad was placed under Lieut. N. W. Sundercombe and was trained in some old Turkish trenches, at the lower end of the Chailak Dere. The members showed such proficiency in their work that in the course of a few days only they were called upon to give a demonstration in method before the other squads of the Division. The members of the squad were Sergt. A. Brown, Corporals A. Gibbons and I. E. Dunkley, Privates J. Connor, S. J. Price, G. B. Brown, F. Congdon, W. G. Green, F. E. Dawkins, H. Thetford, F. Parker, H. Denton, F. Ball, A. Kelly, H. G. Haynes, D. McDonald, and D. W. Cunningham. Several of these bombers earned considerable distinction in the later campaigns in Belgium and France.

The 15th October marked a change in the command of the 7th Brigade. Colonel Burston's health had for some time past been far from robust, nevertheless he had stuck to his post with determination until ultimately compelled to give in. He was sent to a hospital on Lemnos Island, and Lieut-Colonel (Hon. Colonel) J. Paton, V.D., the C.O. of the 25th Battalion, was directed to assume command. Colonel Paton had been an infantry brigadier in New

South Wales, and had also taken a prominent part in the naval and military expedition to occupy German New Guinea. Sickness brought other changes in the brigade staff. Captain G. B. Rowan-Hamilton was appointed Brigade-Major. He had been adjutant of the 1st Black Watch and shared in the opening campaign in France and Belgium. A new Staff Captain was found in Lieut. S. S. Bond, 25th Battalion, who performed the duties until succeeded by Captain W. F. N. Bridges—a son of the original commander of the 1st Australian Division.

About the middle of the month the Battalion received its first supply of canteen stores. A small party had been sent to Imbros to buy "luxuries" and had returned with neither the quantity nor quality they sought. Nevertheless, their arrival in the Battalion area was signalised by the formation of a queue as for an early door at a theatre. Sweets, cake, and notepaper were in greatest demand, and after these, in popularity, came soap and handkerchiefs.

Sir Ian Hamilton had been striving for months to institute this system of canteens. He desired that the troops in the Eastern Mediterranean should be placed on the same footing as those in France. General Birdwood had written to him conveying the medical opinion that the sameness of the food was making the men sick. The rations were A1, but the men loathed the look of them after having had nothing else for months. "If we could only get this wretched canteen ship along, and if, when she comes she contains anything like condiments to let them buy freely from her, I believe it would make all the difference in the world. But the fact remains that at present we cannot count on anything like a big effort from the men who have been here all these months."* The first canteen ship did eventually arrive about the end of August, and then brought only £10,000 worth—amongst over 100,000 troops! The Commander-in-Chief sent it to Anzac. Later arrivals brought very little more and, finally, early in December, the supplies petered out altogether. Parties sent to Imbros foraged over the island, but soon exhausted even that source, which produced only fruit, eggs, Turkish delight, candles, and canned goods.

To pay for these extras the Australians had ample resources. Periodically the field cashier appeared on the Peninsula with English silver and notes. The adjutant drew from him, and company commanders paid their men in accordance with their requirements—within the credit which the Pay Book (always carried on the person) disclosed they possessed. The British Treasury note for 10s. became known as a "Bradbury"—a name derived from a signature

---
* Gallipoli Diary.

thereon. Those issued to the Mediterranean Expeditionary Force at the time were endorsed in Turkish so that they might have currency in Constantinople when the Straits were forced.

The 16th October witnessed the return to the Battalion of the Machine Gun Section from the Apex. It was arranged that at 4 a.m. this day an attempt should be made to compel the enemy to disclose his gun and machine gun positions. At that hour a rocket went up from Russell's Top. Immediately our guns, and the machine guns to either flank of the 28th, opened fire. The Battalion had been ordered to man the trenches, show their fixed bayonets over the parapets, and cheer lustily. All these things were done and the effect added to by throwing clods of earth down amongst the bushes in the Dere to give the impression of the noise of troops advancing. All came to nought. The Turk uttered not a sound, and after the firing ceased the West Australians, appreciating some humour in the situation, went about their day's work with broad smiles on their faces.

Aeroplanes occasionally made their appearance above the contending armies. To the man in the trench it seemed that some arrangement existed whereby our aviators should not use the same days in the week as the Turk. Never were the two seen in the air at the one time and the infantry, who were spoiling to witness an aerial combat, were greatly disappointed. An appearance was usually the signal for a little practice by the anti-aircraft guns, one of which was located in the 1st Division's sector. The enemy gunners had better luck than ours, for twice during the Battalion's stay they succeeded in winging our men—one of whom made a forced landing on Suvla Lake and the other in the sea, not far from the shore, about half a mile further south. Here they provided a target for the field guns and, in the former instance, the machine, viewed from the Apex, soon resembled a fly whose wings had been burned off. Whilst at Cheshire Ridge the 28th observed a hostile aviator traverse the line from right to left, flying at an altitude of a few hundred feet only. The pilot leaned over the side of the car as he passed over the West Australians and waved his hand to them. The rifle fire directed at him apparently did no harm and in a few seconds he disappeared in the direction of Suvla.

Between the 17th and 20th of the month the Battalion suffered four casualties (wounds) from shrapnel. On the evening of the 25th the Turks landed in the Chailak Dere several heavy high explosive shells. At 11 a.m. on the 27th they opened a brisk fire all along the brigade sector and up towards Suvla. The beach behind was also shelled by the big guns. The "stand to" was ordered but, as usual, firing died down without further development. The rest of the brigade had a number killed and wounded but the 28th escaped unscathed. For the remainder of the month the enemy was comparatively quiet.

Lieut. J. F. Quilty arrived from Egypt on the 24th and brought seven men as a reinforcement.

"A" COMPANY.
Getting ready to move from the Reserve position at Cheshire Ridge.
Photo. lent by Mr. T. Pritchard.

Sickness increased during the month and seriously affected the officers. The Adjutant (Captain Lamb), Captains Montgomery and Stroud, Lieutenants Davey, Hargraves, and Carter were taken to the hospital. Captain Menz also became alarmingly ill and had to be carried away on a stretcher. On the way down the Dere a shell came along and killed one of his bearers and wounded the other. He escaped with a bad fall and the loss of the heel of his boot. A few days later Major J. A. C. Wilson left the Battalion. He had been obviously suffering from jaundice for some time but had clung to his command until he had to be ordered to hospital. As "A" Company had lost both its O.C. and 2nd-in-Command, Lieut. N. F. Macrae from "D" Company was appointed temporarily to command.

Lieut. H. E. C. Ruddock was selected to carry on as adjutant until the return of Captain Lamb. Reg. Sergt.-Major P. T. C. Bell was promoted to commissioned rank.

The weather changed on the 22nd October and turned as cold as the coldest days in Western Australia, involving bleak conditions in the trenches at night. On the 27th there was a very unpleasant wind and dust storm which lasted for hours.

THE Q.M's. STORE OF "A" COMPANY
at Cheshire Ridge.
Photo. lent by Mr. T. Pritchard.

The Battalion having been in the firing line for about seven weeks, the Brigadier ordered the 26th Battalion, which had not yet been in the trenches, to relieve it. On the 30th October "A" Company of the Queenslanders and Tasmanians took over from "B" Company of the 28th. On the following day, however, the return to the Peninsula of the 4th Brigade being imminent, the order was cancelled. Nevertheless, on the 1st November, "C" Company proceeded to join "B" Company at Taylor's Hollow (in Bauchop's Hill, just north of Waterfall Gully). "D" Company followed on the next day and, on the 3rd, Lieut.-Colonel J. M. A. Durrant, with the 13th Battalion, took over the sector. The Machine Gun Section was again temporarily detached from the Battalion and joined the 8th Light Horse near Sazli Belt Dere. Whilst there they had a duel with a Turkish gun and came out victorious—finally calling upon our field artillery to blow up the enemy's emplacement. This was done very effectually.

During the month of October the Battalion had suffered a loss of five killed, four died of wounds, 27 wounded, and 137 sick.

Located at Taylor's Hollow the Battalion now became the divisional reserve. The 26th Battalion had proceeded to rejoin the 2nd Australian Division and was followed on the 10th November by the 25th and 27th Battalions. Nominally the Battalion was withdrawn for a rest, but actually the divisional reserve's main function was to supply parties for all manner of work behind the front line.

For the sake of convenience these parties were placed near Hell Spit, in Reserve Gully, and other features which afforded the necessary cover. They worked under their own officers, who received their instructions from the Beach Commandant, from the Commanding Royal Engineer of one of the divisions, or from a member of the Corps Staff.

One party was engaged in building a series of terraces to receive the marquees of a Casualty Clearing Station. This necessitated the free use of explosives and the removal of many tons of earth. The work was carried out in such an efficient manner as to excite the surprise and admiration of the Royal Engineers. To finish it off an elaborate retaining wall was built with material from the shore. This wall contained a large corner stone upon which was placed the inscription "A Coy. 28 Bn. didit."

Some platoons were employed on the engineer, ordnance, and supply dumps. Others assisted in unloading lighters at the piers and transferring loads from storeships into lighters. Generally the work was without incident except for occasional casualties from "Beachy Bill," which from the Olive Grove sprayed the beach with its shrapnel. The great storm of November 27th was, however, productive of some experiences of interest and not without danger. Several of the ships upon which the men were working had to make for shelter—refuge being taken at Suvla, Imbros, and even as far away as Lemnos. To this latter place went Lieut. T. O. Nicholls and his team, who found themselves on a craft that dragged her anchors and was short of water and stores. Fourteen days elapsed before they were able to return to Anzac. Those who suffered from sea-sickness certainly did not enjoy these involuntary trips.

At 5 p.m. on the day of the storm, all hands and the cook were summoned to Anzac Cove for salvage work. On arrival it was found that the piers had been washed away. Big baulks of timber were being thrown about by the sea, in a most disconcerting manner, amongst all sorts of stores. The first duty assigned the party by the Beach Commandant was to restore some semblance of order amongst the members of a certain Labour Corps who had run wild. This was achieved in an expeditious though somewhat violent manner. The next duty was salvaging amongst the flotsam and jetsam which, with the timber charging about and the water at a very low temperature, was a decidedly unpleasant task. Night put a stop to the operations, and the Beach Commandant congratulated the party on the work done. This officer was no lover of the "Aussies," owing—so rumour had it—to some of them "pinching" his fattening fowls, but on this occasion he contributed, voluntarily, a double issue of rum—an act which was undoubtedly popular and timely.

Speech, accent, and manner counted for a good deal when working in conjunction with British troops. An incident which illustrates this occurred in connection with a fatigue party which was required by the British Army Service Corps for night work on the beach. This party was commanded by an officer who possessed neither size in stature or feature in voice. His second-in-command was a corporal with very marked characteristics. With the N.C.O. in rear the two set out for the A.S.C. dugout, at the entrance to which the officer announced his arrival. The A.S.C. officer emerged into the night and asked the question "Where have you got your men?" The corporal gave the answer in his deepest stentorian tones and with faultless accent, "They are anchored just abaft the stack of Fray Bentos." The "Tommy" officer immediately came over towards him and remarked, "Oh! I'm sorry, Old Chappie, I didn't know there was an officer here, I thought this little N.C.O. was in charge of the party." The corporal wasn't quite clear as to what followed, but had a distinct recollection of receiving an order in good Australian, "Corporal! Go back and bring the men along to the cheese stack, *at once!*"

From the Beach, where men of all units met, came the daily crop of "furphies" or rumours. Some of these, it was suspected, were set going by the Intelligence Section of the General Staff, but many of them were the deliberate creation of a few people with a rather perverted sense of humour. Others developed from the chance remark of some individual speculating on what might be, or what he hoped would be. The "Anzac Liar," as the unknown person was designated, dealt with many subjects, from an advance to a retirement, from the landing of a Greek or Italian Army Corps on the north to the forcing of the Straits by the Navy. This last, it was said, was to be achieved by the 2nd November, and the sailors were prepared to make handsome bets on it. With experience the ordinary soldier came to regard this news as a topic for conversation only, remaining incredulous and accepting actual facts with the best grace possible in view of his rapidly developing fatalistic spirit.

The Beach was also the hunting ground of those who sought to improve their lot. One night a well-known Signaller, a noted hunter with an eagle eye, observed a case of rum—for the moment unattended. The situation obviously required action and P—— possessed the necessary initiative. Five seconds later he was being pursued down the Beach. After successfully losing his pursuers he humped the case to Russell's Top and opened it before a crowd of thirsty and expectant Signallers—to find that it was lime juice. In the opinion of the Section this incident was the one black spot in P——s long career of usefulness.

Authentic news from the outside world came from two or three different sources. General Headquarters at Imbros issued a weekly sheet, entitled the "Peninsula Press," which published notes on the doings on other fronts and gave alarming accounts of the winter conditions on Gallipoli. The Navy had, apparently, their own sources of information, for signallers would often gather items of interest by watching the flashing of the helios by day or the blinking of the signal lamps by night. Then there were the mails. In this, as well as in many other respects, the army treated the soldiers well. Mails came at irregular intervals, but never more than three weeks elapsed without bringing the ever-welcome letter and newspaper from Australia. The 28th mail comprised a large portion of that for the whole brigade. Some of the members would receive as many as 13 or 14 letters each.

Parcels also came to hand. These contained a great diversity of articles, ranging from woollen goods to chewing gum and safety pins.

The Battalion Postal Orderly, Private J. H. Mann, was most conscientious and energetic in his work. He usually installed himself in some dugout away from the company lines and where he had room to cope with his thousands of packets. When the Battalion moved, new quarters were necessary, and Mann was sometimes seen, bared to the waist, working hard with pick and shovel in the excavation of a new post office. Sometimes ill fortune befel the mails. Twice during the November storms lighters containing hundreds of bags were swamped and sunk. One of these was carrying the outward Christmas mail and disappeared within sight of the beach.

As a rule letters for Australia were despatched once weekly and, in spite of the local distractions, many found ample opportunities for writing home. A few wrote with an eye to the publication of their letters in their town Press. When these newspapers were subsequently received by the Battalion, the scribes came in for a good deal of chaff. Private E. St. I. Bilston of "C" Company made little essays into verse—some of the results appearing in the Perth and Kalgoorlie Sunday papers. At times writing paper was very scarce, and the New Zealand Divisional Sanitary Officer complained that he was unable to continue certain necessary issues because the supplies were disappearing into the mail bags. In November a case of stationery was received by the Battalion. This was the result of the kind and thoughtful action of Mrs. Lohoar of Fremantle, who had arranged a "Stationery Tea" amongst her friends.

The attention of the men in the firing line was by no means always centred on the imminence of danger. Except during actual bombardments, or when on sentry, they had some leisure, which was filled by diversions of various kinds. Sleep—when possible, letter writing, and card playing, passed many hours pleasantly away. Those in the reserve areas found other amusements, in which figured largely the games of "Banker" and "Two-up," upon which had been placed an official taboo. In the hollows and gullies groups of men were often noticed, and the observer would see the faces momentarily turned towards the sky and then towards the earth again—actions denoting interested eyes following the flight of the spinning coins. Some men brought considerable sums of money to their officers for safe custody. A good deal of this the owners subsequently remitted to their homes.

Again, others found an interest in watching the flocks of wild geese that passed over during the autumn migrations. The appearance of these birds whetted the appetites of the "dog-fed" soldiers, but no rifle bullet seemed to be able to find them. During the first week in December starlings passed over in flocks of thousands—flying low and following the line of hill and vale, whilst emitting a curious sound from the movement of so many wings. In the Deres would be seen an occasional blackbird and thrush, which were later on joined by the robin. On one occasion a visitor from the Balkans—an eagle with a very large spread of wings—hovered over Cheshire Ridge and, by a few, was thought to be an aeroplane flying at great altitude.

Nor was the sea unpleasant to the eye. The wonderful blue of the Mediterranean, the storms, and the sunsets and clouds behind and above the sharp peaks of the island of Samothrace—some 40 miles away—made believers of those who had seen copies or prints

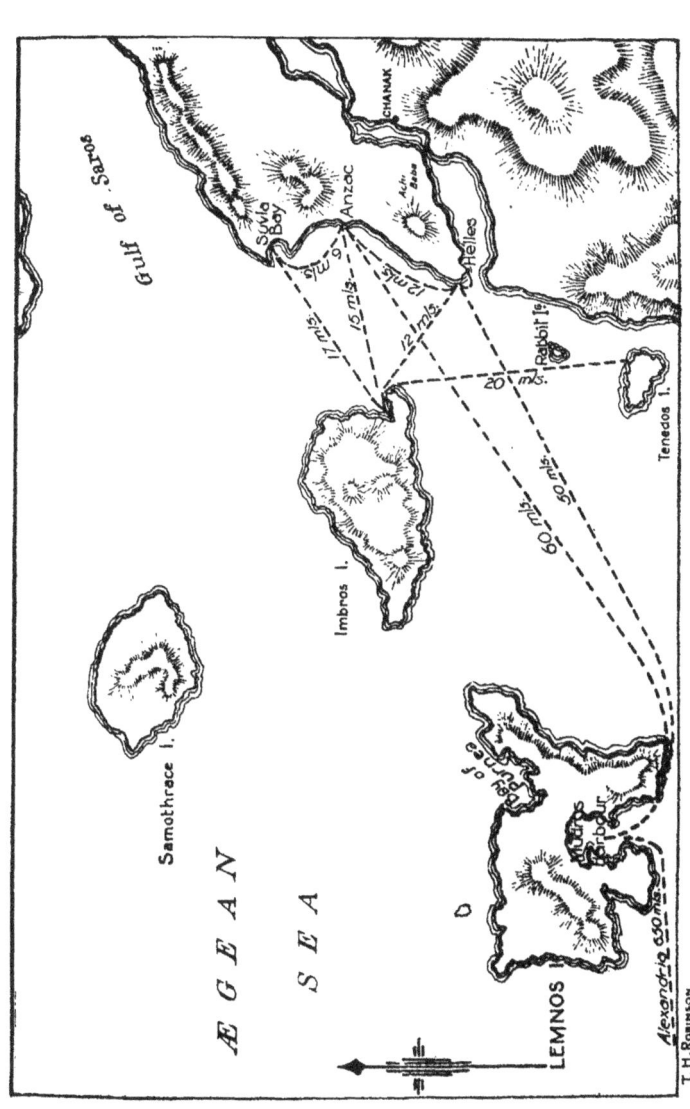

LEMNOS, IMBROS, AND SAMOTHRACE.

Lent by Mr. C. E. W. Bean.

of Turner's pictures. Farther south, and 12 or 15 miles distant, lay the less mountainous island of Imbros, where Sir Ian Hamilton had his headquarters. Kephalos Bay was on the east side, and there, on a clear day, could be discerned the anchored shipping.

Nearer at hand trawlers were engaged in mine sweeping. Others were lying at anchor, just beyond the range of the Turkish guns, waiting for darkness in order to discharge or take in cargo. Occasionally these craft came in too close and afforded a target for enemy "whizz-bangs" or salvos of "4.2's." These latter made a whining progress through the air and landed in the sea, throwing up fountains of water as they burst. Seldom did the Turk score a hit, and only once during the Battalion's stay was a shell noticed to reach its intended destination.

Other vessels could be seen. An occasional destroyer proceeded at full speed on some errand or in search of a hostile submarine whose presence had been rumoured. Once a huge battle cruiser approached Suvla with a watching destroyer keeping station on each bow and quarter. Low-lying monitors, standing a long way off shore, with their one or two guns trained at high angles, made practice at some inland target near Achi Baba or at the northern end of the Peninsula. One of these, the "Peninsula Press" reported, secured four direct hits on the flour mills at Galata at a range of 19,400 yards.

Close at hand was the ever-present "Grafton," which, when the evening sun lighted up the north-western slopes of Sari Bair, would loose her guns, the firing of which gave forth a peculiar long-drawn-out double echo.

With the fall of night sight failed except in regard to the flashes of the naval guns and the red and green lights of the waiting hospital ships.

Whilst in Taylor's Hollow the Battalion was not immediately concerned with the operations of the front line. It was, however, still under fire, for numerous shells fell at the entrance to the Hollow and bullets came thickly at night all over the area. The sole casualty was a donkey killed. On the beach near-by a lighter had been blown ashore. In its vicinity some of the men were in the habit of bathing. The Turks shelled the locality one afternoon and the bathers took cover under the distant side of the boat. From this they emerged rather hurriedly when a shell lobbed right into the craft. But instead of forsaking the neighbourhood they lay about under the sand ridges, and when a shell landed were seen to rush out and "souvenir" the copper driving band, from which interesting mementos were manufactured by the artificers of the adjacent howitzer battery.

Advantage was taken of the relatively quiet period to pay a visit to the IX. Corps. A party of officers traversed the front line as far as the headquarters at Suvla. In doing so they not only had the opportunity of surveying the positions, but also of meeting a great number of the units who had been so sorely tried in the August fighting and who did so well later in Palestine and Mesopotamia. London and County Regiments, Ghurkas, Sikhs, Welsh miners, and Scottish and Irish units, were all represented and received the Australians with evident curiosity.

CHAPTER IX.

GALLIPOLI (continued).

On November 4th, at 9 p.m., an unusually heavy outburst of firing commenced on the extreme right and rapidly spread along to Russell's Top. Flares were seen to be ascending freely. Later on came the news that the Turks had made an attack near Chatham's Post and had been successfully repulsed.

November 11th saw the return of the miners from the Apex, also the Machine Gunners and Lieut. Phillips' platoon from Canterbury Slope. This was preparatory to a junction with the 2nd Division, which was effected the following night. As the last of the 7th Brigade was now leaving the N.Z. and A Division area, General Godley forwarded to the Brigadier a message expressing his complete satisfaction with its fighting qualities, work, and promise. Subsequent events amply justified this proof of his goodwill and judgment.

During the night of the 12th the headquarters of the Battalion were moved to Happy Valley. This feature formed the northern side of Walker's Ridge and ran up to Russell's Top, then occupied by the 26th Battalion. Prior to the August advance 3,000 troops had been successfully concealed there. The sides of the valley were steep and composed mostly of loose soil rendering excavation for cover difficult. There were also disagreeable evidences of the previous occupants and the ground was freely scattered with tins of preserved meat.

Here the 28th became a support for the garrison above. It had also to provide a patrol to connect with the 1st Light Horse Brigade now on the Battalion's left and on the opposite side of Malone Gully. Between Happy Valley and Malone Gully ran a razor-edged spur—descending from Turk's Head, the extreme left of the Russell's Top position. At the summit Lieut. Shaw took charge of two machine guns already in position there. The remainder of his section, now 60 strong, engaged in training on the hinter slope. The spur itself was known officially as "Wild Cat Sap," but more popularly as the "Ghost Walk." During the hours of darkness, up and down the footway that had been cut, toiled and slipped a patrol, whilst in the valley itself a platoon was kept in a state of constant readiness as an inlying picquet.

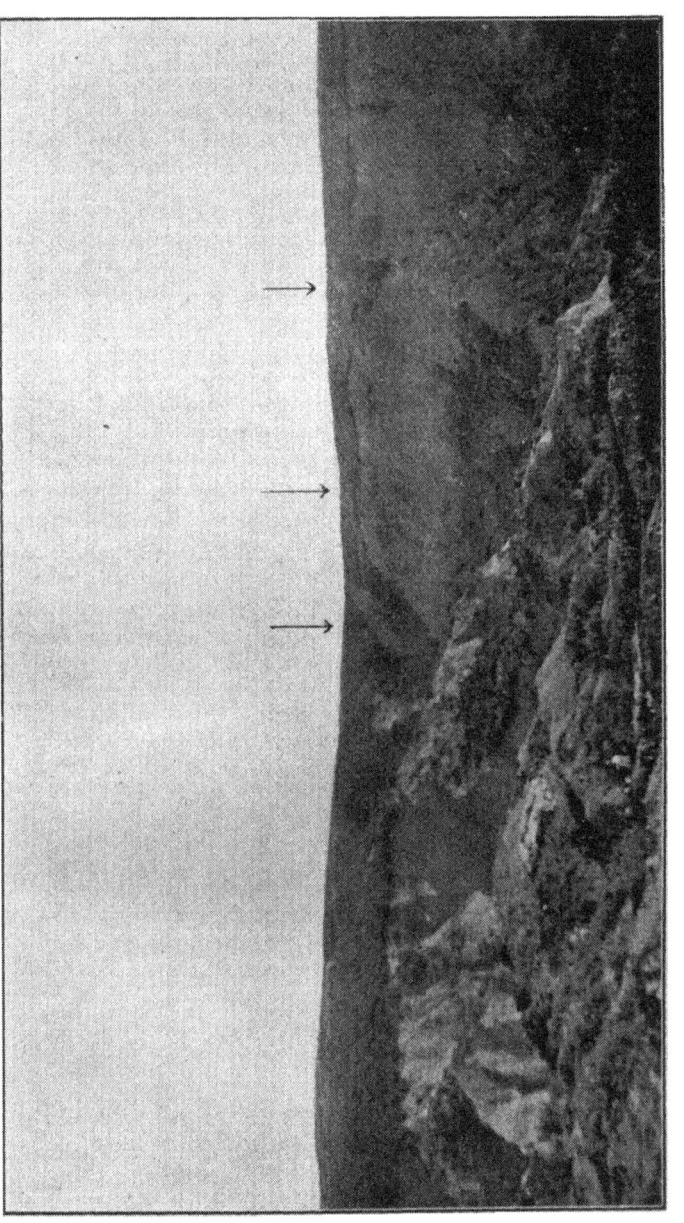

THE SARI BAIR RIDGE.

Showing Baby 700, the Nek, and Russell's Top. The Nek is shown in the centre of the picture at the head of the dark patch. The opposing trenches are to the right of it.

Photo. lent by Mr. C. E. W. Bean.

Copyright by Australian War Museum.

During the afternoon of the 13th November, the sounds of cheering, coming from the direction of the beach, indicated some unusual happening. Shortly afterwards Lord Kitchener, accompanied by Generals Monro, Maxwell, and Birdwood, was seen ascending the slope to Walker's Ridge. He had spoken to the men who had "reviewed" him on landing and had given them a gracious and flattering message from the King. One of the Battalion "rumourists" returned from the vicinity with the report that the words spoken included, "Well, boys, you will all be in Egypt for Christmas." The stay of the Secretary of State for War was brief and he left Anzac again in a small launch which did not attract even a single shell from the enemy's guns.

Sickness continued to make its levy on the officers. Lieut. Ruddock went down with pneumonia on the 13th November, and was succeeded as Adjutant by Lieut. G. A. Read. Captain Montgomery, who had returned to duty, had again to be sent away and was followed a few days later by Lieuts. G. A. F. Smith and H. J. Bowra. Dean Brennan, who had fallen a victim to jaundice, was also evacuated. Major Leane became ill, but as the Battalion was in reserve he was granted his plea to be allowed to remain with his company, and eventually pulled round.

The weather was now becoming cold and unsettled. A third blanket was issued to each man. These blankets were of varied colours and when spread out to dry or air gave the landscape an appearance that must have puzzled any hostile aviator. On the 15th the wind began to rise early in the morning and blew clouds of dust about. The sea also became troubled. Two days later the atmospheric conditions got worse. Several boats were blown ashore and the piers damaged. About 8 p.m. rain descended and drenched those whose dugouts afforded little protection. During the worst period the enemy became "jumpy" and opened a heavy fire on the hill above. The prospect of having to ascend the slippery tracks was forbidding. However, quiet returned and daybreak revealed the sea rapidly subsiding.

About this time, the Battalion witnessed an enemy aeroplane pass over our positions—dropping several bombs and arrows. One bomb fell near to the main ammonal magazine, but, very fortunately, failed to explode. This was the first of many similar experiences in other theatres of war.

That the war had not destroyed the humane instincts of the soldiers was evidenced by an incident which occurred near the beach and was witnessed from Happy Valley. Two mules, secured together by neck chains, were being led northwards by a native attendant. Inadvertently, it would seem, the man left the cover of the excavated road, which was used for traffic and took his charges out into the open. Here they came into full view of the enemy snipers, who promptly killed one of the animals. The attendant immediately took to his heels and left the live mule anchored by the chain to his dead companion. Bullets began to throw up the dust around him—and it seemed to be only a matter of seconds before he would go too—when a Light Horseman ran out from cover, some 50 yards away, undid the chain, and, under an increasingly rapid fire, led the second animal to safety.

At the head of Malone Gully there was a small projecting cliff, which was in the possession of "Jacko." This and the ground behind it gave a command over a limited portion of the beach, which was only a few hundred yards away. In order to clear out the Turk and strengthen the hold on Russell's Top, a plan for an advance in this direction was considered during the month of November. It was proposed that the 28th Battalion should carry out the operation and, with that object in view, a preliminary reconnaissance was made. This, however, revealed that the enemy had so placed his machine guns as to sweep the whole of the area concerned. It was, therefore, decided to abandon the idea, as the probable losses would be quite out of proportion to the benefit to be gained.

The policy of the Anzac Corps, as given out at this time, was, in view of the strength of the defences, to invite the Turk to attack. It was anticipated that the losses inflicted on him would be so heavy that he would be compelled to remain quiescent for the whole of the winter. During that period the Australians would be able to hold their ground with a greatly reduced garrison; thus simplifying the question of supply and enabling the surplus troops to be sent away for rest and refit. On the 22nd November, a Divisional Order was received directing that as little firing as possible should take place and that no offensive on our part was to be attempted. A further Order laid down that from 6 p.m. on the 24th the Australians should not only hold their fire, but should also refrain from displaying periscopes above the parapets. Proceeding, it stipulated that the enemy was to be allowed to show himself, but this latter provision subsequently gave way to an imperative injunction that no opportunity of killing a Turk was to be missed.

This period of inactivity was continued until midnight on the 27th November, and was facetiously termed the "close season for Turkey." In the early portion, the unusual quietness on our side had a weird effect. The enemy continued his ordinary activity for a time and then audibly slackened, only to resume again later on. At night time he sent over patrols to investigate, but these were not allowed to return. A story was told of a solitary individual crossing over from the opposite lines and quietly removing some filled sandbags from our parapet in order to repair his own. The Turk was very short of this useful article and his trenches always presented a spectacle of many materials and colours.

The ruse having failed in its expressed purpose, the normal defensive was resumed.

On the 24th November, the 25th Battalion, then in Reserve Gully, was ordered to be in readiness to embark for Lemnos Island for a rest. The following day the 27th Battalion, at Mule Gully, received a similar order. Both these orders were subsequently countermanded—much to the disgust of the units concerned, who were employed in heavy pick and shovel work and were far from being in a healthy condition.

Running from the bottom of Happy Valley to the main traffic trench, the Battalion had excavated a new roadway. In honour of the first officer casualty, this was named the "Jensen Sap" (Division took this as a compliment to the then Minister for the Navy). In this was found, one morning, the remains of a labour company of the Army Service Corps. It was composed of men, recruited in England, too old for ordinary line service and intended for work on the beach and piers. It was quickly proved that they were quite unable to withstand the rigors of the local climate. After losing many from the ranks through shell fire near Hell Spit, they had been moved to the north. There at first they wandered helplessly about, apparently quite unable to do anything for themselves. The 28th men, who dubbed them "the Old and Bold," took pity and assisted them to make their little bivouacs in protected places. The old gentlemen were very grateful. One of them was the originator of a now well known story. Seeing a Light Horseman passing along the main sap, and wearing the distinctive head-dress, he hailed him— "Say, choom, be them kangaroo feathers in your 'at?"

A few days of sunshine had followed the storm of the 17th November. Then came cold and colder winds, which chilled to the bone. The sea was rough and the landing of stores became impossible. Rations were cut down to biscuits and bully beef, and water to ¼ gallon per diem. In spite of these privations, Battalion Headquarters had fresh "lamb" chops for breakfast on one day. Having on the previous day seen the meat ration of the Native Labour Corps browsing on the slope of Walker's Ridge, the staff asked no questions, but made a mental note of a very self-conscious batman and an imperturbable quartermaster.

During the night of the 27th/28th November, snow began to fall and daylight revealed the whole country covered as with a white pall. Many of the Australians had never seen snow before and were greatly attracted by this new experience. A few indulged

HEADQUARTERS OF "C" COMPANY,
Happy Valley, 28th November, 1915,
Showing signs of the Blizzard.
Photo. by Major R. C. Phillips.

THE GREAT TRAFFIC TRENCH.
This ran along behind the left centre of the Corps line.
Photo. lent by Mr. T. Pritchard.

in snowballing, others gathered the new element and melted it with a view to supplementing the water supply, but it soon became apparent that the visitation was going to have very serious effects. Traffic turned the snow into mud and the inclines used by the mules became almost impassable. Snow continued to fall until midday, and towards evening, with the thermometer down to 24°, a hard frost set in, accompanied by a keen wind. This removed the mud difficulty for the time being, but rifle actions became rigid and machine guns refused to work. On Turk's Head for twelve hours the garrison was almost defenceless.

These severe conditions existed until the last day of the month, when the sun re-asserted itself, gave off some warmth, melted the ice, and, for a period, restored the muddy conditions. The visitation of the blizzard had dire consequences, especially to the men in the trenches, where there was such little room for movement. Cases of frost-bite were numerous—a few only in the 28th—whilst many men who had been bravely hanging on to duty now found their last ounce of vitality forsaking them and were impelled to parade sick. The troops to the north of Anzac fared the worst. The snow had been preceded by heavy falls of rain, converting the low-lying trenches into watercourses and in some cases obliterating them altogether. With the advent of the frost, men previously wet through had their garments frozen on them. Two hundred deaths followed from exposure and exhaustion. Some sentries were found still at their posts with the last spark of life departed. Altogether some 10,000 sick were evacuated from the Peninsula, one British Division losing 50 per cent. of its strength. Nor did the enemy, it is believed, fare much better, as many of his dead were washed down the deres into our trenches near Suvla.

The month closed for the Battalion with a record of five died of wounds and 111 evacuated sick. In consequence of further casualties in the commissioned ranks, Sergt. F. Sears was promoted to be a platoon commander.

Since near the middle of November there had been a noticeable increase in the enemy artillery fire. The beach received special attention. Not only was there an increase in the number of rounds fired, but it seemed that more large calibre guns were being brought into use. Intelligence reports also, from time to time, mentioned additional heavy German guns reaching the Turks *via* Bulgaria.

The dawn of the 29th November revealed a series of small flags flying from the parapet of the enemy front line trenches. Soon there commenced a heavy bombardment of Russell's Top and a heavier one of the Lone Pine position. At this latter place serious casualties were suffered by the 6th Brigade. Many men were buried alive by the collapse of the covered saps. Part of the 7th Brigade was sent up as a reinforcement and to assist in the restoration of the works.

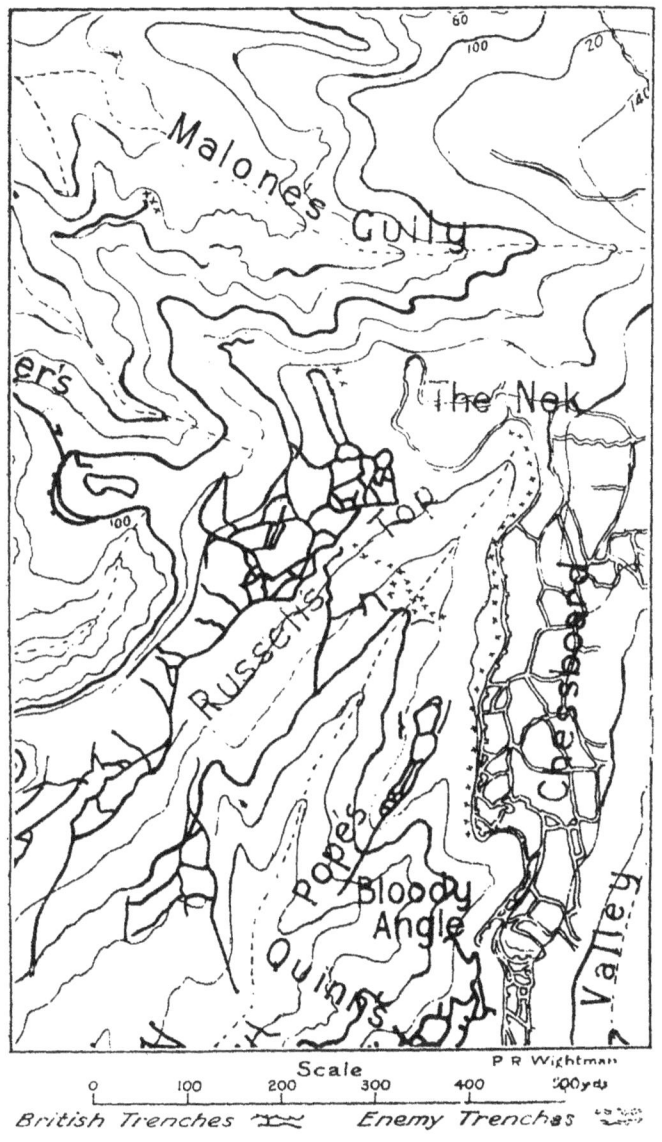

THE TRENCHES ON RUSSELL'S TOP.
Map by Australian War Museum.

Happy Valley received many of the "overs" intended for Russell's Top and also much spent shrapnel. Little or no damage was done.

Noon of Sunday, the 6th December, witnessed the coming into action of the much talked-of German guns. Heavy and ear-splitting crashes in the direction of old No. 2 Post attracted attention and the observer saw geyser-like columns of earth ascending. Seemingly the enemy was endeavouring to reach the headquarters of the N.Z. and A. Division, but his shells either fell short or, unfortunately, went in amongst the marquees of the 13th Casualty Clearing Station, which was situated near-by. Men could be seen running for cover, some bearing in their arms, or on their backs, other men who were unable to help themselves. Many, already wounded, were killed in their beds.

On the 3rd December a conference took place on Walker's Ridge between the Army Commander and the Corps, Division, and Brigade Commanders, at which the C.O. was present. The 2nd Division was now commanded by Brig.-General W. Holmes in place of Major-General Legge who, in ill-health, had left the Peninsula towards the end of November. General Godley had taken General Birdwood's post, the latter having moved to Imbros to assume direction of the whole of the forces on the Peninsula, which were now grouped as the "Dardanelles Army." At this conference certain special defence measures were discussed and a plan of relief decided upon whereby the 26th Battalion was to be replaced by the 28th.

During the day following, "A" Company moved up. "D" Company left Happy Valley on the 6th, Headquarters and "B" Company on the 7th, and "C" Company made the Battalion complete on the 8th. Lieut. Shaw took over charge of all the machine guns in the position. There were two reasons for the time taken over this relief. The first, the difficult approach to and intricate nature of the defences; and, secondly, the necessity of withdrawing men gradually from the beach fatigues so that they might be replaced from the relieved battalion without causing a break in the continuity of the services.

Russell's Top was another "Apex" and a cockshy for any enemy guns that were within range. The possession of it denied to the enemy observation of the beach and piers. The ascent to it was by a winding road cut in the feature which separated Happy Valley from Mule Gully. Its flanks rested on precipices 150 to 200 feet high and away to the right rear ran a long narrow tongue of cliff terminating at "The Sphinx." In front lay "The Nek" across which our Light Horse had so gallantly attempted to charge on the 6th August.

Both sides had pushed forward their trenches until very little space separated them from one another. Mining and countermining had been very active, and galleries, on three different levels, ran forward under the Nek. The 26th Battalion had broken through into the Turkish workings in one or two places, and some spirited bombing and revolver shooting had taken place in the bowels of the earth. At the rear of the position a large gallery had been commenced with a view to tunnelling right under the Turkish works on Battleship

A CONFERENCE ON WALKER'S RIDGE.
December, 1915..
Generals Birdwood, Godley, and Holmes, Colonel Paton, and Lt.-Colonels Ferguson, Collett, and G. H. N. Jackson.

Hill. Such progress had been made that at the beginning of December the head of the drive was underneath the enemy's second line of trenches. Into these different workings went the 28th mining party under Sergt. Arundel, whilst sentries stationed at various points were charged with the duty of listening for countermining and to act in case of a sudden break-through.

"B," "C," and "D" Companies were in the front line in that order from the right. "A" Company was in reserve. The first-named unit had a considerable length of trench to deal with—part of which was known as "Bully Beef Sap," and ran down into Monash Gully opposite to Pope's Post. From the top of this sap a magnificent view of the southern part of the Peninsula could be obtained, and it was to that point that Lord Kitchener was brought on the occasion of his visit. Behind the right flank of the position, and leading down into Reserve Gully ran a deep wide trench known as "Broadway." This constituted the main traffic road for the bringing up of supplies and reinforcements. Behind this again, and on the edge of the cliff, was a pile of stores containing seven days' supply of biscuits and preserved meat together with ammunition. Inspections by Generals Birdwood and Godley, and the Divisional Commander, at frequent intervals, were an index to the importance of the position in their eyes.

The Battalion now came under bombardments which were indulged in by the enemy three or four times daily. Six-inch shells, filled with black powder, were common but did little damage—except to the earthworks. Some of these could be observed in flight as they traversed the position and fell over into one or other of the ravines. "Whizz-bangs" were more deadly, and shrapnel accounted for a number of casualties which, during the stay in the line, amounted to two killed and 11 wounded. One of these smaller shells tore away the tarpaulin which covered the Quartermaster's stores and was followed immediately by a heavy shell which landed right amongst them and scattered biscuits and tins of bully beef broadcast.

At 8 o'clock on the night of the 9th December an explosion occurred in one of the enemy's deep-level tunnels. No damage was done to our garrison or works. The Turk followed this up with such a concentrated rifle and machine-gun fire across the Nek as had never before been experienced by the Battalion. An hour later all was normal again, and the indications seemed to point to the subterranean eruption having been accidental and attributed by the Turk to our side as the precursor of an attack.

The 28th did not submit tamely to the frequent bombardments. Our artillery, from both land and sea, replied in a spirited manner. Hand bombs were also thrown, and the small trench mortars, catapults, and Japanese trench mortar, were brought constantly into play. One of the bombs of this last-named weapon was observed to penetrate into a trench, and the explosion which followed threw into the air various articles of personal apparel. Shortly afterwards a Turk was seen to emerge barefooted from the trench, walk deliberately into No-Man's Land, and remove a pair of boots from the feet of a dead body lying there. He returned to his shelter without having been observed by the snipers.

THE 28th: A RECORD OF WAR SERVICE, 1915-19. 131

The 11th December brought a surprise for the Battalion. It was informed that in accordance with the policy of reducing the garrisons during the winter months, the 7th Brigade would embark on the following day. The Divisional Commander's plan included the relief of the garrison of Russell's Top by the 20th Battalion. That afternoon a party of the New South Wales unit, consisting of the C.O., three majors, and the Adjutant, came along Broadway with the intention of making preliminary arrangements for the next day's move. Unfortunately they were caught by a burst of shrapnel and the three majors were killed.

THE VIEW FROM RUSSELL'S TOP, LOOKING INTO MALONE GULLY.
Official Photo. No. G. 1879.   *Copyright by Australian War Museum.*

By noon of the 12th December the 20th Battalion had taken over the line, and the Western Australians moved down to Happy Valley. Here preparations were commenced for the impending move. These included, apart from the assembly and packing of baggage, the collection and destruction of all scraps of letters, documents, or newspapers. Whilst engaged in this task shrapnel "overs" slightly wounded Captain J. Kenny, the Regimental Medical Officer, and Lieut. E. G. Glyde.

During the afternoon the real object of the move was explained to the C.O. by the Divisional Commander. He stated that the evacuation of the Peninsula had commenced, and that Colonel J. Paton had been selected to command the rear guard.

For the previous two months rumours of pending advances and retirements had been rife. All ranks had gleaned from the newspapers that the wisdom of further prosecuting the campaign had been openly debated in the British Parliament. That it seemed impossible to expect any further substantial support from England or her Allies, and that the defection of Bulgaria in October had opened the way for German aid to the Turks, who had been in a critical situation up to that time. Further, the heavy losses sustained during the August fighting, and the alarming inroads of disease, had so weakened the force as to raise the question of whether it would be able to hold on should the enemy take the offensive. On top of all came the prospect of the long winter with its rains and blizzards, against which there was such little protection available, and which would turn the ravines and hollows into veritable death traps.

On the other hand, the departure of Sir Ian Hamilton in October, the publication of his farewell order, the appointment of his distinguished successor—who also had a reputation for doing things—the visit of Lord Kitchener, the increased naval force and gun activity noticeable after the three days' silence of November, and the removal of troops to rest stations, all pointed to a renewal of the policy of action as soon as circumstances permitted. Nor was this theory discounted by the obvious departure of troops from Suvla, and guns and wagons from Anzac, "to reinforce Salonika"—the allied force at that time being hard pressed.

The first suspicion that all was not going well was caused the day before the 28th Battalion left Russell's Top, by the spectacle of men hurling boxes of rifle ammunition into deep pits and the receipt of the order that rations must be drawn from the reserve located on the position.

Now when the truth was known, all ranks were exercised by feelings partly of relief and partly of disappointment. Relief at the thought that the apparently useless sacrifice of life was to cease, and disappointment that in spite of the streams of blood that had been shed, and notwithstanding the performance of feats of arms not previously equalled in history, Australia had failed to achieve complete success in her first undertaking as a nation.

In this state of mind the Battalion quietly completed its arrangements for embarkation. It had been ordered that an officer

THE 28th: A RECORD OF WAR SERVICE, 1915-19. 133

and 17 other ranks of the Machine Gun Section were to be left to man the guns on Russell's Top. Lieut. Shaw, on calling for volunteers for a "stunt," received responses from the whole of his men and had difficulty in choosing the right number from so much excellent material.

After dark the Battalion, which had assembled in the main saps, moved down to Williams' Pier. Through over-anxiety on the part of the Divisional Staff to avoid delay, the arrival of the unit was premature. The 27th Battalion, having been ordered to embark earlier, was only just commencing the operation. About 1,200 to 1,500 men were now crowded at a point that the Turk constantly shelled. By one of those coincidences which had been witnessed when Lord Kitchener landed at the same spot, and was frequently noticeable when General Birdwood visited the front line trenches, not a shot was fired by the enemy.

By 10 p.m. the last man had been taken off by the "beetles" and transferred to the Khedivial Mail Steamer "Osmanieh." This vessel was of some 4,000 tons and was now packed with the 27th, 28th, and some of the 26th Battalions. The baggage had been left behind on the beach under guard, and was to follow the unit. Ultimately it was placed on another transport and never seen again by its owners. Some valuable regimental records and very interesting personal souvenirs were thus lost.

The policy in regard to the evacuation, as a tactical operation, was the gradual withdrawal of the troops over a period of several days. Each day the garrisons of posts would become weaker, and each day would make a corresponding extra demand upon those remaining to keep up a display of strength and activity. On the last day would be left a mere screen of men and guns, known as the "C Party," who themselves were again subdivided into three divisions. The men of the "C3" party were to be the last to leave—were to be all volunteers—and were known as the "Die-hards." To Lieut. G. D. Shaw and his men fell the task of defending with their machine guns one of the last posts to be vacated in the Anzac sector.

The guns were four in number and four men constituted the crew of each gun. Each man did two hours on duty and two off. In this latter period he had to cook his food and get what rest was possible. In contrast with the previous three months the men were fed well and given many kinds of articles extra to the rations. They received socks which were worn over the boots so as to deaden the sounds of movement.

Commencing on the 15th December, each gun fired 10,000 rounds nightly. This expenditure of ammunition was broken by irregular periods of silence during which nobody showed lights, fired, or talked, and so gave the place an air of having been deserted. The Turk was at first puzzled and then became apprehensive. He was seen to be putting out fresh wire and strengthening the already existing defences. To the fire he replied in a spirited manner, but did little damage the first day.

On the following day the garrison observed ten men-of-war heavily bombard the hostile lines near Hellas. Our aeroplanes were also busy and kept unwelcome observers away. At 5 p.m. a heavy bombardment killed Private E. Morrow and wounded Sergt. G. Moore. Private N. A. Munro was killed and Private H. W. Greenwood slightly wounded by a bullet which entered through a loophole. Five hours later a fire broke out on the beach amongst the surplus stores. This burned all night. Flames shot up 60 feet and the valleys became filled with smoke.

Dawn of the 17th witnessed the fire still burning. That night the enemy guns three times demolished one of Shaw's gunpits, and the gun was finally placed near the parapet so as to fire over the top if necessary.

The following day the final instructions were issued to the garrisons. The activity continued, and that night the men in the Russell's Top position numbered 300 only. Lieut. Shaw's guns were reduced to three.

The 19th December. The last day. The sunny spring-like weather of the previous fortnight continued and the sea remained calm. At 6 p.m. all but 100 men came down to Williams' Pier and embarked. Sergt. Waddingham and Lance-Corpl. M. F. Newnes took their guns to the lower slopes of Walker Ridge to cover the retirement from the left flank. Lieut. Shaw, with the remaining gun team, then roved about from post to post in the front trench making as much display as possible with the solitary weapon and getting very hot replies. At midnight the "C1" party retired. About an hour later a report was received that the enemy was moving down Monash Gully. On investigation this proved to be a wiring party only. At 2 a.m. on the 20th December the "C2" party left, and now in the key position there remained only 37 officers and riflemen, four machine gunners, and two signallers.

The embarkation proceeded more rapidly than was expected, and at 3 a.m. Lieut. Shaw, in moving around, met the remainder of the 20th Battalion in movement. He and his party had been forgotten. Five minutes later—being the last to leave the front line in this sector—he joined his other two guns lower down and came into action

CAPTAIN T. O. NICHOLLS, M.C.
Who commanded the 7th Machine Gun Company.

CAPTAIN G. D. SHAW, M.C.
Machine Gun Officer.

again. At 3.35 a.m. he was ordered to retire to the boats. This he did and got his remaining men and material safely on board.

Mines had been placed in the galleries that knew the men of the 28th at the Apex and Russell's Top. At 3.45 a.m. these were exploded with great effect. The Turk was silent for a moment or two, and then opened a tremendous but harmless fire all along the line. At 4.30 a.m. a fascinating display was afforded those now on the boats when smaller mines were discharged and fires broke out at different points on the beaches amongst the stores that it had been impossible to bring away.

The Machine Gun Section, as a parting gift to their friends the enemy, had laid a table and set thereon porridge and cocoa ready for the first who came into the evacuated trenches.

The names of the 28th men who took part in the final phase of the evacuation are as follows:—

Lieut. G. D. Shaw.
Sergt. G. Moore (wounded).
Private J. Adams.
Private C. G. Graham.
Sergt. F. H. Waddingham.
Lance-Corpl. M. F. Newnes.
Private M. M. Fitzpatrick.
Private H. W. Greenwood (wounded).
Private A. Harris (1st Rft.).

Private W. A. Johnstone.
Private E. Morrow (1st Rft., killed).
Private G. B. Neilson.
Private T. W. Spencer (1st Rft.).
Private H. K. de W. Harvey.
Private C. McKail.
Private N. A. Munro (killed).
Private E. S. Smart (1st Rft.).

CHAPTER X.

LEMNOS ISLAND.

The crowded "Osmanieh" left the anchorage opposite Anzac early in the morning of the 13th December. Removed, for the time being, from the everlasting noise and risk of battle, feeling also that the morrow would bring real rest and a life of comparative ease, the troops slept well in spite of their uncomfortable surroundings.

After daylight the transport entered Mudros Bay and before noon the disembarkation had been carried out at a pier near the northern end of Port Mudros.

The Battalion formed up and then moved off by a military road, made by Turkish prisoners of war, which ran through the lines of the 2nd Australian Stationary Hospital, the 3rd Australian General Hospital, and a Canadian General Hospital, all of which were accommodated in marquees. The staffs, and some of the patients, of these establishments stood by the roadside as the new arrivals passed. Many friends and acquaintances were recognised and the C.O. of the 2nd Stationary Hospital (Major G. W. Barber) invited the officers of the Battalion staff to a dinner, to be held the following evening, to mark the first anniversary of the medical unit's departure from Australia.

Seen on the line of march for the first time for over three months, the Battalion presented a sorry spectacle as compared with that witnessed when it left Heliopolis on the 3rd September. Equipment fitted anyhow and clothes were torn and stained. Few hats remained, their place being taken by caps of various sorts and even woollen comforters. But the most pitiful feature was the appearance of the men themselves. Emaciated bodies, colourless faces, and lack-lustre eyes, revealed the effects of the privations undergone, the continuous exposure to shell fire, and—most of all—the inroads of disease.

The route the Battalion now followed led around a shallow inlet of the sea to a camp near the little village of Sarpi. The distance was little more than three miles in all, but so weak were the majority of the men that they could not carry their packs and at the same time keep their positions in the ranks. The camp site was eventually approached in a kind of skirmishing formation of many lines. Numbers of men had fallen out on the way—catching up again as best they could—whilst some, game to the end on the Peninsula, had at last to give in and were handed over to hospitals on passing through.

It was understood that the halt at Sarpi would be only temporary. The area belonged to the 1st Division and was already occupied by the 3rd Brigade. Communication was very soon established with the members of the 11th Battalion—notwithstanding the fact that they were in quarantine on account of an outbreak of measles.

The accommodation in the camps was that furnished by tents only. In this instance they were not very plentiful at the moment and a good proportion of the men had to sleep out in the open. However, the air was still warm and another mild hardship at this stage was neither here nor there.

Having noticed a large canteen near the landing pier, the C.O. decided that the Battalion's long divorce from good ale might reasonably, and with great advantage, be brought to a close. Transport was the difficulty. The canteen was over three miles away and the unit possessed neither horse nor cart. Recourse was had to an officer of considerable powers of initiative who, in civil life, held a master mariner's certificate. He knew little about horses but a saddled one was borrowed from the 3rd Brigade and given to him with instructions to purchase the beer and bring it back to camp. He disappeared at a gallop over the skyline and returned about two hours later with a wagon load of full barrels. He had discovered a detachment of the Royal Army Service Corps and, posing as an orderly officer or a.d.c., had told its officer a distressing story of a brigadier who for several hours had been separated from his personal baggage. The arrival of the wagon was greeted with cheers and after its load was taken off, the men came up and gazed reverently on the barrels until they were tapped and the contents distributed.

Lieut.-Colonel G. H. Ferguson now being temporarily in command of the Brigade, Major C. R. Davies was detached to succeed him in command of the 26th Battalion.

On the 15th December the Battalion moved down the western side of the bay to a locality termed "Z Valley"—near the entrance to the harbour. The adjacent area was now known as "South Camp" and was destined for occupation by the 2nd Division.

Tents were pitched and a neat little camp soon made its appearance. Some difficulty was encountered in making the floors of the tents comfortable. There existed a superabundance of stones of the size of emu eggs which had first to be removed. These also littered the parade ground spaces and large parties had to be set to work clearing them up before exercises could be commenced. Water was scarce and the supply had to be augmented by sinking wells which later yielded a fair return.

Other camps appeared as units continued to arrive from the Peninsula. The 25th Battalion marched in on the 18th, and on the

THE 28th: A RECORD OF WAR SERVICE, 1915-19.

20th Colonel Paton rejoined the Brigade, bringing the surprising intelligence that the evacuation had been completed with the loss of scarcely a single man. That evening the survivors of the Machine Gun Section appeared and were heartily welcomed, the more so as they had been given up for lost.

During the first two or three days after arrival at Z Valley little but absolutely necessary work was performed. The men were allowed to rest. Many of them went down to the adjacent beach and bathed, or sat down on the rocks and ate large quantities of oranges and chocolates purchased from Greek boatmen.

As soon as the Ordnance branch of the army had established itself near-by, the process of refitting was commenced. However, supplies were short and not even the demands for bare necessaries could be fully met. Nevertheless, the Battalion was able to change and wash its clothes, cut its hair, and indulge in a daily shave.

At this period the 28th had been long enough on service to begin to appreciate the axiom "We are here to-day and gone tomorrow." No sooner had the members settled down in their new camp then they began to ask themselves "How long shall we be here?" and "Where are we going to?" They knew that the evacuation of Anzac was merely the end of a phase of the war. They were anxious as to how the news would be received at home and hoped that it would not cause the people of Australia to be despondent. They speculated on a possible return to Gallipoli—now that it was discovered that Helles was being held. They considered Salonika once more; dealt with the rumours of unrest in Egypt and the threat of another Turkish attempt on the Canal; and, finally, discussed the campaign on the Western Front where troops lived in billets, got good food in quantity, and now and then received leave to go home.

The 28th left Gallipoli with a strength of 25 officers and 660 other ranks. It had been thirteen weeks under fire and, although not taking part in any "stunt," had held the line in such a manner as to add considerably to its prestige and earn the reputation of being a solid battalion. This duty had been carried out at a cost of 50 dead, 84 wounded, and 355 evacuated through disease.

The discipline had been excellent and, where all had behaved and done their work so well, it was difficult to discriminate between one individual and another. Nevertheless, in response to the inquiries of the Divisional Commander, the following were selected for special mention: Major A. W. Leane, Captain J. Kenny, A.A.M.C., Sergt. W. T. Dawson, Lance-Sergt. G. M. Hammond, Corporal A. Jerry, Lance-Corporal A. W. Curran, and Privates H. A. Franco and D. McAuliffe. Four of those so named were subsequently awarded the Military Medal "for bravery in the field."

The condition of the Battalion on arrival at Lemnos Island was such that it was almost totally unfit to take the field again without being reinforced, refitted, and the *personnel* given an opportunity of regaining its normal health and strength. Inquiries as to reinforcements resulted in 72 men arriving, on the 29th December, from details camped on the island. Fifteen of these were individuals rejoining after sickness, etc. Larger numbers, it was understood, were being trained in Egypt.

The health began to improve with the rest the members now received, the better quality and variety of food supplied, and the institution of a graduated system of physical exercises, drill, and marches, intended to re-invigorate their mental and physical faculties. Within a fortnight the effect was most noticeable. Colour came to the faces, the bodies filled out, and individuals moved with an alertness strikingly different from that when landing on the shores of the bay.

The second morning after arriving at Z Valley, the Assistant Director of Medical Services of the Division attended at the "sick parade." Being a very humane man, he was concerned at the appearance of the soldiers present and told them that they ought all to be in hospital. This thought was attractive. The vision, obtained a few days before, of real beds and clean white sheets, combined with the prospect of being waited on by the comely nurses of the Australian and Canadian services, could only have one result. On the following sick parade the attendance was trebled. But disappointment followed. The A.D.M.S. was not about, and a far-seeing regimental medical officer pronounced his verdict—"Medicine and duty"—on all but a few.

The drill exercises commenced with the squad formations, and here arose the rather ludicrous situation of N.C.Os. not being able to describe the movements required. This was brought about by the promotion on the Peninsula of men who fulfilled the requirements there and got things done by giving orders in a few terse phrases of their own coining, but had never handled a section on parade or seen inside the cover of a text-book. The position was aggravated by many of the officers being "rusty" themselves and not having books of reference handy. However, the difficulty was got over by forming a class of instruction in each company, and the desired result was obtained in a few days. Five hours daily were given to parades and a half-holiday observed on Wednesdays and Saturdays.

THE CAMP AT SARPI,
Lemnos Island.
Photo. lent by Lieut. H. V. Woods.

THE SHIPPING IN MUDROS BAY, 1915.
Photo. lent by M. Rene de Marigny, Paris.

Although cold winds blew occasionally, and rain fell intermittently, the climate of the island was not unpleasant at this time of the year. Members of the Battalion, in their leisure hours, visited the neighbouring villages of Portianos, Mudros, and Kondia, although this latter place was subsequently placed out of bounds owing to an outbreak of typhoid fever amongst the inhabitants. At Portianos occurred one of those incidents the like of which is not altogether foreign to army life—even in peace time. A solitary Australian encountered a "Tommy" town picquet commanded by a tyrannical corporal. For a breach of certain orders, of the existence of which he was unaware, the Australian was rather roughly abused and handled by the picquet. Retiring discomfited from the scene he met several of his countrymen. A brief conference was followed by a return to the village and resulted in a very successful "clean-up" of the original aggressors.

Some men walked considerable distances and penetrated to the western side where is situated the principal town, Kastro—a place of some 3,000 inhabitants. Here they were able to inspect the Genoese fortress which stands on a rocky peninsula and has an eminence of some 400 feet above the sea. Souvenirs were obtained in the form of small roundshot from the ancient cannon which formerly surmounted the walls.

Lemnos has an area of some 175 square miles and, before the war, boasted of a population of some 27,000, of which number 3,000 or 4,000 were Turks, and the remainder Greeks. In ancient times, it was part of the Athenian Empire. The 15th Century saw it occupied by the Turks, in whose possession it remained practically up to the close of the Balkan War of 1913. On the outbreak of hostilities in 1914, the question of ownership was still under consideration by the Great Powers, but early in 1915 the Greek Premier, Venizelos, offered the island to the Allies as an intermediate base for their operations in the Eastern Mediterranean.

The island has many rugged barren hills—the highest near to where the Australians were camped being Mt. Therma, which attained to 1,130 feet. In wandering about the valleys and villages, the West Australians noted the quiet demeanour of the inhabitants. The males had a somewhat brigandish appearance in their dress of top boots, divided skirts, sheepskin coats, and astrakan caps. With so many strangers about, it would seem that great care was taken of the younger women. Very few of those between the ages of 16 and 30 were seen. The few that were visible had rather fine eyes, but otherwise were quite unattractive. Their usual dress was European, but made up of cheap prints with a shawl or coloured material tied round their heads as a covering.

The houses are square-built of stone, with no verandahs and little window balconies in some of those of two stories. In a few cases, the exterior walls were plastered and whitewashed or else painted with colour of a violent blue. The windows and doors are small and the rooms scarcely high enough to permit of one standing upright. The building stone is granitic and of several colours, which, combined with the tint of the moss on the roof tiles, gives an unusual effect to the general appearance of the dwellings. In Kastro, the streets are of the width of a Perth right-of-way and have shops on either side. These business houses vary in size from half that of a street coffee stall to the dimensions of the little grocery shops on the corners in our suburbs. Here, besides fruit, might be bought a lot of cheaply made English and German goods at prohibitive prices. Local wine and brandy were procurable, also "Black and White" whiskey, which had been made in Greece and bore a spurious label. This last was brought under the notice of the military police, who compelled its withdrawal.

The products of the island seemed to be grapes and a few other fruits, walnuts, wheat, barley, and a little cotton. Poultry were reared in some numbers, and the eggs mainly went to the monasteries on the mainland, at Mt. Athos, where the rules of the Order resident there forbade the admission of females of any species. At one time the authorities on the island derived a considerable revenue from the sale and export of a certain red earth which, with much religious ceremony, was dug out at stated times of the year and sealed in small packets. This, applied internally and externally, was regarded as an antidote to poison and a cure for snake bite.

A few flocks of long-wooled sheep roamed the hillsides. Many of these were black. For tilling, primitive wooden ploughs, fitted with an iron share, were used. These were drawn by oxen or, sometimes, by an ox and a donkey, both animals usually in a very decrepit condition. The ordinary means of conveyance was a curious old covered cart—also drawn by donkeys.

Dotted about on the lower hills were windmills, with long wooden arms, carrying the sails. The internal fittings and cog wheels were also wood. These mills were used for grinding the corn that was not exported to the mainland.

The island seemed to be well watered. One or two streams ran into the Bay, and springs were plentiful. Some of these latter were built over and provided with appliances for filling the carrying vessels. The villages also had their wells, but the water in these was reported to be polluted and to be the cause of outbreaks of fever.

There was almost a complete absence of trees, the natives having to secure their fuel from the neighbouring islands. Animal life seemed to consist of black and grey crows, jackdaws, a few hares, and moles, whose mounds were numerous.

Like unto Egypt, each little village on the island had its cafés, where the menfolk gathered and drank the thick sweet coffee. The 28th men frequented these when desiring a rest in their walks. Sometimes they visited the Greek churches—mostly old places, whitewashed, poorly furnished, and with a good deal of tawdry decoration in the way of pictures and tinsel. To the building at Portianos was an annexe half filled with human skulls and leg and arm bones. Some of these were ranged on shelves, whilst others were tied up in cloths, like bundles for the laundry. The general impression was that these were the remains of victims of Turkish massacres, but close inquiry revealed the fact that they were the relics of the priests of the church—the custom being to disinter the bones from the cemetery three years after the burial of the body.

But the excursion most in favour with the Australian was to the hot springs, on the slope of Mt. Therma. Round these had been built a rest house. The springs fed into two marble baths about three feet deep and six feet long. The water left the rocks at a temperature of 100 degrees Fahrenheit, and to the man who had not had a decent wash for nearly four months, the opportunity was revelled in. They used the baths in twos and threes, covered themselves in soap and washed it off, and repeated the process until the proprietor of the establishment knocked loudly at the door to announce that other customers were waiting.

The harbour and bay at this time presented a spectacle not likely to be again seen by many Australians. In addition to portions of the Allied navies, and smaller vessels such as trawlers, there were assembled some 13 hospital ships and at least 70 transports of 4,000 tons and over. Besides these, during the stay of the Battalion on the island, there arrived the "Aquitania" (45,600 tons), "Mauretania" (31,900 tons), and "Britannic" (50,000 tons), the latter vessel seeming to almost fill the entrance to the harbour as she steamed slowly in.

Christmas Day was now approaching, and preparations for making the season as enjoyable as possible were taken in hand. Tents were decorated and the ground around laid out in designs formed with the aid of the stones from the sea beach. A competition had been arranged and prizes were given for the parties securing the best results. One man constructed from the soil some models of kangaroos and swans. A supply of beer was ordered from the Canteen, and a consignment of Swallow & Ariell's tinned plum puddings having been received were issued in the proportion of one tin to every two men.

On the afternoon of the 24th December arrived the "Christmas Billies." These were two-quart cans which had been filled with comforts by the people of Australia and despatched for the use of the troops. Each can contained a card whereon the sender had written a seasonable greeting. By a touch of irony, painted on the outside of the receptacle was a representation of an Australian kicking a Turk off the Peninsula. Beneath was inscribed a line from "Dryblower's" well known song, "This bit of the world belongs to us." The contents of the "billies" covered a fairly wide range of articles, and an inventory made of one gave the following result:—

1 tin shortbread.	1 tube toothpaste.
1 tin cheese.	1 toothbrush.
1 tin tobacco.	1 packet prunes.
1 pack playing cards.	1 packet boracic acid.
1 corkscrew.	1 writing pad with envelopes.
1 mouth organ.	1 pipe.
Safety pins.	6 cigars.
1 piece soap.	

Although each State of the Commonwealth sent its proportion of gifts, the whole lot were pooled and distributed *pro rata*. The 28th thus received mostly Victorian gifts, but they were none the less welcome, and many men answered by letter the greetings of the senders.

The receipt of these gifts excited considerable interest and gave infinite pleasure. The scene when the cans were being opened was absorbing. Men were behaving like children, exhibiting the articles to one another, exchanging when not quite to taste, rendering impromptus on the mouth organs, and laughing over their own interpretations of the messages. In these last, as might be expected, little incongruities were discovered, and the commanding officer of a neighbouring battalion, who admitted an age of 40 and a weight of some 200lbs., felt flattered when he read the enclosed inscription, "To my dear little soldier boy."

That night went pleasantly enough—the men singing and talking until a late hour. Next morning, in beautiful weather, the Battalion paraded for divine service, which was conducted by the Rev. S. McBain, a chaplain of the 6th Brigade, in a manner that interested and pleased all. The dinner was a feast as compared with the meals of the previous months, and afterwards the Western Australians played their first, and a victorious, game of football in the A.I.F.— on this occasion against the 24th Battalion. A visit was also received from Colonel Burston, who was now located on the island in command of a large reinforcement camp. That evening in his own Mess he very pleasantly entertained some of the officers. Boxing Day was also observed as a holiday and passed without incident except for a visit from a hostile aeroplane which passed over the camp travelling eastwards at a considerable height.

Probably owing to the dislocation of the services brought about by the evacuation, the Battalion received no Australian mails for some time, and its latest news from home was quite two months old. About the 20th December, however, information was received that several thousand bags were in the vicinity. Later, curious members located these on the east side of the Bay. Representations made to higher authority failed to secure delivery, the statement being made that no transport was available but that battalions would receive their portions on reaching the next theatre of operations. This answer not proving satisfactory, a mild conspiracy was indulged in which covered the chartering of a local fishing boat and a trip across the Bay. Lieut. Nicholls was master, the owner pilot, and 28th men formed the crew. This and other measures were successful, and the Battalion got its letters just before the end of the month.

As time went on the Battalion so far improved in health and training that unit and Brigade route marches were undertaken. Here the Western Australians came under the eye of the Divisional Commander (Brig.-General W. Holmes, D.S.O.), who complimented them on their march discipline. On the 31st December he inspected them in close order drill and the practice of formations when under artillery fire. So pleased was he with their performance that he characterised the unit as "a damned fine battalion. I have never before seen such good work done in the Division."

On the 27th December was received, and read on parade, a message from the King congratulating the troops on the successful evacuation of the Peninsula. About this time arrived news of the deaths at Alexandria of Captain H. B. Menz and Lieut. H. E. C. Ruddock, both of whom had succumbed to disease.

A series of evening open-air concerts, arranged in the Brigade, concluded on New Year's Eve with that given by the 28th. Visitors from other units attended in considerable numbers and all enjoyed the following programme:—

28TH BATTALION.
Camp Concert—Programme.

Song	...	"The Deathless Army" ...	Private Allanson.
Song	...	... ...	Private "Sport" Edwards.
Song	...	... ...	Private Bolt.
Recitation		"Voice of Gallipoli" ...	Private Carr.
Song	...	"Queen of Angels" ...	Private Rolfe.
Song	...	... ...	Private Allanson.
Song	...	... ...	Private Piggott.
Sketch	...	"Chrysanthemums" ...	Corpl. Haydock.
Song	...	... ...	Private Carr.
Recitation...	...	... ...	Lieut. Field.
Song	...	... ...	Private Vicaridge.
Song	...	... ...	Private "Sport" Edwards.
Song	...	... ...	Private Thomas
Chorus	...	"28th Anthem"	
Chorus	...	"Auld Lang Syne"	

Lemnos Island, 31st December, 1915.

Many sat awake in their tents that night awaiting the arrival of the New Year and wondering what their future lot would be. At midnight whistle and siren sounds, so familiar, came from the vessels in the Bay.

About the 28th December instructions were received that the troops would re-embark within a few days and that a small party would precede each battalion in order to make the preliminary arrangements at the next assembly point. Captain E. A. Coleman was placed in command of the 28th details, and marched out on the 31st of the month.

January 1st was observed as a holiday, but training was continued on the following days, when the weather, which was now becoming broken with rains and cold winds, permitted. Definite instructions were issued to embark on the 5th, but these were cancelled later on account of heavy seas. However, at 7.30 a.m. on the 6th the camp ground was vacated, and two hours later 24 officers and 667 other ranks of the 28th began to file along North Pier and embark on the "Ansonia" (7,900 tons)—another Cunard boat.

The transport also took on board 3 officers and 53 others of the 2nd Divisional Train, under Captain S. Walker, and 6 officers and 717 other ranks, details of various units, under Lieut.-Colonel R. A. Crouch.

No difficulty was encountered in regard to quarters, and when the transport left the harbour next morning at 7.30 everybody had settled down.

The danger from submarines had become more acute recently, consequently special precautions were taken. No lights were exposed, and all life belts were kept handy. However, the voyage was without incident and, travelling rather slowly down through the Grecian Archipelago, Alexandria harbour was entered during the afternoon of the 9th January.

CHAPTER XI.

BACK TO EGYPT.

The Battalion disembarked at 10 a.m. on the 10th January and at once boarded a train. Little of Alexandria could be seen except the sea front and the southern and eastern portions which the railway skirted in its way out between the large shallow lakes, Mariut and Abukir, into the Libyan Desert. The route lay across the Rosetta and Damietta branches of the Nile and through the railway junctions of Tanta, Benha, and Zagazig, to Tel-el-Kebir, a station on the Sweet Water Canal some 16 miles west of Zagazig. Here there was a large military siding and signs of an extensive camp.

Leaving the train the Battalion proceeded to its camp site eastwards for some distance along a new military road. There, standing conspicuously on a little knoll, the first object to catch the eye was a bulky figure which had last been seen at Blackboy Hill and was now recognised, with ironical cheers, as belonging to the Camp Provost Corporal—the terror of all newly-joined recruits.

Near the camp site was parked the Regimental Transport which, under Lieut. T. D. Graham, had for over four months been impatiently awaiting orders to rejoin its parent unit. Men, horses, and vehicles were in fine condition and showed the benefit of the hard training that had been undertaken in anticipation of an advance after the enemy had been dislodged. In the care of the Transport were Australian mails, which had been accumulating for four weeks. These were very welcome.

Judging by the appearance of the lines of the neighbouring units, tents were not plentiful. Thanks, however, to a thoughtful Quartermaster and an unsuspecting Ordnance Officer at Alexandria, the Battalion had brought with it on the train a supply sufficient to house all ranks and allow a few over for the rest of the brigade. Beyond tents and a limited water supply, drawn from a neighbouring main, none of the ordinary conveniences, such as were found at Abbasia, were available. All these had to be provided by the Battalion's own efforts.

The greatest difficulty was encountered in connection with the kitchens, which could not be satisfactorily constructed in mere sand and gravel without other aids. To some extent relief was obtained by secretly requisitioning some of the loose railway material. When,

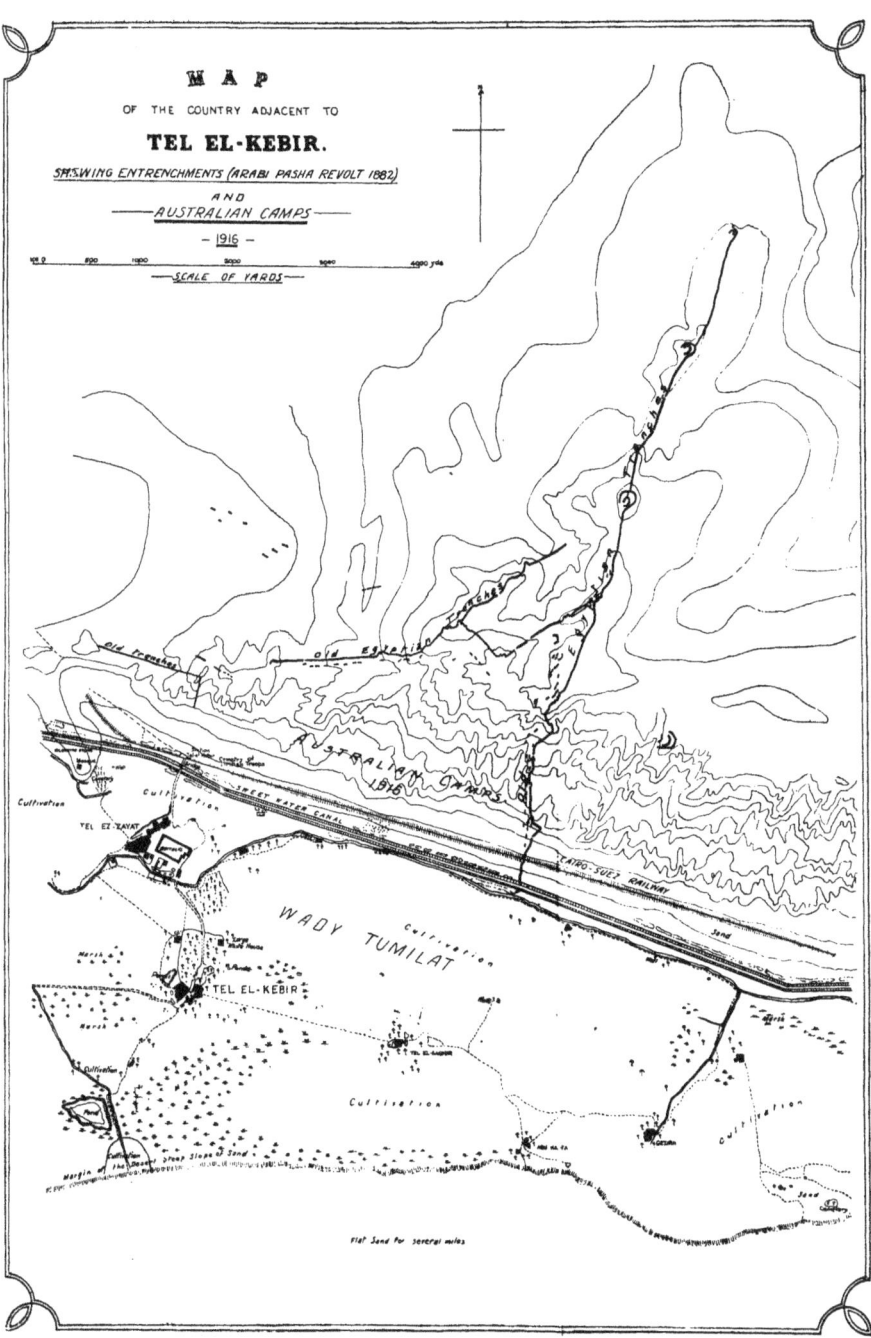

however, some newly wrought points, which were required for an additional siding, disappeared, the railway engineers and divisional staff descended in wrath upon the battalions and compelled the broken-hearted Sergeant-Cooks to dismantle their improvised establishments. Notwithstanding this discouragement, the cooks stuck to their tasks with that faithfulness which always characterised their attitude to the remainder of their comrades. They never let the men down.

At Tel-el-Kebir had been concentrated the 1st and 2nd Australian Divisions. The N.Z. and A. Division was at Moascar (near Ismailia). The 8th Infantry Brigade, which had arrived in Egypt from Australia about the middle of December, was covering a wide front on the eastern bank of the Suez Canal. The three brigades of Light Horse had recovered their mounts and were stationed near Cairo.

The camp of the 1st and 2nd Divisions ran for some two or three miles along the north bank of the Wady Tumilat, through which in ancient days had flowed the waters of the Nile to an outlet in the chain of lakes, of which Timsah was the nearest. The stream bed is some two miles wide and is dotted about with small villages and extensive cultivated tracts, whose edges are sharply defined by the sand and gravel of the Arabian Desert. On the south bank are traces of a canal excavated about 600 B.C., whilst on the north bank runs the Ismailia, or Sweet Water, Canal. This is also a work commenced in ancient times, re-opened some 60 years ago and continued to Suez originally for the purpose of supplying those engaged on Lesseps' great work.

The camp backed on to the railway line and faced towards the open desert, to the north. The 28th was on the extreme right of the infantry, but still further to the right lay the three brigades of the artillery of the 2nd Division, which had recently arrived from Australia. The neighbouring ground was historical. On it had been camped Arabi Pasha's rebel army of 25,000 Egyptians and 5,000 Bedouins to oppose Sir Garnet Wolseley's flank march on Cairo from Ismailia. About 1,000 yards to the east of the 28th, was a line of earthworks—ditch, rampart, bastion, and redoubt—which, commencing at the Sweet Water Canal, extended about due north for nearly five miles. Other and smaller works lay to the west of this line. At dawn on the 13th September, 1882, the British, 17,000 strong with 61 guns, had attacked the Egyptian Army by storming the fortifications. Within an hour the enemy was routed with heavy loss, including 58 guns, and at the small cost to the assailants of 57 killed and 412 other casualties. The following night Cairo had been entered and the submission of Arabi Pasha and his followers received.

150   THE 28th: A RECORD OF WAR SERVICE, 1915-19.

The first necessity, after the arrival of the Battalion at Tel-el-Kebir, was to complete the refitting of the *personnel* where it left off at Lemnos Island. Here began in earnest the system of charging individuals for losses of Government property. Up to date, these losses had been attributed to active service conditions and considered almost inevitable. But now a kit inspection revealed a deficiency of over £1,000 worth of articles that had been delivered to members of the Battalion less than a month before. This condition of affairs could only be set down to carelessness, and as a corrective, those in authority ruled that the individual must pay. Then followed little debit entries in the Paybooks. These annoyed the owners, but had the desired effect.

The refitting was spread over many days, the greatest difficulty being experienced with hats, which were scarce, the requisite numbers not arriving until many weeks later.

The return to Egypt involved a reversion to conditions regarding rationing which were far from satisfactory. The 8½d. per diem per man for groceries and extras was quite inadequate. Prices were higher and supplies more difficult to obtain. The soldiers could not be fed properly and grave trouble was threatening although all ranks were loyal and recognised that the best possible was being done to improve conditions. Eventually the Corps Commander, paying heed to the strong representations made, issued orders that the whole matter of supplies should be taken over by the Australian Army Service Corps and units provided direct with what was required. An immediate and vast improvement was the result.

The climate was found now to be very different from that of four months earlier. It closely resembled September in Western Australia, with occasional light showers of rain and nights cold enough to make at least two blankets desirable.

During the afternoon of the 15th January the 1st and 2nd Divisions were inspected by General Sir Archibald Murray, the Commander-in-Chief in Egypt. The Brigade was drawn up in a line of battalions in mass and mustered some 3,000 of all ranks. The General rode along the front of the Brigade and commented in very favourable terms on the appearance and steadiness of the Western Australians. In connection with this parade the Divisional Commander (General Legge had by now returned to duty) had been emphatic in regard to the dress of the troops. As a consequence company commanders were instructed to take especial pains to see that their men were correctly "turned out." When the unit was assembled the C.O. also inspected them and apparently found nothing to complain of. However, when the distinguished visitor arrived at the front of the 28th, there, standing in the centre of the front rank, could be seen a soldier wearing on his head nothing less than a yellow cap comforter. After the parade was over the Divisional Commander said what he had to say to the Colonel and, in accordance with the custom of the service, the Colonel passed the good words on.

ON THE BATTLEFIELD OF TEL-EL-KEBIR,
January, 1916.
Captain Rowan-Hamilton, Lt.-Col. J. Walker, Brig.-General J. Paton, Lt.-Cols. W. Dollman, G. A. Ferguson, and H. B. Collett.

At Tel-el-Kebir camp visits were exchanged between the various W.A. units. Members of the newly-arrived 32nd Battalion also called in on their way to Cairo. Brig.-General, J. J. T. Hobbs, from the 1st Division, found time to look in on his fellow-countrymen.

Leave to visit Cairo was now granted to a percentage of all ranks. As the majority of the pay accounts were substantially in credit this privilege was made use of freely, and a very pleasant and well-earned holiday of two or three days' duration spent in the city. Some men could not wait for their turn. They evaded the police for the time being, only to return later on, perhaps under escort, and face "Orderly room." There they usually pleaded guilty to the charge against them—convinced that in this instance the game had been worth the candle.

For some months past many complaints had been made at the front, and in Australia, in regard to the parcel post. Parcels intended for soldiers or their relatives had failed to reach their destinations. Where the leakage was occurring it was impossible to say. However, about the beginning of 1916 a change and reorganisation took place in the Army Postal Service and a tremendous improvement resulted. That this change was not viewed altogether without apprehension may be gathered from the remark attributed to some individual—"Everybody but the rightful owners has now been supplied with woollen underclothing, socks, pipes, tobacco, and cigarettes for the next twelve months, as well as with cigarette holders and wristlet watches. Why should we again have to go without whilst a new lot of people are being equipped?"

Training was resumed immediately the Battalion had settled down into its new camp. The General Staff still, apparently, held the opinion that the Turk, reinforced by the German, would advance on Egypt. In consequence, exercises in defence and in desert and night operations were constantly practised. The Battalion also studied those portions of the textbooks relating to savage warfare, to movements in echelon of companies, to the formation of squares to resist hordes of barbarian cavalry, and to suitable dispositions to counter the effects of artillery fire. During the dark hours movements on astral and compass bearings were tried and met with uniform success. Once a route march to an oasis some six miles to the north-east was attempted, and the hard smooth gravel in the desert in these parts made the "going" comparatively easy. Usually the training was carried out on the scene of the battle of 1882 and the feet, or inquisitive entrenching implement, of the soldier displaced many relics of that engagement which was sometimes referred to in short talks given when resting.

On the 22nd and 30th January, the whole Battalion, under Major Davies, crossed the neighbouring canal and the Wady Tumilat and, in conjunction with the 27th Battalion, engaged in a tactical exercise in which ball ammunition was used. The enemy was represented by tiles suitably arranged in the desert to the south.

Shortly after its arrival at Tel-el-Kebir the Battalion was notified that volunteers were required for a new unit—the Imperial Camel Corps—which was to be formed for operations in the desert. A number of names were given in, and a few days later Lieuts. T. D. Graham, H. R. Denson, and J. F. Quilty, with a goodly party of men, took train to Abbasia to report to the I.C.C. Depôt. Regimental Quartermaster-Sergeant R. G. Sexty was promoted to fill the vacancy caused by Lieut. Graham's transfer.

Inquiries in regard to reinforcements revealed that several hundred men, intended for the 28th, were in Zeitun Camp, where they were being trained on a system intended to fit them to take their place in the ranks of the parent unit. Sir Archibald Murray had promised that these should be sent to join the Battalion. On the 19th January 281 men arrived. This number included 53 sick and wounded returned to duty.

The 27th January brought the news that Colonel Paton, for his services during the Evacuation, had been rewarded with the rank of Brigadier-General. This promotion, apart from being popular, brought additional prestige to the 7th Brigade.

Notwithstanding the improved conditions of climate and surroundings, the 28th still suffered a few casualties from sickness. During the first month of the year three officers and 56 other ranks were sent to hospital. Shower baths were badly needed, and although the waters of the adjacent canal looked attractive they were reported to be infested with the bilharzia worm and bathing was forbidden.

The last day of January was spent in brigade work in close formation. This was not quite a success and, beyond traversing a considerable area of ground and raising a great deal of dust and sweat, secured little result. On the following day an exercise in the brigade in defence, and the occupation of a position by night, were more practical and interesting.

About this time it was decided, owing to the increasing number of Turks in the Sinai Peninsula, to strengthen the defences of the Suez Canal. The orders which followed directed that the 1st and 2nd Divisions should cross the waterway and establish a new line of defence in the desert on the east side. The 8th Brigade was to be relieved.

On the evening of the 3rd February, the Battalion, now 17 officers and 891 other ranks strong, climbed into a rake of trucks and was hauled down to Ismailia—a journey of some 30 odd miles. Detraining at Moascar, on the west side of the town, a march of some four miles, along a first-class road, brought the 28th to the bank of the Suez Canal. A crossing was effected by means of a pontoon bridge constructed by the Engineers. As the east bank was reached, Signaller Yeldon was heard to exclaim in tones of great satisfaction, "Well, this is another bally country I can say I've been in." The march continued for another mile to a camp (Staging Camp) in which the remainder of the Brigade was already assembled.

For the comparative ease and order with which this move was carried out, the Battalion was specially mentioned by the Divisional Commander. Some two months later, on the return march, General Legge held up the discipline of the 28th Battalion to the rest of the units in the Division as an example for them to follow. This is not to imply that the marches were enjoyed by anybody. No march with full equipment up ever is, and when dust and heat are added to weight and distance, there is little reason to rejoice.

The 7th Brigade was now a reserve for the 5th and 6th Brigades. A reconnaissance of the route to the front line was therefore made. A military road under construction had already run some miles out into the desert. On this were working numerous gangs of Egyptian labourers and many strings of camels. These animals in this part of the country seemed to be as numerous as cattle in Australia.* Quarries had been opened at the few places near by. A pipe to carry water to the advanced positions was also being laid alongside the road at the rate of over a mile a day.

The desert is almost pure sand, and very trying for man and beast. Numerous hills, some of which are over 300 feet high, make the going difficult. The summits of these hills present a razor-like edge, and the wind keeps the sand continuously in motion in the form of a miniature cascade stretching along the whole of the crest.

The line occupied by the troops was some 12,000 yards out from the Canal. Trenches, heavily revetted with sandbags and protected by barbed wire, had been dug and were thinly manned, the main portions of the garrisons being sheltered in tents pitched in convenient hollows. Here the Australians led a dolorous existence, without even the distraction of shell fire or an adjacent enemy. Away out in front detachments mounted on camels, and an occasional aeroplane, looked for signs of a Turkish approach.

The 28th did not remain long at Staging Camp. On the 6th February it moved back to the Canal bank near the crossing point—Ferry Post—and took over from the 30th Battalion the duties connected with the inner defences at this part.

The defences consisted of a bridgehead system, the earthworks of which had been constructed in the spoil taken out during the excavation and dredging of the Canal. The southern flank rested on the shore of Lake Timsah, whilst the northern flank terminated on the Canal bank some two miles above Ferry Post. At this extremity of the line "A" Company was located and had, with the support of the Machine Gun Section, to garrison two posts named Bench Mark and Ridge Post. Here they led a life of comparative ease. At night time the trenches were thinly manned, and at all times a guard was maintained on a neighbouring dredge. But for the rest, bathing and fishing were the main diversions of Captain Macrae's men. A small pontoon, left by the Turks twelve months earlier, was on charge to the post. There was also considerable interest evinced in the passing vessels—feluccas and barges carry-

---

* It was reported that 50,000 camels were requisitioned for the operations in the Sinai Peninsula.

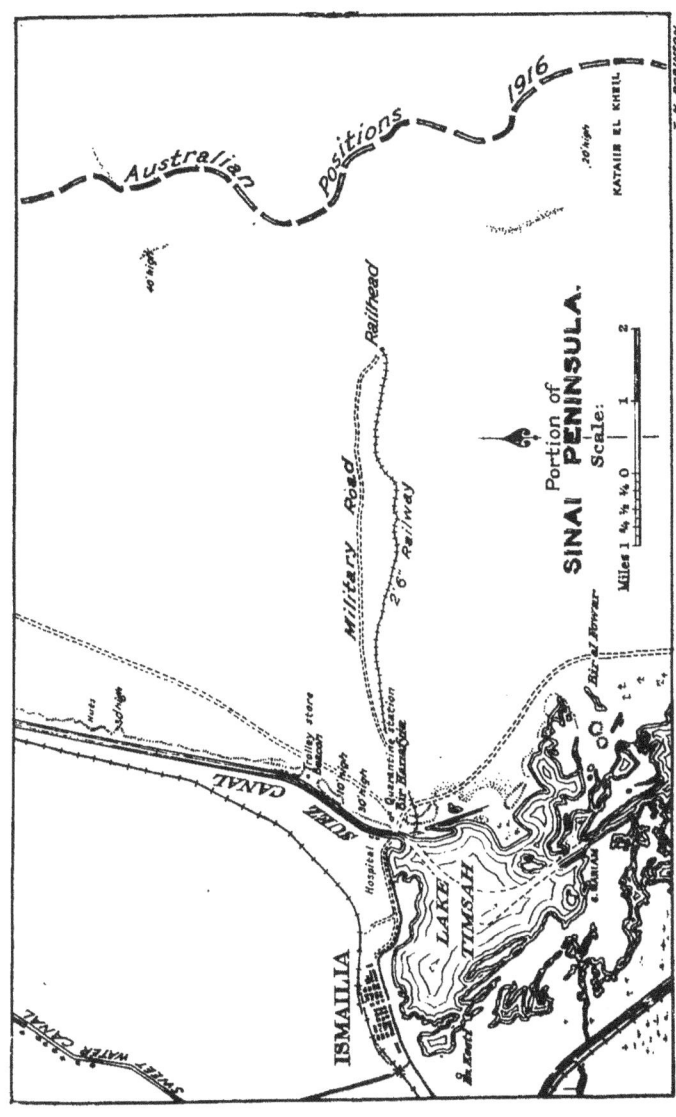

THE AUSTRALIAN POSITION IN DEFENCE OF THE SUEZ CANAL, 1916.

Map by Australian War Museum.

ing stone and stores to Ferry Post, transports, and steamers bound for or returning from Australia. With these last news was exchanged *viva voce*, and passengers sometimes threw ashore tins of cigarettes, tobacco, and chocolates.

Attached to the 28th was a section of the Hongkong-Singapore Royal Garrison Artillery, manned by Sikhs, and a detachment of the Bikanir Camel Corps—a force composed of the subjects of India, which had been raised and was maintained in the field by the Maharajah of that State. An additional force was the Royal Australian Naval Bridging Train, under Captain Bracegirdle, which had been present at Suvla Bay and marched into Ferry Post a few days after the 2nd Division arrived in the vicinity. This unit was to assist in the management of the bridge and ferry traffic.

The Battalion was accommodated partly in tents and partly in wooden rush-roofed huts. Its duties were many. Training was almost impossible. A guard had to be furnished for a large Ordnance Depôt located on the west bank. Men had to be found to work the ferry on which, when the pontoon bridge was drawn back, troops and horses were hauled across the Canal. Police to regulate the traffic over the bridge and maintain a check on the passes, without which no person was allowed to cross the waterway. Then again, the natives who fished the lake were not allowed to ply their trade except with a written permit and the presence in the boat of a soldier. This escort duty was not unpopular, for the reason that nearly every man who performed it returned to camp with several pounds' weight of excellent fish.

But the foregoing were the light duties. Others, more arduous, were attached to the handling of the hundreds of tons of supplies which were daily dumped on the wharf at Ferry Post and taken away to the forward area by horse wagons. On Gallipoli the soldier became also a navvy. At Ferry Post he was changed into a wharf labourer. Few who were there will forget the task of handling the iron water mains which had to be cleared from the barges, without the aid of cranes, and which ruined the clothing by contact with the tar with which they were covered. Then again, the adjacent dump absorbed many men, and what clothing the pipes had failed to destroy was dealt with in moving coils of barbed wire and other material equally destructive. A light railway had been commenced for the purpose of supplying the front line with its needs. Here once more the Western Australian found his services in demand and he went along to do work which the native labourers could not be trusted with. Through it all he "groused," but he applied himself earnestly to the task in hand and seriously complained only about his spoiled clothes. One Engineer officer said he had never had men who had worked so hard and effectively.

At the Headquarters of the Battalion was established an Examining Post. Through this passed numerous secret service agents employed by Army Headquarters for the purpose of gaining information within the enemy lines. Fierce-looking ruffians some of them were, and they responded none too willingly to the few questions put to them through the Syrian interpreter—a graduate of an American college at Beyrout—attached to the Post.

Traffic through the Canal was dependent to some extent also upon Battalion Headquarters. As has already been mentioned in an earlier chapter, one ship had been mined. Other mines had been located, and proof existed that enemy agents, under cover of darkness, were endeavouring to block the waterway. One method utilised to counter these measures was to sweep a track along the sand of the eastern bank. By means of a horse harnessed to logs and other material this was done daily before nightfall. At dawn patrols would examine the swept area, and if tracks of man or beast crossed it at any point these would be closely followed until their origin and purport had been explained. Reports were then sent to the Adjutant, and by 8 a.m. an "all clear" message went forward to Army Headquarters, which, in turn, informed the Canal officials that traffic could proceed without risk. Should, by any chance, this report be delayed the effect at Army Headquarters was remarkable, and the life of the responsible people at Ferry Post very unenviable for the next few hours.

The Canal at Ferry Post was some 70 yards wide, and the depth believed to be something over 30 feet. Just below the ferry the water ran into Lake Timsah, which was irregular in form and measured about three miles from side to side. In this lake a few vessels were anchored, some of them being men-of-war—French and British—as auxiliary to the defence. On the bank opposite Ferry Post is a rocky plateau, upon which was a convent, or monastery, and some buildings used by the management of the Canal. Here, during February, Sir Archibald Murray established his headquarters.

The town of Ismailia is situated near the north-western edge of the lake, and in 1916 contained about 12,000 inhabitants, one-fourth of which were foreigners, mostly French and Italians. The Australians found the place quite attractive, taking especial delight in the gardens, some of which contained the familiar bougainvillæa in full bloom, and in the shade afforded by the fine avenues of lebboks and magnolias. The native bazaar attracted those who had money to spend on local manufactures; whilst a very fine clubhouse afforded means for rest and refreshment to those officers whom leave or duty brought across the Canal.

FERRY POST.
Showing the Suez Canal where it enters Lake Timsah. Ismailia in the distance.

Photo. lent by Mr. Yeldon.

FERRY POST.
The landing place on the East bank. General Legge waiting for the High Commissioner.

At varying times during the 24 hours vessels passed north and south along the waterway. Freighters, transports bringing reinforcements from Australia (including the 8th/28th), or troops to augment the army in Mesopotamia, and well known mail steamers such as the "Osterley," all came into view and in a few minutes travelled beyond. Often news was exchanged with those on shore and sometimes occurred the mutual recognition of friends. At night time sleepers, awakened by the flash of a search light in their faces, sat up and observed the approach of the larger craft, with the assistance of powerful arc lights affixed to their bows, cautiously navigating the channels.

From the foregoing description of the life and environment of those who dwelt at Ferry Post, it may be gathered that, although their daily lot was a hard one, it was sufficiently full of incident to banish monotony. Without such incident existence would have been intolerable. Nature herself seemed to be almost somnolent in these parts, for, besides a few chameleon-like lizards, a stray jackal or hawk, and a plentiful supply of small black beetles which stood on their heads when interfered with, all other forms of life were absent. Even vegetation was reduced to a few rushes and a very occasional stunted bush.

At Tel-el-Kebir an increase in the popularity of gambling had been noted. Greater leisure and consequent opportunity probably accounted for this. At night time, when training was not in progress, numerous knots of men could be observed between the rear of the camp and the railway line gathered around two or three candles stuck in the ground. There "House" and some of the unlawful games were played with relatively high stakes. The military and regimental police broke up some of these "schools," but this action had, apparently, no deterrent effect. After the move to Ferry Post the craze became even greater. A favourite haunt of the gamblers was on the ramparts of those parts of the defences which were not occupied by posts. There after dark some hundreds of men would assemble—the illuminations spreading for half a mile down towards Lake Timsah. The authorities took action. Raids were made, plants confiscated, and some of the offenders punished. At other times the judiciously circulated rumour of an intended raid also had a desirable effect and the ramparts that night would be deserted. On the whole the spread of the evil was arrested but, as in civil communities, it was never possible to completely eradicate it.

Despite the severer conditions, the health of the Battalion was not materially affected during the month of February. There was a slight increase in the number sent to hospital—the total reading one officer and 73 other ranks. Unfortunately two deaths from disease

THE CAMP OF THE 28TH AT FERRY POST.
Lake Timsah in the background.

THE SUEZ CANAL.
A liner in the fairway and feluccas tied up to the banks.

occurred, and with the loss of Company Sergt.-Major R. Wolstenholm and Private E. M. Edwards, Australia was deprived of two very promising and popular soldiers. Cerebro-spinal meningitis was reported to have broken out in Australia and, despite the precautions taken, a few cases made their appearance on the Canal. As a preventive against the threatened epidemic, the Regimental Medical Officer caused each company to parade daily and indulge in a little gargling exercise with a mouthful of Condy's fluid.

The proximity of Army Headquarters and Corps Headquarters (at Ismailia) led to fairly frequent visits from Generals Murray, Birdwood, and Godley, and their staffs. Other visitors were Sir Arthur Henry M·Mahon, the High Commissioner for Egypt, accompanied by Lady M·Mahon and members of the family. On one occasion the Commander-in-Chief was escorted by a number of frock-coated gentlemen, wearing tarbooshes, who constituted some of the "notables" of Egypt and had been invited to witness a display by the Air Service of the Army.

CHAPTER XII.

PREPARING FOR FRANCE.

Early in 1916 the Australian Government decided to raise and maintain three new Divisions of the Australian Imperial Force. One of these—the 3rd—was to be recruited in Australia and the other two—4th and 5th—found from *personnel* available in Egypt. By this decision Australia was committed to providing, straight off, a new formation of 20,000 men and, in addition, to increasing her monthly flow of reinforcements by 150 per cent., in order to adequately maintain the five divisions in the field.

When the 1st and 2nd Divisions moved down to the east bank of the Suez Canal, the 4th and 8th Brigades were taken back to Tel-el-Kebir camp to form the nuclei of the 4th and 5th Divisions, respectively. As a means of preserving the admirable spirit of the A.I.F., and also to ensure a backing of trained and experienced *personnel*, 50 per cent. of the new infantry brigades, technical and departmental units, was secured by splitting up the four original infantry brigades and their attendant auxiliaries. The balance was furnished from the accumulating reinforcements at the training camps, near Zeitun. By this means, the two original Western Australian Battalions—11th and 16th—became the parent units of the 51st and 48th Battalions, respectively.

Following on this very important addition to the forces, the A.I.F. was now divided into two Corps. General Birdwood remained in supreme command, but personally directed the operations of the 1st Anzac Corps, whilst to General Godley fell the 4th and 5th Divisions which, added to his own New Zealanders, formed the 2nd Anzac Corps. The main body of the Light Horse became a separate Division under the command of Major-General H. G. Chauvel.

In consequence of the necessity for filling up the ranks of the new formations, a goodly portion of the body of reinforcements—officers and others—intended for the 28th Battalion was diverted to the 51st Battalion.

Following on the action taken in regard to the creation of the new Divisions, steps were taken to form several new units. These included a Cyclist Battalion for the Corps, a Pioneer Battalion for each Division, and a Machine Gun Company for each Brigade. Heavy calls were made on the infantry to man these, and the transfers which ensued made serious gaps in the ranks of the 28th.

Lieut. J. J. S. Scouler, the Signalling Officer, was selected to command a company of the Cyclists and secured his third star. Lieut. G. D. Shaw and 2nd Lieut. A. M. Hope went to the 2nd Pioneers and were accompanied by many well tried N.C.Os. and men.

To the Machine Gun Company Lieuts. T. O. Nicholls and C. R. Field went together with the whole of the Machine Gun Section which had done such sterling work on Gallipoli. For the future, in order to ensure a tactical use more in keeping with their fire power, machine guns were to be grouped under the Brigade Commander. Their place with the Battalion was taken by two Lewis Guns—an automatic rifle and a new weapon. These were given into the care of 2nd Lieut. F. Sears who, with a newly formed Section, was sent to attend a School of Instruction in that arm.

In connection with the new formations, Major C. R. Davies was selected for promotion, and on the 28th February left Ferry Post to take over the command of the 58th Battalion.

Towards the end of February some modifications were made in the establishments of the infantry battalions. For reasons unknown, provision for Signalling and Transport Officers was omitted and the duties had henceforth—until some time after arrival in France—to be carried on by subaltern officers taken away from their platoons.

Further changes in the Battalion were necessitated by the attachment to Brigade Headquarters of Lieut. N. W. Sundercombe, as Brigade Bombing Officer, and Lieut. G. A. Read, as a Staff Trainee. The necessary adjustments were made. Major A. W. Leane became second in command, and was succeeded in "C" Company by Captain A. S. Isaac. Lieut. C. M. Foss took up the duties of Adjutant. 2nd Lieut. R. G. Sexty remained in charge of the Transport, whilst the Signallers were supervised by Lieut. A. E. C. Gepp —a Duntroon graduate, who was posted to the Western Australians at this stage. The remaining vacancies for officers were filled by the promotion of Sergt. A. Brown, whose good work on Gallipoli had brought him especially under notice, Company Sergeants-Major B. A. Bell, J. McIntyre, and Sergt. H. C. King.

About the middle of February, the General Staff seemed to have formed the opinion that the situation in regard to the Canal no longer gave cause for anxiety. The strength of the forces available for its defence, the backward condition of the enemy preparations, the route of the Senussi's army, and the approach of summer, all pointed to the improbability of active operations for at least some months to come. At this time also Sir Archibald Murray, in an official document, referred to the A.I.F. as the "Imperial

Strategical Reserve." Those persons who grasped the meaning of this phrase expected early developments, and the various foreign theatres again came under discussion. Nor were indications as to the new field of service long in coming. The institution of a certain type of tactical exercise; the overhauling of gas helmets and the constant practice in

PRIVATE H. A. FRANCO, M.M.
A well-known member of the Battalion, who died of illness in France on 16th February, 1918.
Photo. lent by Mr. S. Jones.

wearing them; lecturettes on the tactics and weight of metal of the German artillery; and leaflets describing the rank, badges, and saluting habits of one of our Allies, all pointed to an early departure for the Western Front. Following on these things came a complete change of rifles—the new ones firing mark VII. ammunition, which gave a flat trajectory for a longer distance than the earlier mark—and instructions to study the regulations regarding the transport of troops by sea.

Before any move took place the A.I.F. indulged in a little introspection. Considering the size to which the Force had grown it was inevitable that some proportion of undesirables must exist in its ranks. Nor is this to be wondered at when it is remembered that in certain cities in Australia magistrates released well known criminals from custody on their undertaking to enlist. The majority of these men had no intention of fighting, and when they eventually joined their units were the cause of endless trouble. In their nefarious operations they were not easily detected, but evidence of their handiwork was forthcoming from the police, who received complaints of

THE PIONEER-SERGEANT AT WORK.
Sergeant J. W. Anderson.

serious assaults and robberies from the villages around Tel-el-Kebir and on the route to Cairo. In cases where arrests were made it was sometimes not difficult for the prisoner to escape from his captors and then the search for him began anew. Later, when the main body of the A.I.F. had officially departed from Egypt, a party had to be left behind to clear up the situation caused by the presence of these individuals in the native community.

The 28th was not altogether free from characters of this sort. On the eve of embarkation for Gallipoli a man was missed from his company. His absence was duly reported in the proper quarter, but nothing more was seen of him by his officers until January, 1916, when he marched into the camp at Lemnos with other details. He remained with the Battalion until the rumours of the Turkish advance began the preparations for the move to the Canal. Once more he vanished, and just prior to the embarkation for France information was received that he had been seen near the Pyramids, dressed as a Light Horseman, armed with a revolver, conducting a "two-up" school. The next indications of his whereabouts came from Etaples, about the middle of 1917. From there he was sent to England suffering from *debility!* He did not return to Australia.

Another original member of the Battalion, whose appearance and demeanour gave a fair indication of his capabilities, could never be satisfactorily brought to book. After the first action at Pozieres he joined the stream of men returning to Sausage Valley, but the contrast between him and those who had taken part in that heroic fight was so marked as to make it fairly safe to say where he *had not* been during those trying hours. Some months later he was found walking down Piccadilly arrayed in a frock coat and top hat. He retired to Lewes for a term, was placed on board a transport after the Armistice, but got ashore at Cape Town and, it is hoped, has not troubled Australia since. One or two other similar types joined the Battalion later in the war and their records varied but slightly.

It was the type of men indicated in the foregoing that neither General Birdwood nor the A.I.F. desired should accompany the troops to France. In order to be rid of them, instructions were issued that all "undesirables" were to be returned to Australia. Unfortunately, in the 2nd Division, it was soon found that the C.Os were not considered to be good judges as to who were the vicious characters. A call was made for the records of the men, and from those who had the greatest number of entries in their "conduct sheets" the selection was made. This was greatly deplored, for the reason that many men who were frequent offenders in a minor way were excellent soldiers in the line. On the other hand, the real undesirable was sufficiently astute to keep free from ordinary military "crime." Nevertheless, his presence in the ranks was a continual menace to the preservation of order and to the peace and property of individuals. Experience later proved that to the failure to thoroughly clear up the situation whilst in Egypt, and to the inability of certain officials in Australia to recognise that the good name of Australia's volunteer army required to be jealously guarded, may be attributed many of the troubles and prejudices which hampered the Force during the remainder of the war and were so costly to the taxpayer.

There were other men whose services it seemed unwise to retain. A few existed in every unit. They were constitutionally unfit for active service and, whilst not requiring medical treatment, were unlikely ever to become fit. It was useless evacuating them to hospital because they always turned up again in a few days or weeks marked "Fit." To deal with them a Medical Board, composed of experienced officers, was assembled. After an examination of the individual, the Board recorded its opinion and, if it was adverse, he was sent down the Line of Communication either for return to Australia or for employment as a "B. Class" man.

During the first week in March the camp at Ferry Post began to get uncomfortable. The heat was increasing and the desert winds brought the "khamsin" or duststorms. For hours on end the air would be laden with the flying sand which got over and into every object in its path. Early one morning 500 men of the Battalion were called out and, armed with shovels, proceeded to uncover the railway track which had been completely submerged during the night.

The "move" commenced on the 5th March. On this date Brigade Headquarters and three battalions marched back to Moascar where a divisional camp existed. From that date for several days there was a continuous stream of troops crossing the pontoon bridge. After a lapse of several months the New Zealanders were encountered again as they came over to the east bank to relieve the 2nd Australian Division.

On the 8th March the 28th joined the rest of the Brigade after a rather trying march in great heat—the last portion being through heavy sand.

It was directed that before embarkation all troops were to be reinoculated against paratyphoid. This unpopular action was duly taken.

By the addition of reinforcements, which had dribbled in, together with officers and other ranks returning from hospital, the strength of the Battalion had been brought up to near the authorised establishment. The last draft marched in on the day before departure for Alexandria. Transport vehicles and bicycles were not to be taken overseas and were transferred to the charge of the New Zealanders.

These preparations took up several days, during which very little training could be carried on. On the evening of the 13th March the Brigade assembled and was addressed by General Birdwood. His principal theme was Australia's good name and Lord Kitchener's message to the British Expeditionary Force on embarkation in August, 1914. Later General Godley rode into camp to say good-bye and wish good luck to those who had served under him on Gallipoli.

The Transport Officer, together with 25 other ranks and the 56 horses of the Battalion, boarded a train near midnight on the 13th, journeyed to Alexandria, and next day embarked on H.M.T. "Minneapolis," which left the harbour early in the morning of the 15th. This last date witnessed the main body of the 28th, climbing on to open trucks at Moascar siding. From 10 p.m. until next morning the train rumbled and jolted through the night. The air was cold but the single blanket, now the sole covering for the soldier, was reinforced by the heat generated by the crowded condition of the trucks. At Tel-el-Kebir there was a brief halt. Here three reinforcement officers, Lieut. R. S. Browne, and 2nd Lieuts. J. Roydhouse and R. H. Gill, reported and were carried on.

Arriving at a wharf at 6.30 a.m., some little delay ensued before the men could file on to the Transport. Besides the 28th Battalion there were to be accommodated 1½ Companies of the 27th Battalion (Major F. R. Jeffrey), and the 2nd Divisional Signal Company (Major R. H. Goold, M.C.). Later in the day Major-General Legge and the Divisional Headquarters were added to the number, making a total complement of 53 officers and 1,533 other ranks. Travelling as a passenger was Major-General W. G. B. Western, who had recently commanded the troops on Lemnos Island.

The Battalion now found itself on the most comfortable ship that, so far, it had been its lot to travel by. Bearing the number "A32," the Transport was the Aberdeen liner "Themistocles," of some 11,000 tons.

The voyage commenced that evening. The usual precautions against fire and submarines were observed. Life belts were always in evidence, and boat stations practised daily. All lights were covered at night. The weather proved to be ideal and the look of content on every soldier's face gave indication of how the change of life, scene, and air was appreciated.

A modified form of training was carried on—prominence being given to anti-gas measures and trench routine and discipline.

During the morning of Sunday, the 19th March, the rather violent "zig-zagging" of the ship gave an indication of the presence of hostile submarines. There were, however, no visible signs of their presence, and it was not until later in the day that the information as to another ship having been torpedoed, not many miles away, was passed down by the ship's staff.

Having passed around the north side of Crete the ship, during the afternoon of this same day, arrived off Malta. Her engines were

THE 2ND DIVISION CROSSING THE CANAL EN ROUTE TO
EUROPE, MARCH, 1916.
Photo. lent by Mr. Yeldon.

THE "THEMISTOCLES" AT ALEXANDRIA.
The 28th waiting to embark, 16th March, 1916.
Photo. lent by Mr. Yeldon.

stopped for a while and those on the decks had a brief glimpse of the narrow entrance to the Grand Harbour, the heavy fortifications whose walls seemed to run down into the sea, and, beyond, the steep slopes, upon which the picturesque city of Valetta is built. A few naval vessels were within sight of the Transport. A wicked looking submarine and a French torpedo boat passed close by.

Receiving fresh instructions as to the route to be followed, the "Themistocles" resumed her course and, passing through the Malta Channel, entered the Sicilian Sea. The Italian possession of Pantellaria Island was sighted and also the elevated headland of Cape Bon on the Tunisian coast. Skirting the western shores of Sardinia and Corsica, the French coast east of Toulon came into view on the morning of the 21st March. Little could be seen of the great naval base, but as the Transport headed north-west, a short lapse of time revealed Marseilles, France's most ancient city, lying within its circle of verdured hills.

Proceeding under slow steam towards a precipitous islet, which with its castle was recognised by some as the Isle d'If, made famous by Dumas' "Count of Monte Cristo," a hail was received from a picket boat, which came racing out from the direction of the shore. In response, the Transport changed her course abruptly, as it seemed she had been on the verge of entering a mine field.

As the harbour was entered all eyes were agaze at this first contact with the civilisation of the Old World. Comments were made on the obvious fertility of the soil, on the apparent prosperity of the community, and on the magnitude of the engineering undertakings, as disclosed by the many docks and their machinery.

A closer approach to the shore revealed sentries posted here and there. These were old gentlemen in battered képis, long coats and baggy trousers, armed with rifles, which were capped by bayonets of an inordinate length. The 28th Band, which had been revived at Ferry Post, came into action and did its best with the "Marseillaise." This was responded to from the wharves, where a number of women and a few men had assembled to see the new arrivals. "Vivas" for France and Australia were exchanged and some of the members of the Battalion let go what they recollected of their schooldays' French.

At 3.30 p.m. the voyage came to an end.

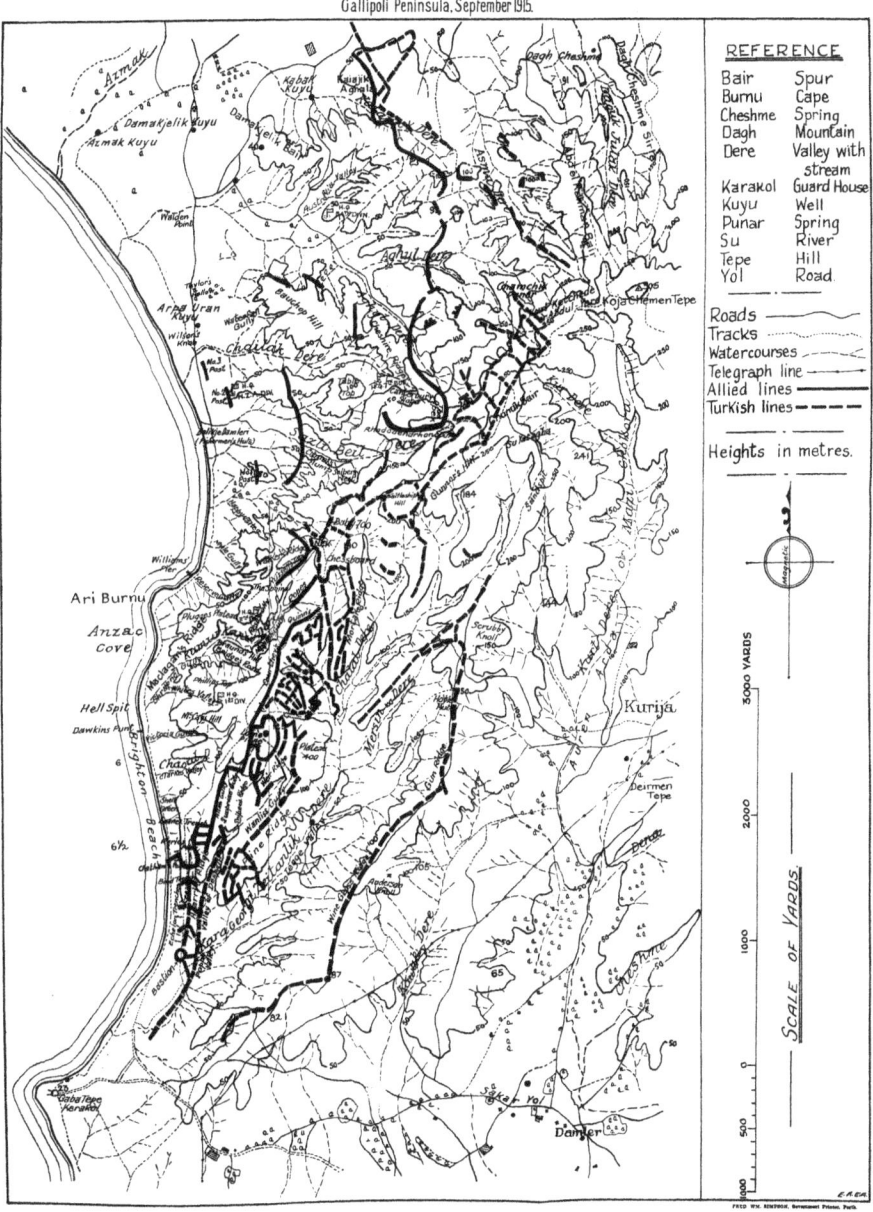

Appendix A.

AUSTRALIAN IMPERIAL FORCE.

LIST OF UNITS RAISED AND RECRUITED BY WESTERN AUSTRALIA.

(Compiled from information supplied by the Defence Department.)

Australian Flying Corps.*
10th Light Horse Regiment.
36th (Australian) Heavy Artillery Group.*
8th Battery, 3rd Field Artillery Brigade.
1st Divisional Ammunition Column.*
3rd Field Company, Engineers.*
6th Field Company, Engineers.*
1st Divisional Signal Company.*
3rd Divisional Signal Company.*
Australian and New Zealand Wireless Signal Squadron.*
3rd Light Railway Operating Company.
4th Broad Gauge Railway Operating Company.*
3rd Mining Battalion.*
6th Tunnelling Company.
11th Infantry Battalion.
12th Infantry Battalion (one company).
16th Infantry Battalion (part from South Australia).
28th Infantry Battalion.
32nd Infantry Battalion (two companies).
44th Infantry Battalion.
51st Infantry Battalion (organised in Egypt).
3rd Pioneer Battalion.*
4th Company Army Service Corps.*
16th Company Army Service Corps.
2nd Depôt Unit of Supply.
7th Depôt Unit of Supply.
4th Squadron Australian Remount Unit.
4th Field Ambulance.*
2nd Australian Stationary Hospital.

* Part only.

Appendix B.

Roll of Honour.

(Those who died between the 16th April, 1915, and the 21st March, 1916.)

AVE ATQUE VALE.

> Hail and farewell! the laurels with the dust
> Are levelled, but thou hast thy sure crown,
> Peace and immortal calm, the victory won.
> Somewhere serene thy watchful power inspires,
> Thou art a living purpose, being dead,
> Fruitful of nobleness in lesser lives,
> A guardian and a guide; Hail and farewell!

Taken from an "In Memoriam" to the late General Sir F. Stanley Maude, the Conqueror of Mesopotamia.

206	Private	Alexander, D.	... Died of wounds, Gallipoli ...	26-9-15
558	,,	Archibald, G. A.	... Died of wounds, Malta ...	3-10-15
562	Sergeant	Ball, F. W.	... Killed in action, Gallipoli ...	14-9-15
1016	Private	Barnsley, W.	... Killed in action, Gallipoli ...	3-10-15
1117	,,	Barrie, A. ...	... Died of wounds, Malta ...	10-10-15
565	L/Corpl.	Bateman, W. H.	... Killed in action, Gallipoli ...	8-12-15
397	Private	Burge, W. ...	... Killed in action, Gallipoli ...	19-9-15
950	,,	Burvill, H. H.	... Killed in action, Gallipoli ...	14-9-15
599	,,	Butt, E. ...	... Killed in action, Gallipoli ...	7-10-15
238	,,	Colgate, O.	... Killed in action, Gallipoli ...	16-9-15
35	,,	Coll, J. ...	... Died of illness, at sea ...	25-9-15
403	.,	Connor, E.	... Died of illness, Malta ...	7-11-15
264	,,	Copley, N.	... Died of illness, at sea ...	1-11-15
826	,,	Cunningham, D. W.	Died of wounds, Gallipoli ...	24-11-15
254	,,	Curwen, F. E.	... Died of wounds, Gallipoli ...	21-9-15
1100	,,	Dale, G. F.	... Killed in action, Gallipoli ...	19-9-15
272	,,	Delaporte, R.	... Killed in action, Gallipoli ...	16-9-15
1193	,,	Duff, R. ...	... Killed in action, Gallipoli ...	26-9-15
989	,,	Earl, A. ...	... Killed in action, Gallipoli ...	22-9-15
1532	,,	Edwards, E. M.	... Died of illness, Egypt ...	12-2-16
1711	,,	Gleeson, S. J.	... Killed in action, Gallipoli ...	15-10-15
985	,,	Gresham, J. D.	... Died of illness, Egypt ...	22-11-15
1545	,,	Hallam, E. J.	... Died of illness, at sea ...	24-10-15
1153	Corporal	Hawley, C. K.	... Died of wounds, Gallipoli ...	23-9-15
954	Private	Height, H L.	... Died of wounds, Gallipoli ...	14-9-15
861	,,	Hodder, G.	... Killed in action, Gallipoli ...	2-12-15
308	Sergeant	Hodgson, J.	... Killed in action, Gallipoli ...	22-9-15

Roll of Honour—continued.

444	Private	Hopkins, F. W.	Accidentally drowned, Blackboy Hill	16-5-15
298	,,	Horrocks, E. J.	Died of wounds, Gallipoli	18-9-15
299	Corporal	Hyde, W. ...	Died of wounds, at sea	18-9-15
306	Private	Hynes, N	Died of wounds, Gallipoli	6-11-15
	Lieut.	Jensen, F. E.	Died of wounds, Gallipoli	13-9-15
887	Corporal	Kennon, A.	Killed in action, Gallipoli	5-10-15
107	Private	Knapp, J. L.	Died of illness, Egypt	12-11-15
1208	,,	Lee, G. C. ...	Died of illness, England	31-10-15
1122	,,	McGill, W. P.	Killed in action, Gallipoli	22-9-15
660	,,	Mackay, D. McK.	Died of wounds, Gallipoli	26-9-15
744	,,	McKenzie, A.	Died of wounds, Gallipoli	30-11-15
994	,,	McNamara, J.	Died of wounds, Gallipoli	3-10-15
	Captain	Menz, H. B.	Died of illness, Egypt	27-11-15
124	Private	Merrick, J.	Killed in action, Gallipoli	30-9-15
1557	Corporal	Morrow, E.	Killed in action, Gallipoli	16-12-15
1111	Private	Munro, N. A.	Killed in action, Gallipoli	16-12-15
496	Sergeant	Pead, S. W.	Died of wounds, at sea	22-9-15
371	Corporal	Quick, J. K.	Died of illness, Egypt	14-8-15
1578	Private	Rainsden, A.	Drowned at sea	6-10-15
584	,,	Reen, C. F.	Killed in action, Gallipoli	11-10-15
1576	L/Corpl.	Roy, J. H.	Died of wounds, Egypt	28-11-15
	Lieut.	Ruddock, H. E. C.	Died of illness, Egypt	22-11-15
1775	Private	Saunders, J.	Died of illness, Egypt	18-2-16
517	,,	Shenfield, E. A.	Killed in action, Gallipoli	22-9-15
524	,,	Snudden, A.	Killed in action, Gallipoli	14-9-15
722	,,	Wilson, A.	Died of wounds, Gallipoli	12-10-15
783	Coy. Sgt.-Major	Wolstenholme, R.	Died of illness, Egypt	24-2-16
727	Private	Wright, F.	Died of wounds, Malta	28-11-15

This be their epitaph : " Traveller, south or west,
Go, say at home we heard the trumpet call,
And answered. Now beside the sea we rest.
Our end was happy if our country thrives :
Much was demanded. Lo ! our store was small—
That which we had we gave—it was our lives."

" L.L." in the " Anzac Book."

Appendix C.

CASUALTIES OF THE 28TH BATTALION, A.I.F., WHILST WITH THE MEDITERRANEAN EXPEDITIONARY FORCE.

(Note.—On arrival at Marseilles the Battalion passed to the British Expeditionary Force.)

	Officers.	Other Ranks.	Total.	
			Officers.	Other Ranks.
Killed in action	...	22		
Died of wounds	1	17		
Died of disease	2	11		
Died from other causes	...	2		
Total deaths	...	...	3	52
Wounded in action	2	82		
Prisoners of War	...	...		
Total wounded and prisoners of war	...	...	2	82
Evacuated sick (from Peninsula only)	...	...	9	346
Total Casualties	...	...	14	480

ERRATA.

Page 175.—Opposite the name of Lamb, C. H., delete "Mentioned in Despatches."

Page 196.—Opposite the name of Rickman, F. O., add "Mentioned in Despatches."

Page 206.—Opposite the name of Fox, J. A., add "Mentioned in Despatches."

Page 207.—Opposite the name of Green G., delete "T. to Y.M.C.A., Ptd. Hon. Lieut. 1/5/18," and insert "Apptd. 2nd Lieut. 6/1/19. Ptd. Lieut."

THE 28th: A RECORD OF WAR SERVICE, 1915-19. 175

Appendix D.

ROLL OF ORIGINAL OFFICERS OF THE 28TH BATTALION, AUSTRALIAN IMPERIAL FORCE.

Appointment.	Rank.	Name.	Memoranda.
Commanding Officer	Lt.-Colonel	Collett, H. B.	Commanded Battn. 23/4/1915 to 29/7/1916 (severely wounded), and from 13/10/1917 to 22/3/1918. Transferred to General List. Mentioned in Despatches. Promoted Colonel. C.M.G., D.S.O. Mentioned by the Secretary of State for War. Promoted Brevet Colonel. Australian Military Forces, for "specially meritorious service."
Second-in-Command	Major	Davies, C. R.	Transferred to 58th Battn., 1916. Promoted Lt.-Colonel. O.B.E. Previously served in the South African War, 1901-1902.
Adjutant	Captain	Lamb, C. H.	Invalided 1915. Returned with 44th Battn., 1916. Wounded. Mentioned in Despatches. Promoted Major. M.C.
Quartermaster	Hon. Lieut.	Dunn, R.	Resigned Commission, 1915.
Signalling Officer	2nd Lieut.	Scouler, J. J. S.	Transferred to Australian Cyclist Battalion, March, 1916. Promoted Captain. French Croix de Guerre.
Transport Officer		Graham, T. D.	Seconded with Imperial Camel Corps, Jan., 1916. Transferred to 4th Pioneer Battn., 1916. Promoted Captain and Adjutant. Killed in action, Belgium, 2/10/1917.
Machine Gun Officer	2nd Lieut.	Shaw, G. D.	Transferred to 2nd Pioneer Battn., 1916. Wounded on two occasions. Mentioned in Despatches. Promoted Captain. M.C.
"A" COMPANY.			
Officer Commanding	Major	Wilson, J. A. C.	Invalided 12/11/1915.
2nd-in-Command	Captain	Montgomery, A. M. P.	Invalided 1915. Returned from Australia with Reinforcements 1916, and rejoined, 1917. Severely wounded, 1917, and again invalided.
O.C. No. 1 Platoon	Lieutenant	Davey, A. H.	Promoted Captain. Invalided 1916.
O.C. No. 2 Platoon	2nd Lieut.	Pugh, C. H.	Wounded. Promoted Captain.
O.C. No. 3 Platoon	2nd Lieut.	Denson, H. R.	Seconded with Imperial Camel Corps, Jan., 1916. Thence transferred to 14th Light Horse. Served in Sinai and Palestine with that Regiment. Promoted Major. D.S.O.
O.C. No 4 Platoon	2nd Lieut.	Read, G. A.	Promoted Lieut.-Colonel. Commanded Battalion from 5/1/17 to 28/9/17. Severely wounded. Invalided. Thrice mentioned in Despatches. D.S.O. Montenegrin Order of Danilo, 5th Class.

Appendix D—continued.

ROLL OF ORIGINAL OFFICERS OF THE 28TH BATTALION—continued.

Appointment.	Rank.	Name.	Memoranda.
"B" COMPANY.			
Officer Commanding	Major	Jeffrey, F. R.	Attached to 27th Battn., 8/6/15. Afterwards transferred to that unit. Previously served in the South African War with City Imperial Volunteers.
2nd in Command	Captain	Stroud, W. G.	Commanded "B" Company until October, 1915. Invalided.
2nd in Command	Lieut.	Jackson, P. E.	Attached from 27th Battn., vice Major Jeffrey. Promoted Captain. Died of wounds, France, 31/5/16.
O.C. No. 5 Platoon	2nd Lieut.	Ruddock, H. E. C.	Acting Adjutant, Oct.-Nov., 1915. Died of pneumonia, Egypt, 22/11/15.
O.C. No. 6 Platoon	Lieut.	Gibbings, C. T.	Commanded "B" Company in 1916. Promoted Captain. Killed in action, France, 29/7/16.
O.C. No. 7 Platoon	2nd Lieut.	Hargraves, G. A.	Invalided Oct., 1915. Rejoined Sept., 1917. Wounded. Invalided Nov., 1917. Promoted Captain.
O.C. No. 8 Platoon	2nd Lieut.	Sundercombe, N. W.	Seconded to command 7th Light Trench Mortar Battery, 1916-17. Rejoined Battn., 1918. Mentioned in Despatches. Promoted Captain. M.C.
"C" COMPANY.			
Officer Commanding	Major	Leane, A. W.	Commanded Battn. from 30/7/16 to 4/1/17. Promoted Lieut. Colonel. Died of wounds, France, 4/1/17.
2nd-in-Command	Lieut.	Isaac, A. S.	Commanded "C" Company, March-July, 1916. Promoted Captain. Severely wounded 29/7/16. Invalided.
O.C. No. 9 Platoon	2nd Lieut.	Jensen, F. E.	Died of wounds, Gallipoli, 13/9/15. Previously served in the South African War.
O.C. No. 10 Platoon	2nd Lieut.	Phillips, R. C.	Promoted Captain. Twice wounded. Transferred to Australian Flying Corps, April, 1917. Promoted Major. M.C. and Bar. D.F.C.
O.C. No. 11 Platoon	2nd Lieut.	Carter, L. J.	Invalided 1915.
O.C. No. 12 Platoon	2nd Lieut.	Smith, G. A. F.	Transferred to 47th Battn., 1916, and afterwards to 15th Battn. Promoted Captain.
"D" COMPANY.			
Officer Commanding	Major	Welch, L. B.	Killed in action. France, 28/7/16.
2nd-in-Command	Captain	Menz, H. B.	Died of enteric fever, Egypt, 27/11/15.
O.C. No. 13 Platoon	2nd Lieut.	Glyde, E. G.	Wounded on four occasions. Promoted Major. Belgian Croix de Guerre.
O.C. No. 14 Platoon	Lieut.	Macrae, N. F.	Commanded "A" Company, 1915-16. Promoted Captain. Killed in action, France, 29/7/16.

Appendix D—continued.

ROLL OF ORIGINAL OFFICERS OF THE 28TH BATTALION, ETC.—continued.

Appointment.	Rank.	Name.	Memoranda.
O.C. No. 15 Platoon...	2nd Lieut. ...	Foss, C. M. ...	Acting Adjutant, 1916. Promoted Captain. *M.C.* Died of wounds, France, 11/8/16.
O.C. No. 16 Platoon...	2nd Lieut. ...	Nicholls, T. O....	Transferred to 7th Machine Gun Company, 1916, and subsequently commanded that unit. Mentioned in Despatches. Promoted Captain. *M.C.* Severely wounded 4/10/17 and invalided.
ATTACHED.			
Medical Officer ...	Captain ...	Kenny, J. ...	A.A.M.C. Transferred from France to Egypt, 1917. Promoted Major.
Chaplain	4th Class ...	Brennan, Very Rev. D. A.	Promoted to Chaplain, 2nd Class.

Appendix E.

ROLL OF OFFICERS PROMOTED FROM THE RANKS, 28TH BATTALION, A.I.F., BETWEEN 9TH JUNE, 1915, AND 21ST MARCH, 1916.

Reg. No.	Rank.	Name.	Promoted to:	Date.	Remarks.
1005	Regtl. Sergt.-Major	Gettingby, J.	Hon. Lieut. & Quartermaster	26-8-15	Invalided April, 1916. Promoted Honorary Captain on Permanent Supernumerary List, 1917.
796	Sergeant ...	Field, C. R.	2nd Lieut.	13-9-15	Transferred to 7th Machine Gun Company, 1916. Adjutant 7th M.G. Bn., 1918. Promoted Captain. Twice mentioned in Despatches.
787	Coy. Sergeant-Major	Bell, P. T. C.	do. ...	3-11-15	Killed in action 29th July, 1916.
1000	Sergeant ...	Sears, F....	do. ...	14-11-15	Wounded. Promoted Lieutenant.
221	Do. ...	Brown, A.	do. ...	8-2-16	Wounded on two occasions. Mentioned in Despatches. Promoted Major. Second-in-Command 1918. *D.S.O., M.C.*
776	Regtl. Quartermaster-Sgt.	Sexty, R. G.	do. ...	1-3-16	Transport Officer, 1916-17. Mentioned in Despatches. Promoted Captain. Invalided.
784	Coy. Sergeant-Major	Bell, B. A.	do. ...	1-3-16	Killed in action, 29th July, 1916.
337	Coy. Sergeant-Major	McIntyre, J.	do. ...	14-3-16	Promoted Captain 1917. *M.C.* Killed in action 28th February, 1917.
461	Sergeant ...	King, H. C.	do. ...	14-3-16	Adjutant 1917-18. Mentioned in Despatches. Promoted Captain. Wounded. *M.C.* Died of wounds 7th April, 1918.

Appendix F.

ROLL OF REINFORCEMENT OFFICERS WHO JOINED THE 28TH BATTALION, A.I.F., BETWEEN THE DATES 9TH JUNE, 1915, AND 21ST MARCH, 1916.

Rank.	Name.	Date joined.	Remarks.
Lieutenant...	Quilty, J. F. ...	17-8-15	Left in Egypt 4th September, 1915. Rejoined 24th October, 1915. Seconded with Imperial Camel Corps, Jan., 1916, and subsequently invalided.
Captain ...	Coleman, E. A.	11-10-15	Commanded " B " Company October, 1915, till June, 1916. Invalided.
2nd Lieut....	Hope, A. M. ...	11-10-15	Transferred to 2nd Pioneer Battn., 1916. Promoted Lieutenant. Severely wounded.
Do. ...	Bowra, H. J. ...	11-11-15	Invalided 4th December, 1915.
Lieutenant	Gepp, A. E. C.	20-2-16	Graduate of Duntroon College. T. from 32nd Bn. Killed in action 5th August, 1916.
Do. ...	Browne, R. S.	15-3-16	Intelligence Officer, 1916. Severely wounded 23rd June, 1916. Invalided.
2nd Lieut....	Gill, R. H. ...	15-3-16	Promoted Captain. M.C. Died of wounds 28th September, 1917.
Do. ...	Roydhouse, J.	15-3-16	Adjutant 1916-17. A brigade-major 1918-19. Wounded on two occasions. Twice mentioned in Despatches. Promoted Captain. M.C.

Appendix G.

Civil Occupations of Original Members of the 28th Battalion, A.I.F., who embarked as Officers or were subsequently promoted to Commissioned Rank.

Profession, Trade or Calling.	Original Officers.	Those promoted from the Ranks.
Accountants	4	...
Assayers	...	1
Bank Clerks	...	2
Barristers	1	1
Blacksmiths	...	1
Bushmen	...	1
Carpenters	...	1
Civil Engineers	...	1
Civil Servants	4	...
Clergymen	1	...
Clerks	4	9
Coachmen	...	1

Appendix G—continued.

Civil Occupations of Original Members of the 28th Battalion, A.I.F.—contd.

Profession, Trade, or Calling.	Original Officers.	Those promoted from the Ranks.
Commercial Travellers	1	...
Dentists	1	...
Doctors	1	...
Draughtsmen	1	2
Electrical Engineers	2	...
Engine-drivers	...	1
Engineers	2	2
Farm hands	...	2
Farmers	1	6
Fitters	...	1
Graziers	1	...
Grocers	...	1
Horse-drivers	...	1
Indent Agents	1	...
Inspector, S.P.C.A.	...	1
Insurance Inspector	1	...
Labourers	...	2
Master Plumbers	1	...
Mechanics	...	1
Miners	1	3
Navvies	...	1
Orchardists	1	1
Painters	...	1
Pearlers	...	3
Policemen	...	1
Postal Assistants	...	1
Railway Assistants	...	2
Sailors	1	1
Salesmen	1	1
School Teachers	...	2
Sheep Overseers	...	1
Sleeper Hewers	...	1
Station Hands	...	1
Station Masters	...	1
Surveyors	1	1
Tailors	...	1
Telephone Operators	...	1
Wool Experts	1	...
No occupation	1	1
Total	34	63

Appendix H.

28TH BATTALION, AUSTRALIAN IMPERIAL FORCE.

NOMINAL ROLL OF ORIGINAL MEMBERS WHO EMBARKED AT FREMANTLE ON H.M.A.T. "A.11" ("ASCANIUS"), 9TH JUNE, 1915, AND ON THE "BOONAH," 12TH JULY, 1915.

ABBREVIATIONS USED.

A/-	... Acting.		Fld. Amb.	... Field Ambulance.
A.A.M.C.	... Australian Army Medical Corps.		H.T.M. Bty.	... Heavy Trench Mortar Battery.
A.A.S.C.	... Australian Army Service Corps.		I.C. Corps	... Imperial Camel Corps.
A.A.V.C.	... Australian Army Veterinary Corps.		K. in A.	... Killed in Action.
			L/Cpl.	... Lance-Corporal.
A.G.H.	... Australian General Hospital.		L/Sgt.	... Lance-Sergeant.
			L.T.M. Bty.	... Light Trench Mortar Battery.
Apptd.	... Appointed.		M. Gr.	... Machine Gunner.
Bgr. ...	... Bugler or Drummer.		M.G. Bn.	... Machine Gun Battalion.
Bn. ...	... Battalion.		M.G. Coy.	... Machine Gun Company.
Bty. ...	... Battery.		M.T.M. Bty.	... Medium Trench Mortar Battery.
Bty. S.M.	... Battery Sergeant-Major.			
C.Q.M.S.	... Company Quarter-Master-Sergeant.		Occ. ...	... Occasion or occasions.
			Pnr. Bn.	... Pioneer Battalion.
C.S.M.	... Company Sergeant-Major.		Prov.	... Provisional.
Cpl. ...	... Corporal.		Ptd. ...	... Promoted.
D.A.C.	... Divisional Ammunition Column.		Pte. ...	... Private.
			R.Q.M.S.	... Regimental Quartermaster-Sergeant.
D. of Ill.	... Died of Illness.			
D. of Wds.	... Died of wounds.		R.S.M.	... Regimental Sergeant-Major.
Div. Hqrs.	... Divisional Headquarters.		Reg. Sig.	... Regimental Signaller.
Div. Sig. Coy.	Divisional Signal Company.		Rft. ...	... Reinforcement.
Dr. ...	... Driver.		Sgt. ...	... Sergeant.
E.R. ...	... Extra Regimental.		St. Bearer	... Stretcher Bearer.
F.A. ...	... Field Artillery.		T. ...	... Transferred.
F.A. Bde.	... Field Artillery Brigade.		T/- ...	... Temporary.
F. Coy. Eng.	Field Company, Engineers.		Wdd. ...	... Wounded.

NOTES.

1. Unless otherwise stated the rank on embarkation was that of Private.

2. Where it has been possible to obtain the information, the letters "Wdd." have been set opposite to the names of those who were wounded.

3. It has not been practicable to show who were evacuated sick. In 1915 severe illnesses accounted for the complete severance from the Battalion of a considerable number of members.

4. Original members of detachments are so recorded in the column headed "Memoranda." This applies to Machine Gunners, Pioneers, Regimental Signallers, Stretcher Bearers, and A.A.M.C. Details. Transport Drivers and Buglers or Drummers are shown as "Dr." and "Bgr." respectively, under the heading "Rank on Embarkation."

5. There may be errors in the various records. In the absence of direct access to the official documents this has been almost inevitable, but the best has been done with what data the compiler could collect from various sources.

THE 28th: A RECORD OF WAR SERVICE, 1915-19. 181

Appendix H—continued.

28TH BATTALION.—NOMINAL ROLL OF ORIGINAL MEMBERS—continued.

Reg. No.	Rank on Embarkation.	Name.	Memoranda.
982	...	Aaltonen, E. A.	
207	...	Abram, R. ...	K. in A., France, 29/7/16.
1013	...	Acres, J. J. ...	T. to 7th M.G. Coy., 11/8/16. Ptd. L/Sgt. Wdd. 2 occ. *M.M.*
193	...	Acton, W. J. ...	Wdd. 1915. T. to 7th F. Coy., Eng., 7/3/16. Apptd. Dr.
590	...	Adams, J. ...	T. to 7th M.G. Coy., 3/3/16. Ptd. L/Cpl.
199	...	Adamson, E. E.	
555	...	Ahnall, K. ...	Apptd, 2nd Lieut., 27/12/16. Wdd. *D.C.M.* K. in A., France, 28/2/17.
1	...	Ainsworth, H. J.	K. in A., France, 29/7/16.
206	...	Alexander, D. ...	D. of Wds., Gallipoli, 26/9/15.
194	...	Alexander, G. ...	D. of Wds., France, 7/11/16.
2	...	Allan, J. W. ...	Wdd.
202	...	Allanson, A. H. C.	T. to 7th M.G. Coy., 3/3/16. Wdd.
3	...	Allen, J. B. ...	Ptd. L/Cpl.
975	...	Allen, L. G. ...	Apptd. 2nd Lieut., 16/8/16.Ptd. Captain. Adjutant 1918. Ment. in Despatches. *M.C.*
4	Dr.	Allen, P. ...	D. of Ill., France, 16/4/18.
557	...	Allen, P. R. ...	Reg. Sig. T. to 2nd Div. Sig. Coy., 14/8/16. Wdd.
1014	...	Allport, A. K.	
5	...	Anderson, A. A.	
1126	Sgt.	Anderson, C. T.	T. to 2nd Pnr. Bn., 11/3/16. Ptd. C.S.M. Wdd.
587	...	Anderson, F. R.	Wdd. T. to A. Provo. Corps, 5/4/17. Ptd. E. R. Cpl.
1184	Sgt.	Anderson, J. W.	Pioneer-Sergeant.
586	Cpl.	Anderson, W. ...	Ptd. Sgt. *M.M.*
1106	...	Andrews, G. ...	D. of Wds., France, 24/4/16.
497	...	Angus, J. B. ...	Apptd. Dr. Wdd.
591	...	Angus, J. C. ...	D. of Wds., France, 6/7/16.
589	...	Annear, K. C. ...	Invalided to Australia, 1915. Returned and T. to 46th Bn., 31/3/16. Wdd. K. in A., France, 18/9/18.
198	...	Anthony, F. T.	Ptd. L/Cpl. T. to 2nd Pnr. Bn., 11/3/16.
792	C.S.M.	Appleyard, W. S.	Ptd. R.S.M. Evacuated 1915. Rejoined Nov., 1917. T. to 11th Bn., 4/1/18.
8	...	Archer, R. ...	Invalided to Australia, 1916. Returned and T. to 46th Bn., 12/8/17. Ptd. L/Cpl. K. in A., France, 5/4/18.
558	...	Archibald, G. A.	D. of Wds, Malta, 3/10/15.
203	...	Armstrong, B. ...	Ptd. L/Cpl. Wdd., 1915.
941	Cpl.	Arundel, E. A.	Ptd. L/Sgt.
201	...	Ashe, E. R. ...	T. to 2nd Pnr. Bn., 11/3/16. Apptd. Dr.
200	...	Ashton, H. ...	Ptd. L/Cpl. Wdd.
588	...	Atkinson, S. ...	Ptd. L/Cpl. T. to 5th F. Coy., Eng., 18/8/15.
205	...	Austin, H. ...	Invalided to Australia, 2/9/15.
995	...	Badcock, G. L.	Wdd.
225	...	Badcock, H. ...	Wdd., 1915. T. to A.A.M.C., 27/8/17.
560	...	Baesjou, R. C.	
1015	...	Bainbridge, A. J.	T. to 13th F.A. Bde., 1/4/16.
992	...	Baker, B. ...	Wdd.
1137	...	Baker, D. J. M.	
990	...	Balcke, W. H. ...	Ptd. Cpl. Wdd.
561	...	Ball, F. ...	Apptd. Dr. Wdd.
562	Sgt.	Ball, F. W. ...	K. in A., Gallipoli, 14/9/15.
9	...	Ballingall, C. T.	T. to H.T.M. Bty., 1916. Ptd. Bty. S.M. *D.C.M.*
594	...	Banks, R. ...	Wdd. K. in A., France, 26/3/17.
10	...	Barbary, L. ...	K. in A., France, 29/7/16.

Appendix H—continued.

28TH BATTALION.—NOMINAL ROLL OF ORIGINAL MEMBERS—continued.

Reg. No.	Rank on Embarkation.	Name.	Memoranda.
228	...	Barge, W.	Ptd. Cpl. K. in A., France, 1/6/18.
208	...	Barker, B.	Ptd. Sgt. Wdd. 1915 and 2 occ. later.
226	...	Barker, F.	Wdd. 1915.
1065	...	Barnes, T.	T. to Aust. Provo. Corps, 1/1/17. Ptd. E.R. Sgt.
600	...	Barnett, C.	Ptd. L./Cpl. Died of Wds., France, 30/5/16.
1016	...	Barnsley, W.	K. in A., Gallipoli, 3/10/15.
1117	...	Barrie, A.	D. of Wds., Malta, 10/10/15.
598	...	Barter, G. M.	Ptd. Sgt.
219	...	Bartlett, W.	Wdd.
209	...	Barton, T. C.	
227	...	Barun, J.	Wdd.
563	...	Basford, T. R.	Ptd. Cpl. Wdd.
564	Cpl.	Bateman, H. P.	Apptd. 2nd Lieut. 30/6/16. K. in A., France, 5/8/16.
565	...	Bateman, W. H.	Ptd. L/Cpl. K. in A., Gallipoli, 8/12/15.
394	...	Batley, A.	Ptd. L/Cpl. Wdd. 1915. K. in A., France, 29/7/16.
11	...	Bear, E.	Apptd. Dr. T. to 5th F. Coy. Eng., 18/8/15.
1154	...	Beggs, J.	M. Gr. T. to 7th M.G. Coy., 3/3/16. Apptd. 2nd Lieut. 2/12/16. Ptd. Lieut.
232	...	Beggs, W.	T. to 2nd Pnr. Bn., 10/3/16.
784	C.S.M.	Bell, B. A.	See Appendix E.
787	C.S.M.	Bell, P. T. C.	See Appendix E.
601	...	Belstead, G. W.	Wdd. 1915.
222	...	Belstead, H. M.	D. of Wds., France, 25/4/17.
567	...	Benarie, M.	T. to 2nd Div. Sig. Coy. 12/8/15.
1204	...	Bennett, G. H.	K. in A., France, 8/4/16.
568	...	Bennett, H. G.	K. in A., France, 29/7/16.
1083	...	Bennett, S. H.	T. to Aust. Postal Corps 19/5/16. Ptd. E.R. Cpl.
13	...	Bent, W. T.	Wdd.
998	...	Benton, J. G.	
223	...	Betts, G. E.	
1018	...	Biggs, C.	T. to 4th Pnr. Bn. 16/4/16. Apptd. Dr. Wd. 1915 and 2nd occ.
210	...	Biles, A. R.	T. to 51st Bn. 2/4/16. K. in A., France, 3/9/16.
570	...	Biles, C. L.	T. to 2nd Pnr. Bn. 10/3/16.
398	...	Bilston, E. St. I.	Wdd. 1915.
14	...	Bingham, A.	K. in A., France, 3-6/11/16.
1019	...	Black, J. K.	Wdd.
1116	...	Blampey, T.	Ptd. C.S.M. Wdd. 1915 and 2nd occ.
571	...	Blechynden, A. G. R.	Invalided 1915. Returned with 12/28th Rfts. Ptd. Sgt. K. in A., France, 28/2/17.
229	...	Blows, O. S.	Reg. Sig. Ptd. Cpl. Wdd.
596	Sgt.	Bodinner, J.	Wdd. 1915.
1166	...	Bolin, P.	Ptd. Sgt. Wdd. 2 occ.
731	...	Bond, R.	Wdd.
393	...	Bond, T.	T. to 7th F. Coy., Eng., 7/3/16.
733	...	Boon, A.	Wdd.
396	...	Boorman, T.	
15	...	Boryss, B.	Wdd.
233	...	Bourne, R. F.	T. to 2nd F.A. Bde. 17/10/15. Ptd. Bty. S.M. Wdd. M.M.
930	Dr.	Bowen, G.	
1054	...	Bowers, W.	
395	...	Bowron, C.	Wdd. 1915.
17	...	Boyle, P. T.	Apptd. Dr.
1017	...	Boys, A. J.	Ptd. Cpl. Wdd.

THE 28th: A RECORD OF WAR SERVICE, 1915-19. 183

Appendix H—continued.

28TH BATTALION.—NOMINAL ROLL OF ORIGINAL MEMBERS—continued.

Reg. No.	Rank on Embarkation.	Name.	Memoranda.
399	...	Brazier, O.	Wdd. K. in A., Belgium, 30/10/17.
1020	...	Brennan, E. J. ...	K. in A., France, 29/7/16.
18	...	Brennan, P.	T. to 11th Bn. Ptd. Cpl. Wdd.
934	...	Brigatti, G.	Ptd. R.Q.M.S. K. in A., France, 20/5/18. Previously served in Sth. African war.
231	...	Briggs, E.	
1200	...	Brisco, G. H.	Ptd. L/Cpl. K. in A., France, 29/7/16.
569	...	Bristow, B. B.	T. to 7th F. Coy., Eng., 7/3/16. Ptd. E.R. Staff Sgt.
211	...	Britten, R. J.	K. in A., France, 29/7/16.
592	...	Broadbent, H. F. ...	T. to 2nd Div. Sig. Coy. 1/9/16. *M.M.*
1127	...	Brock, H.	Wdd. 1915.
218	...	Brooks, G. H.	Ptd. R.S.M. Mentioned in Corps Orders, 13/12/16. Wdd. 2 occ.
19	...	Brooks, H.	K. in A., France, 29/7/16.
20	...	Brooks, J. H.	T. to 2nd Pnr. Bn. 11/3/16. Ptd. L/Sgt.
21	...	Brooks, S.	T. to I.C. Corps 30/1/16. Ptd. Cpl. Wdd. 2 occ.
221	Sgt.	Brown, A.	*See* Appendix E.
958	...	Brown, F. E.	Ptd. Cpl. Wdd. 2 occ.
809	...	Brown, G. D.	Wdd. 1915. T. to 2nd Pnr. Bn. 10/3/16. Ptd. L/Cpl.
1145	...	Brown, G. J. R. ...	T. to H.T.M. Bty. 22/4/16. Returned to Bn. 10/8/17. Wdd. 1915 and 2nd occ. *M.M.* K. in A., Belgium, 4/10/17.
22	...	Brown, J. McL. ...	T. to 51st Bn. 2/4/16. Accidentally killed, France, 27/6/16.
217	L/Cpl.	Brown, J. W.	A.A.M.C. Detail. Ptd. L/Sgt. *M.S.M.*
220	Sgt.	Brown, R.	Apptd. 2nd Lieut. 29/7/16. Ptd. Captain. Wdd. 2 occ. Mentioned in Corps Orders 13/12/16. *M.C.*
597	...	Brown, W. T.	Invalided to Australia 25/9/15. Returned and T. to 46th Bn. 18/3/17. *M.M.*
213	...	Bruce, H.	T. to 7th M.G. Coy. 3/3/16. Ptd. Sgt. Wdd.
593	...	Bruce, W. O.	Wdd. 1915. T. to 7th M.G. Coy. 3/3/16.
595	...	Bryant, J. B.	
812	...	Buck, H. V.	Ptd. L/Cpl. K. in A., France, 29/7/16.
963	...	Buckingham, A. E. ...	St. Bearer. T. to 7th Fld. Amb. 6/5/17.
913	Dr.	Bullen, H. J. S.	
212	...	Burdon, G.	Wdd. 1915.
397	...	Burge, W.	K. in A., Gallipoli, 19/9/15.
935	...	Burgoyne, V. J. ...	St. Bearer. T. to 17th Coy., A.A.S.C., 21/11/17.
810	...	Burke, J. L.	Ptd. Cpl. Wdd. 2 occ. D. of Wds. France. 19/5/17.
230	...	Burley, R. A.	K. in A., France, 29/7/16.
811	...	Burns, H.	Wdd. 2 occ.
224	Cpl.	Burns, T. A.	T. to Royal Flying Corps, Nov., 1916. Ptd. Lieut.
23	Dr.	Burridge, A. T.	
009	...	Burton, A. P.	T. to 2nd Div. Sig. Coy., 1/9/15.
216	...	Burton, O. C. H. ...	Ptd. Cpl. K. in A., France, 29/7/16.
814	Cpl.	Burton, W. N.	T. to 2nd Div. Sig. Coy., 12/8/15.
950	...	Burvill, H. H.	K. in A., Gallipoli, 14/9/15.
215	...	Butcher, T.	T. to 2nd Pnr. Bn., 11/3/16.
24	...	Butler, M. F.	T. to I.C. Corps, 31/1/16.
25	...	Butler, P. L.	
599	...	Butt, E.	K. in A., Gallipoli, 7/10/15.
26	...	Cadee, T.	Apptd. Dr. Invalided to Australia, 25/9/15.

Appendix H—continued.

28TH BATTALION.—NOMINAL ROLL OF ORIGINAL MEMBERS—continued.

Reg. No.	Rank on Embarkation.	Name.	Memoranda.
256	...	Cahill, J.	
816	...	Cahill, W. J.	Wdd.
817	...	Cailes, H. N.	K. in A., France, 29/7/16.
407	...	Calder, J. L.	Wdd.
825	...	Campbell, A. M.	Ptd. Sgt. Wdd.
259	...	Campbell, E. A.	Ptd. L/Cpl. Wdd. 1915.
943	...	Campbell, J. C.	Reg. Sig. T. to 2nd Div. Sig. Coy., 12/8/15. Ptd. Cpl.
824	Cpl.	Campbell, R. F.	Wdd. Invalided to Australia. Rejoined, 1/9/16.
1021	...	Carder, F. S.	St. Bearer. Wdd. 1915. T. to 4th M.G. Bn., 25/5/18. Ptd. Cpl. D. of Wds., France, 21/9/18.
410	...	Carlisle, R.	Apptd. 2nd Lieut., 7/4/17. Ptd. Lieut. Wdd.
50	Sgt.	Carroll, C.	Sig. Sgt. Wdd.
28	...	Casey, R.	M.Gr. Invalided, 1915. Returned with 44th Bn. Apptd. 2nd Lieut., 5/3/17. Ptd. Lieut. M.C. D. of Wds., France, 7/4/18.
234	...	Castles, W. H.	Wdd. T. to 51st Bn., 15/10/17.
29	...	Cave, A. J.	Wdd.
607	...	Cerini, A. V.	Wdd.
235	...	Chalkley, J.	T. to 8th F. Coy., Eng. Apptd. Dr. K. in A., France, 25/9/17.
1157	Bgr.	Chaloner, D.	Wdd., 1915.
30	...	Chamberlain, P.	Ptd. Sgt. Wdd.
261	...	Chamberlin, B. G. S.	Wdd.
1187	...	Chandler, S. A.	
236	...	Chapman, F. B.	Ptd. Cpl. D. of Wds., France, 4/3/17.
960	...	Chapman, W. E.	
404	...	Chappell, W.	Ptd. Sgt. Wdd.
611	...	Charlton, R. L.	Pioneer. T. to 2nd Pnr. Bn., 13 3/16.
405	Dr.	Chipper, G.	T. to 2nd Div. Sig. Coy., 12/8/15.
250	...	Chorlton, O.	Ptd. Sgt. Accidentally killed, France, 17/10/18.
609	...	Christensen, H.	T. to 2nd Div. Hqrs., 16/8/15.
402	...	Christie, J. R.	Ptd. Sgt. Wdd. 2 occ. K. in A., France, 3/10/18.
820	...	Churchard, A.	D. of wds., France, 29/7/16.
828	...	Clairs, G. C.	Ptd. Cpl.
610	...	Clark, A. W.	Ptd. C.S.M. Wdd. Ment. in Despatches. D.C.M.
32	...	Clark, C. C.	
1063	...	Clayton, A. L.	Apptd. Dr.
409	...	Clayton, E.	
33	Bgr.	Clayton, W.	K. in A., France, 4-6/8/16.
257	...	Cleaver, H.	Wdd., 1915.
1144	...	Clegg, P. J.	T. to 11th Bn., 24/1/16. Ptd. L. Sgt. Wdd.
775	...	Clifton, G. L. C.	T. to 2nd Div. Sig. Coy., 12/8/15. Afterwards to Royal Flying Corps. Ptd. Lieut.
248	...	Cobbold, B. W.	
34	...	Coburn, A. P.	Apptd. 2nd Lieut., 7/4/17. Ptd. Lieut. Wdd. 4 occ. Ment. in Despatches. M.C.
258	...	Cockroft, R.	
818	...	Coe, L. A.	K. in A., France, 3-6/11/16.
238	Bgr.	Colgate, O.	K. in A., Gallipoli, 16/9/15.
35	...	Coll, J.	D. of Ill., at sea, 25/9/15.
1163	...	Collett, L. E.	Ptd. Staff Sgt.
36	...	Collins, A. S.	
37	...	Collins, C. P. H.	D. of Wds., France, 4/5/17.

Appendix H—continued.

28TH BATTALION.—NOMINAL ROLL OF ORIGINAL MEMBERS—continued.

Reg. No.	Rank on Embarkation.	Name.	Memoranda.
603	...	Collins, F. W.	Invalided to Australia, 25/9/15. Returned and T. to 59th Bn., 8/10/16. K. in A., France, 11/5/17.
265	...	Collins, P.	Wdd.
263	...	Compston, W.	T. to 10th L.H., 23/10/16. Apptd, Dr.
401	Cpl.	Congdon, F. H. A. ...	T. to 7th L.T.M. Bty., 22/4/16. Wdd.
403	...	Connor, E.	D. of Ill., Malta, 7/11/15.
1022	...	Connor, J.	
237	...	Connor, T.	T. to 2nd Div. Hqrs., 18/8/15. Apptd. Dr.
249	...	Conway, E.	Ptd. L/Cpl. K. in A., Belgium, 2/10/17.
406	...	Cook, F. R.	Ptd. L/Cpl. Wdd.
1072	...	Cooke, M. L.	Wdd.
606	...	Coolahan, A.	Reg. Sig. Ptd. Sgt. D. of Wds., France, 9/11/17.
252	...	Coombe, H. J.	T. to 51st Bn., 2/4/16. Wdd.
1055	...	Coomer, D. C.	Ptd. L/Cpl. Wdd.
38	Cpl.	Cooper, A. S.	Ptd. Sgt. K. in A., France, 29/7/16.
246	...	Cooper, G. B.	St. Bearer. Ptd. Cpl. Wdd. 2 occ.
605	...	Cooper, H. W.	Wdd. D.C.M.
255	...	Cope, H. J.	Ptd. Cpl. Wdd.
264	...	Copley, N.	St. Bearer. D. of Ill., at sea, 1/11/15.
262	...	Coppard, S.	Ptd. L/Cpl. K. in A., France, 29/7/16.
1198	...	Corbett, C. W.	T. to 7th L.T.M. Bty., 6/4/16. Wdd.
247	...	Cordierr, C. W. V.	
786	Sgt.	Corr, O. R	Invalided, 1915.
1086	...	Cottingham, D.	T. to 7th M.G. Coy., 11/8/16. M.M. D of Wds., France, 26/3/17.
40	...	Couchman, R.	K. in A., France, 29/7/16.
822	...	Coulter, F. C. L.	
821	...	Coulter, L. T.	K. in A., France, 4-6/8/16.
41	...	Counihan, G.	Wdd.
819	...	Courtney, M. J.	Wdd.
798	C.S.M.	Cousins, H. M.	
251	...	Cowell. A. W.	D. of Wds., France, 12/8/18.
253	...	Cox, F.	Ptd. Sergt.-Shoemaker.
823	...	Cox, F.	K. in A., France, 29/7/16.
602	...	Cox, H. C.	
42	...	Cox, J.	Wdd.
408	...	Cox, J.	
43	...	Cox, L. D.	T. to 7th L.T.M. Bty. 22/4/16. Wdd.
1118	...	Crabb, G.	Ptd. L/Cpl. K. in A., France, 3-6/11/16.
239	...	Craske, H.	Wdd. 3 occ.
44	...	Creighton, R. A. ...	Wdd.
241	...	Crerar, W.	M. Gr. Wdd. 1915.
260	...	Crofts, S.	Reg. Sig. Ptd. Cpl. Wdd.
45	...	Crorkan, P.	K. in A., France, 29/7/16.
46	...	Cross, A. E.	K. in A., France, 29/7/16.
47	...	Cross, M.	Reg. Sig. Ptd. Sgt. Wdd. M.M
242	...	Crouch, F.	T. to 7th L.T.M. Bty. 19/4/16.
48	...	Crump, J.	Wdd. 1915.
49	...	Cumming, H. A. ...	Ptd. L/Cpl. Wdd. 1915. K. in A., France, 29/7/16.
826	...	Cunningham, D. W. ...	D. of Wds., Gallipoli, 24/11/15.
243	...	Cunningham, P. ...	Wdd. 1915. K. in A., France, 3-6/11/16
1178	...	Curran, A. W.	Reg. Sig. Apptd. 2nd Lieut. 30/8/16. Wdd. 2 occ. Ment. in Despatches.
815	Dr.	Curran, J.	
919	...	Curtis, G. N.	Ptd. Cpl. K. in A., France, 10/6/18.
254	...	Curwen, F. E.	D. of Wds., Gallipoli, 21/9/15.
1070	...	Cutts, R. W.	T. to 48th Bn. 26/4/16.
271	...	Daines, A. C. C.	
1100	...	Dale, G. F.	K. in A., Gallipoli, 19/9/15.
1046	...	Dalton, R.	

Appendix H—continued.

28TH BATTALION.—NOMINAL ROLL OF ORIGINAL MEMBERS—continued.

Reg. No.	Rank on Embarkation.	Name.	Memoranda.
1095	...	Davidson, J. S.	Wdd.
52	...	Davies, A.	D. of Wds., France, 29/7/16.
838	...	Davies, E. S. T.	Wdd. T. to 2nd M.G. Bn. 1/7/18.
839	...	Dawkins, F. E.	Wdd. 1915
1114	Sgt.	Dawson, W. T.	Apptd. 2nd Lieut. 29/7/16. Wdd.
266	...	Deacon, H. S.	
414	Cpl.	Deering, J. B.	Wdd.
833	...	Deery, D.	
834	...	Deery, G.	Wdd. T. to 4th M.G. Coy. 2/12/16.
272	...	Delaporte, R.	K. in A., Gallipoli, 16/9/15.
1023	...	De Lury, F. J.	
830	...	Delury, W.	Wdd. 1915.
1119	...	Dennison, R.	Wdd. 1915. D. of Wds., France, 9/4/16.
942	Bgr.	Deverell, W. F.	T. to 7th M.G. Coy 14/8/16. Wdd
835	...	Devine, A. F.	K. in A., France, 3-6/11/16
54	...	Devine, M. J.	Wdd.
836	...	Dewar, F. L.	Ptd. L/Cpl.
613	...	Dickson, E.	
831	...	Dixon, J. A.	T. to 5th F. Coy. Eng., 18/8/15. Apptd. Dr
832	...	Dobson, J.	Pioneer. T. to 2nd Div. Sig. Coy. 12/8/15. Ptd. 2nd Cpl.
267	...	Dolbear, F.	
55	...	Donaldson, H.	Ptd. Sgt. D. of Wds., France, 10/11/16.
412	...	Donaldson, N. F.	Wdd. K. in A., Belgium, 4/10/17.
268	...	Donovan, D.	Wdd.
614	...	Doran, J.	
56	...	Doust, J. A.	Wdd. 1915 and 2nd occ.
1096	...	Dowdle, W. G.	T. to 2nd Pnr. Bn. 12/3/16. Ptd. L/Cpl.
1053	...	Drew, V. C.	D. of Wds., France, 3/6/16.
57	...	Drock, C. A.	D. of Wds., Belgium, 23/9/17.
617	...	Drummond, W.	Wdd. 2 occ.
58	...	Ducie, W. F.	Ptd. Armourer-Sergt. T. to A. Army Ordnance Corps, 12/2/18, but remained attached to Bn.
794	Cpl.	Ducksbury, J. H.	Ptd. Sgt.
841	...	Ducrow, C.	Wdd.
842	...	Dudley, A.	T. to 48th Bn. 26/4/16.
59	...	Duff, J.	K. in A., France, 29/5/16.
1193	...	Duff, R.	Pioneer. K. in A., Gallipoli, 26/9/15.
612	...	Duffield, A. F.	T. to 7th M.G. Coy. 3/3/16.
837	...	Duncanson, G.	Ptd. Sgt. Wdd. Mentioned by the Secretary of State for War.
1080	...	Dunn, W.	T. to 2nd Div. Sig. Coy. 1/12/15.
996	...	Dunn, W. W. R.	T. to 7th M.G. Coy. 3/3/16. K. in A., France, 4/7/18.
269	...	Dunne, M.	Ptd. Cpl. M.M.
60	...	Dunphy, G. P.	Wdd. 1915. K. in A., France, 29/5/16.
270	...	Dunstan, S. A.	Wdd. 1915. K. in A., France, 3-6/11/16.
989	...	Earl, A.	K. in A., Gallipoli, 22/9/15.
418	Cpl.	Eatough, J.	Ptd. Sgt. K. in A., France, 28-29/7/16.
274	...	Edema, F. W.	
417	...	Elliott, G. L.	T. to 7th M.G. Coy. 14/9/16. Ptd. T/-Cpl.
275	...	Emery, A.	Apptd. 2nd Lieut. 1/8/18. Ptd. Lieut.
273	...	Esmond, M. F.	
619	...	Etty, R.	Wdd. 1915 and 2nd occ.
416	...	Evans, G.	Pioneer. Wdd.
844	...	Evans, H.	Wdd. 2 occ. T. to A.A.V.C. 31/7/17.
415	...	Evans, H. J.	
61	...	Evenis, G. R.	Wdd.
62	...	Fagan, J. M.	Wdd.
625	...	Fairhead, L. C.	T. to 7th M.G. Coy. 13/11/16. K. in A., Belgium, 3-10-17.

THE 28th: A RECORD OF WAR SERVICE, 1915-19. 187

Appendix H—continued.

28TH BATTALION.—NOMINAL ROLL OF ORIGINAL MEMBERS—continued.

Reg. No.	Rank on Embarkation.	Name.	Memoranda.
1155	...	Fairweather, C. L. ...	T. to I.C. Corps 1/2/16. Ptd. T/-Sgt.
1128	...	Falkner, E. ...	T. to I.C. Corps 1/2/16. Wdd. Ptd. Sgt.
422	...	Farmer, H. ...	Ptd. L/Cpl. Wdd. 2 occ. D.C.M.
421	...	Farmer, L.	
621	...	Farmer, L. ...	K. in A., France 4-6/8/16.
63	...	Farris, E. T. ...	Wdd. K. in A., France, 19/5/18.
622	...	Farris, R. P. ...	Wdd. 2 occ. D.C.M.
932	Sgt.	Faulkner, M. L. ...	Transport-Sergt.
424	...	Fawkner, E.	
279	...	Felton, F.	
969	...	Fenn, C. C. ...	T. to 7th M.G. Coy. 3/3/16.
64	...	Ferris, D. ...	K. in A., France, 29/7/16.
479	Sgt.	Field, C. R. ...	See Appendix " E."
845	...	Fingland, G. ...	K. in A., France, 10/6/18.
276	...	Firby, T.	
951	...	Fitzgerald, M. ...	T. to 48th Bn. 26/4/16.
846	Dr.	Fitzpatrick, J. J. ...	Ptd. Cpl. K. in A., France, 16-18/11/16.
623	...	Fitzpatrick, M. M. ...	M.Gr. T. to 7th M.G. Coy. 3/3/16. Ptd. Sgt. Wdd. M.M.
928	Dr.	Flanagan, W. E.	Ptd. Cpl.
277	...	Fleming, B. G.	Ptd. L/Cpl. Wdd. 2 occ.
66	...	Fleming, R.	
805	Sgt.	Fletcher, P. H. ...	Wdd.
847	Sgt.	Flower, C. C. ...	Apptd. 2nd Lieut. 16/8/16. Ptd. Lieut. Wdd. 2 occ.
620	...	Floyd, J. G. ...	T to Aust. Provo. Corps 12/1/18. Ptd. E.R. 2nd Cpl. Wdd. 1915 and 2nd occ.
420	...	Folland, G. ...	Wdd. 2 occ.. Invalided to Australia 29/2/16. Rejoined 19/2/17.
938	...	Ford, G. H. ...	A.A.M.C. Detail. T. to A.A. Pay Corps 29/2/16.
624	...	Ford, J. E. ...	T. to 30th A.A.S.C. 14/3/17.
390	Dr.	Foster, G. ...	Wdd.
1186	...	Foster, H. M.	
795	Sgt.	Foster, M. J. ...	T. to 7th L.T.M. Bty. 22/4/16. Apptd. 2nd Lieut. 31/1/18. Ptd. Lieut.
977	...	Fox, F. H. ...	K. in A., France, 4-6/8/16.
67	...	Francklyn, C. ...	K. in A., France, 29/7/16.
1098	...	Franco, H. A. ...	Wdd. 1915. M.M. and Serbian Silver Medal. D. of Ill., France, 16/2/18.
68	...	Frank, J. C. ...	T. to 5th Bn. Wdd.
278	...	Franklin, T.	
1205	...	Fraser, D. ...	T. to 8th F. Coy., Eng. Ptd. Far. Sgt.
1194	...	Frayne, C. S.	
1105	...	Freeman, J. R. ..●	Wdd. 1915. T. to I.C. Corps 1/2/16.
997	...	Fuller, F. G. ...	A.A.M.C. Detail. Ptd. L/Sgt.
69	L Cpl.	Fulton, W. J.	
857	...	Gallagher, J. ...	Wdd. 1915.
426	...	Galway, J.	
1190	...	Gardiner, A. W. G.	
281	...	Gardner, J. ...	Wdd. 4 occ.
859	...	Garrity, H. W. ...	K. in A., France, 3/5/17.
851	...	Garsden, W.	
782	Sgt.	Garth, T. J. ...	K. in A., France, 3-6/11/16.
1005	R.S.M.	Gettingby, J. ...	See Appendix E.
71	...	Gibbons, A. R. ...	Ptd. Cpl. D. of Wds., France, 14/10/16.
855	...	Gibbons, L. W. ...	Wdd. 1915.
627	...	Gibson, E. T. ...	T. to 7th F. Coy., Eng., 7/3/16. D. of Wds., France, 2/8/16.
72	...	Gibson, W. ...	Ptd. R.Q.M.S. Ment. in Despatches.
1094	...	Gillett, E. A.	
429	...	Gipp, R.	
849	...	Girvan, J. ...	Ptd. Sgt. K. in A., France, 26/3/17.

188   THE 28th: A RECORD OF WAR SERVICE, 1915-19.

Appendix H—continued.

28TH BATTALION.—NOMINAL ROLL OF ORIGINAL MEMBERS—continued.

Reg. No.	Rank on Embarkation.	Name.	Memoranda.
850	...	Gleeson, A. J. ...	Wdd. 2 occ.
856	...	Gleeson, D.	
854	Cpl.	Gleeson, M. W.	Wdd. 1915. D. of Wds., Belgium, 5/10/17.
73	...	Glover, J. A. ...	T. to 7th L.T.M. Btv., 22/4/16. Rejoined 30/10/16. Wdd. 2 occ.
1050	...	Gobey, C. N. ...	Wdd. T. to 2nd M.G. Bn. 23/3/18.
1056	Bgr.	Godfrey, G. A. T.	
282	...	Goffin, J.	T. to 2nd Pnr. Bn. 16/3/16. Ptd. Sgt. M.S.M.
1182	...	Goodall, J. S.	
285	...	Goodfield, W. ...	Wdd. 1915. D. of Wds., France, 22/5/17.
432	...	Goodlet, J. T. ...	Ptd. L/Cpl. Wdd. 2 occ.
1104	...	Gordon, J.	Wdd. 2 occ.
1049	...	Gordon, W. ...	Wdd.
289	...	Goullet, E.	
912	...	Graham, C. G. ...	M.Gr. T. to 7th M.G. Coy. 3/3/16. Ptd. Sgt. K. in A., France, 5/2/17.
778	C.Q.M.S.	Graham, N. ...	Apptd. 2nd Lieut. 24/1/17. T. to 7th L.T.M. Btv. Ptd. Lieut. M.C.
428	...	Graham, R. T.	K. in A., France, 29/7/16.
1004	Sgt.	Graham, T. R. ...	Sergeant Cook.
425	Cpl.	Gramkie, F. J. ...	T. to A. Army Postal Corps, 5/8/18.
287	...	Granger, W. G. R.	Ptd. Cpl. K. in A., Belgium, 2/11/17.
438	...	Greay, H.	Ptd. L/Sgt. K. in A., France, 29/7/16.
961	...	Greay, S. ...	K. in A., France, 29/7/16.
286	Sgt.	Green, A. T. V.	Wdd.
74	...	Green, G. D. ...	Wdd. T. to 48th Bn., 25/4/16.
75	...	Green, J. T. W.	K. in A., France, 29/7/16.
1170	...	Green, W. E. ...	Wdd. 1915.
853	...	Green, W. G. ...	T. to 7th L.T.M. Bty., 2/12/16. Wdd. 2 occ.
852	...	Greene, G. A. ...	Wdd.
76	...	Greenwood, H. W.	T. to 7th M.G. Coy., 3/3/16. K. in A., Belgium, 20/9/17.
283	...	Gregson, J. A. ...	Apptd. 2nd Lieut., 3/1/19. Ptd. Lieut.
985	...	Gresham, J. D.	D. of Ill., Egypt, 22/11/15.
628	...	Guidera, E. ...	K. in A., France, 29/7/16.
779	C.Q.M.S.	Gunn, J. R. ...	Apptd. Hon. Lieut. and Quartermaster, 2/6/16. Ptd. Hon. Captain. O.B.E.
848	...	Gunson, J. ...	Wdd. Invalided Feb., 1916. Rejoined 18/1/17.
448	...	Hadden, W. ...	K. in A., France, 29/7/16.
77	...	Haines, J. F. ...	Ptd. Sgt. K. in A., France, 3-6/11/16.
964	...	Hale, H. G. ...	Wdd. 1915. K. in A., France, 5-6/8/16.
78	...	Hale, W. W. A.	T. to 7th L.T.M. Bty., 19/4/16. Wdd.
1168	...	Haley, D. ...	D. of Ill., Egypt, 26/4/16.
873	...	Hall, B. ...	Ptd. Sgt. Wdd.
79	...	Hall, J.	T. to 7th. L.T.M. Bty., 21/12/16. Ptd. Cpl. Wdd. D.C.M.
1024	...	Hamilton, J.	
309	...	Hamley, J. V. ...	Reg. Sig. Ptd. Cpl.
80	Cpl.	Hammond, M. G.	Apptd. 2nd Lieut., 29/7/16. Ptd. Captain. Ment. in Despatches. M.M. M.C. and Bar. Wdd. 2 occ. D. of Wds., France, 14/6/18.
862	Sgt.	Hanlin, R. A. ...	Apptd. 2nd Lieut., 18/12/16. Ptd Lieut. Wdd. 2 occ.
863	...	Hann, H. N. ...	T. to 31st Bn. Ptd. C.Q.M.S.
905	Dr.	Hansen, F. N. ...	
81	...	Hardey, J. ...	Ptd. Cpl. K. in A., France 29/7/16.

THE 28th: A RECORD OF WAR SERVICE, 1915-19.

Appendix H—continued.

28TH BATTALION.—NOMINAL ROLL OF ORIGINAL MEMBERS—continued.

Reg. No.	Rank on Embarkation.	Name.	Memoranda.
1195	...	Hardwick, R. W. G. ...	Apptd. 2nd Lieut., 16/8/16. Ptd. Captain. Wdd.
1139	...	Harman, J. J.	Invalided to Australia, 31/8/15. Returned and T. to 1st Pnr. Bn., 7/9/16. K. in A., Belgium, 21/9/17.
914	Dr.	Harmour, H.	T. to I.C. Corps, 1/2/16. Ptd. Farrier-Sgt.
642	...	Harris, H. E.	Ptd. L/Sgt, Wdd. 2 occ.
870	...	Harris, H. M.	T. to 15th M.G. Coy., 27/5/16. K. in A., France, 3/5/18.
986	Bgr.	Harrison, C. L. E.	
83	...	Harrison, J.	
101	...	Harrison, J.	Ptd. C.Q.M.S.
439	...	Harrison, J. L. ...	Ptd. L/Cpl. K. in A., France, 29/7/16.
1173	...	Harrison, M.	Ptd. Cpl.
864	Dr.	Hart, G. J.	T. to 7th L.T.M. Bty., 22/4/16. Wdd.
84	Cpl.	Harvey, H. K. de W. ...	Ptd. L/Cpl. T. to 7th M.G. Coy., 3/3/16. K. in A., France, 25/4/16.
874	...	Hassard, R.	St. Bearer. Wdd.
303	...	Hatfield, H.	Wdd.
1120	...	Hatton, F. E.	T. to 7th M.G. Coy., 3/3/16. Wdd.
640	...	Hawkins, E.	Wdd. 2 occ.
1153	Cpl.	Hawley, C. K.	D. of Wds., Gallipoli, 23/9/15.
898	...	Hawtin, V. V.	Reg. Sig. Ptd. Cpl. Wdd.
454	...	Haydock, R.	M.Gr. T. to 7th M.G. Coy., 3/3/16. Apptd. 2nd Lieut., 7/11 17. Ptd. Lieut.
290	...	Hayes, E. T.	Ptd. L/Cpl. Wdd. T. to Dental Unit, A.A.M.C. 20/8/18.
643	...	Hayes H. A.	T. to 32nd Bn., 6/4/16. Ptd. Sgt. Wdd.
310	...	Hayes, J. F.	Wdd. 1915.
1180	...	Hayton, A. N.	Reg. Sig. T. to Army Pay Corps. Ptd. Cpl.
871	...	Hayward, W.	Ptd. Cpl. Wdd. 3 occ.
85	...	Hazlitt. C. J.	Reg. Sig. T. to 11th Bn., 25/1/16.
301	...	Head, W.	Ptd. Sgt. Wdd.
445	...	Heaney, M. J.	Wdd. T. to 3rd M.G. Bn., 13/4/18.
657	...	Hearne, C. R.	T. to 7th M.G. Coy., 3/3/16. Apptd. 2nd Lieut., 16/8/16. Ptd. Lieut. Wdd.
1011	...	Hearty, H.	Invalided 1915. Returned with 44th Bn., 1916. Apptd. 2nd Lieut., 1/3/18. Ptd. Lieut.
291	...	Heasman, F.	K. in A., Belgium, 26/9/17.
87	...	Hedgley, A. E.	K. in A., France, 29/7/16.
954	...	Height, H. L.	D. of Wds., Gallipoli, 14/9/15.
1138	...	Henderson, A. M.	
639	...	Henderson, C. A. ...	T. to I.C. Corps, 30/1/16.
983	...	Henderson, J. N.	
88	...	Hendrick, T. J. ...	Ptd. Sgt. M.M.
447	...	Hendry, C.	Wdd. T. to 3rd M.G. Bn., 14/6/18.
302	...	Henson, M.	K. in A., France, 29/7/16.
89	...	Herbert, H. R. ...	Wdd.
903	Dr.	Herdsman, W. E. ...	Wdd.
878	...	Hewitt, A. C. S. ...	Invalided to Australia, 2/9/15. Returned and T. to 5th Pn. Wdd. 2 occ.
294	...	Hewson, W. A.	
442	...	Hicks, E.	K. in A., France, 16/11/16.
865	...	Hicks, V. C.	K. in A., France, 29/8/18.
443	...	Hilder, W.	T. to 2nd M.G. Bn., 12/4/18. Wdd. 1915 and 2 occ.
90	...	Hill, A. N.	T. to I.C. Corps, 1/2/16. Apptd. 2nd Lieut. 14th Light Horse, 4/1/19. Ptd. Lieut. M.M.
91	...	Hill, L. L.	Wdd.

Appendix H—continued.

28TH BATTALION.—NOMINAL ROLL OF ORIGINAL MEMBERS—continued.

Reg. No.	Rank on Embarkation.	Name.	Memoranda.
92	...	Hilliard, J.	Wdd.
441	...	Hitchcock, H.	
452	...	Hobbs, F.	Invalided 3/1/16. Returned with 16th Rfts. 4/3/17. Ptd. L/Cpl. Wdd. 2 occ.
451	...	Hobbs, J.	Wdd. 3 occ. K. in A., France, 29/8/18.
1183	Sgt.	Hocking, W. J. ...	Sergt.-Drummer. Wdd.
861	...	Hodder, G.	K. in A., Gallipoli, 2/12/15.
308	...	Hodgson, J. ...	Ptd. Sgt. K. in A., Gallipoli, 22/9/15.
102	...	Hodgson, T. W. ...	Wdd. 1915. T. to I.C. Corps, 1/2/16.
948	...	Holden, J. W. ...	A.A.M.C. Detail. Wdd. 2 occ.
94	...	Holford, R. G. ...	T. to 15th A.A.S.C., 15/11/15. Ptd. Cpl.
295	...	Holland, J. ...	T. to 7th M.G. Coy. 3/3/16. Ptd. Sgt.
633	...	Holmes, H. H. ...	Reg. Sig. K. in A., France, 4–6/8/16.
95	...	Hood, A.	Ptd. L/Cpl. K. in A., France, 29/7/16.
96	...	Hopkins, J.	Apptd. 2nd Lieut. 9/12/16. Ptd. Lieut. Wdd. 2 occ. Ment. in Despatches. M.M.
298	...	Horrocks, E. J.	D. of Wds., Gallipoli, 18/9/15.
292	...	Horrocks, S. H.	Ptd. Cpl. D. of Wds. whilst prisoner of War, Germany, 2/8/16.
1060	...	Hortin, J. C. ...	D. of Wds., France, 10/8/16.
781	...	Horton, E. W. ...	St. Bearer. Wdd.
1203	...	Howes, A. H. W.	Wdd. 1915. T. to 2nd Pnr. Bn. D. of Wds., France, 4/8/16.
293	...	Howieson, G.	
876	...	Huckstep, V. ...	Wdd.
638	...	Huddleston, J.	
97	...	Hudson, F. E. J.	Wdd.
98	...	Hull, R.	K. in A., France, 29/7/16.
860	...	Hulls, A. H. ...	T. to 2nd Pnr. Bn., 3/5/16. K. in A., France, 29/7/16.
1199	...	Humberstone, H.	Wdd.
99	...	Hume, R.	
866	...	Humphreys, W. J.	Wdd. 2 occ.
305	...	Hunt, E. R. ...	K. in A., France, 29/7/16.
904	Dr.	Hunt, J.	Wdd.
446	...	Hunter, R. ...	T. to 1st Div. Sig. Coy., 16/3/16.
300	...	Hurst, W. W. ...	Pioneer
1025	...	Hutchins, A. ...	T. to 48th Bn., 28/4/16.
307	...	Hutchins, C. ...	Wdd.
1068	...	Hutchinson, H.	Wdd.
634	...	Hutchinson, H. V.	Ptd. L/Cpl. K. in A., France, 29/7/16.
299	Cpl.	Hyde, W.	D. of Wds., at sea, 18/9/15.
100	...	Hyman, J.	
306	...	Hynes, N. ...	D. of Wds., Gallipoli, 6/11/15.
311	...	Illing, W. G. ...	K. in A., France, 29/7/16.
879	...	Innes, G. W. R.	T. to 2nd M.G.Bn. 30/3/18. Wdd. 2 occ.
644	...	Iveson, C. ...	Wdd.
880	...	Jackson, J. W.	K. in A., France, 4–6/8/16.
1172	...	Jackson, T. ...	Wdd. 1915. Apptd. Dr.
953	...	Jacobsen, C. ...	Wdd. 1915. T. to 51st Bn. 3/4/16. D. of Wds., Egypt, 12/5/16.
1129	...	Jacques, G. ...	T. to 7th M.G. Coy. 3/3/16. Wdd.
1202	...	James, C. A. C.	D. of Wds., France, 27/2/17.
1074	...	Jamson, J. ...	Ptd. Sgt.
457	...	Jeffery, C. H.	
1052	...	Jeffery, W. T. ...	Ptd. L/Cpl. K. in A., France, 29/7/16.
312	...	Jerry, A. ...	Apptd. 2nd Lieut. 23/10/16. M.M. D. of Wds. France, 26/3/17.
316	...	Job, P. F. ...	Invalided to Australia 2/9/15.
645	...	John, J. ...	Wdd. 1915. K. in A., France, 29/7/16.

THE 28th: A RECORD OF WAR SERVICE, 1915-19. 191

Appendix H—continued.

28TH BATTALION.—NOMINAL ROLL OF ORIGINAL MEMBERS—continued.

Reg. No.	Rank on Embarkation.	Name.	Memoranda.
317	...	Johnson, F.	
881	...	Johnson, K. L.	Apptd. 2nd Lieut. 25/1/17. T. to 16th Bn. Ptd. Lieut. Wdd.
882	...	Johnson, R. A.	K. in A., France, 4-6/8/16.
313	...	Johnston, R.	Ptd. C.Q.M.S. Wdd.
885	...	Johnston, S.	Apptd. Dr. Wdd.
1092	...	Johnstone, W.A.	T. to 2nd Pnr. Bn. 13/3/16. Ptd. C.Q.M.S.
456	...	Jones, A. W.	T. to 47th Bn. 4/5/16.
884	...	Jones, G. B.	T. to 5th F. Coy., Eng., 18/8/15. Apptd. Dr. M.M.
314	...	Jones, H. S.	Ptd. Cpl. Wdd. 1915 and 2nd occ.
103	...	Jones, J.	
777	C.Q.M.S.	Jones, S.	Apptd. Hon. Lieut. and Quarter-master. 8/11/17. Twice Ment. in Despatches
104	...	Jones, W. P.	Ptd. C.S.M. D. of Wds., France, 12/11/16.
883	...	Joyce, C.	Wdd.
1146	...	Kahan, H. K.	Reg. Sig.
1175	Dr.	Kay, A.	T. to 7th M.G. Coy. 13/11/16.
788	Sgt.	Keay, R. E.	
926	Cpl.	Keefe, H. R.	A.A.M.C. Detail. Ptd. L/Sgt. T. to 7th Fld. Amb. 29/9/16.
322	...	Keelan, M.	
324	...	Keeley, W. J.	Ptd. Sgt. Wdd. M.M.
988	...	Kelley, B.	Ptd. Sgt. K. in A., France, 10/6/18.
647	...	Kelly, A.	K. in A., France, 29/7/16.
320	...	Kelly, J.	
318	...	Kelly, J. J.	
1188	...	Kelly, R.	
1625	...	Kendall, F.	T. to 5th F. Coy., Eng., 18/8/15. Apptd. Dr.
1010	Sgt.	Kennedy, G. F.	K. in A., France, 20/9/17.
887	...	Kennon, A.	Ptd. Cpl. K. in A., Gallipoli, 5/10/15.
319	...	Kenny, W.	
323	...	Kent, G. A.	K. in A., France, 1/6/18.
105	...	Kenyon, J. H.	
462	...	Kerr, J.	
889	...	Keyte, T. N.	T. to H.T.M. Bty., 22/5/16. K. in A., France, 26/5/16.
321	...	Kidner, A. W.	T. to A.A.M.C. 28/10/17.
463	...	King, C. F.	Wdd. 2 occ.
106	...	King, G. A.	
461	Cpl.	King, H. C.	See Appendix E.
888	...	Kingman, G.	Wdd.
1112	...	Kingsbury, P. F.	T. to 2nd Pnr. Bn. 10/3/16.
978	...	Kingsbury, V. E.	Ptd. L/Cpl.
1162	...	Kinshela, I. W.	Wdd.
107	...	Knapp, J. L.	M.Gr. D. of Ill., Egypt, 12/11/15.
108	...	Knapp, M. S.	M.Gr. Ptd. L/Cpl. K. in A., France, 29/7/16.
646	...	Kolby, R. A.	M.Gr. T. to 7th M.G. Coy., 20/5/17.
915	Dr.	Lafferty, W.	Wdd.
918	...	Lamb, E. A.	M.O.'s Orderly. T. to 7th Fld. Amb.
325	...	Lamb, W. L.	T. to 2nd Pnr. Bn., 13/3/16. Apptd. Dr.
1001	Cpl.	Lang, J. R.	K. in A., France, 29/7/16.
109	...	Langridge, H. W.	Ptd.T/-Sgt. Wdd.
110	...	Langridge, J. H.	K. in A., France. 29/7/16.
653	...	Langton, S. A.	M.Gr. Wdd. 1915. T. to 7th M.G. Coy., 3/3/16. Apptd. 2nd Lieut. 23/10/16. Ptd. Lieut.
111	Cpl.	Lanyon, R. J.	Apptd. 2nd Lieut., 7/4/17. Wdd. 2 occ. K. in A., France, 3/5/17.

Appendix H—continued.

28TH BATTALION.—NOMINAL ROLL OF ORIGINAL MEMBERS—continued.

Reg. No.	Rank on Embarkation.	Name.	Memoranda.
112	...	Latham, A.	
652	...	Latham, R. J. C.	Ptd. Cpl. Wdd. 2 occ.
330	...	Lauder, J.	
113	...	Lawn, H. D.	Wdd.
326	...	Lawrence, A.	T. to 2nd Pnr. Bn., 14/3/16. Wdd 2 occ.
1176	Bgr.	Lawrence, J.	
327	...	Lawson, A.	Wdd. 1915.
920	Bgr.	Lawson, R.	T. to 2nd M.G. Bn., 23/3/18.
467	...	Leaver, W. A.	Apptd. 2nd Lieut., 27/12/16. Ptd. Lieut. Wdd. M.M., M.C.
908	Dr.	Lebovetz, E.	T. to I.C. Corps, 1/2/16. Wdd.
1208	...	Lee, G. C.	D. of Ill., England, 31/10/15.
466	...	Lee, J.	T. to 5th F. Coy., Eng., 18/8/15.
891	...	Leggett, H.	Reg. Sig. Ptd. T/-Sgt.
1078	Bgr.	Lenegan, J. W.	T. to 2nd Div. Sig. Coy., 12/8/15. M.M.
806		Lester, E. C.	
328	...	Lester, V.	T. to A.A.S.C., 14/6/17.
114	...	Levy, F.	T. to I.C. Corps, 31/1/16. Ptd. L/Cpl. K. in A., Palestine, 19/4/17.
115	...	Lewis, C. S.	Wdd. 1915. T. to 7th M.G. Coy. D. of Wds., France, 14/8/16.
925	Sgt.	Lewis, L. C.	Armourer-Sergt. Wdd. T. to A.Army Ordnance Corps, 11/5/18.
890	Dr.	Leyshon, W. E.	Wdd.
332	...	Linden, G.	St. Bearer. K. in A., France, 3-6/11/16.
893	...	Long, R.	K. in A., France, 29/7/16.
1207	...	Longmore, T.	K. in A., France, 16-18/11/16.
651	...	Longson, E.	T. to 7th F. Coy., Eng., 7/3/16. Wdd.
774	...	Lukin, L. R.	Ptd. Cpl. Wdd. K. in A., France, 10/6/18.
329	...	Lunnon, W. E.	Apptd. Dr. T. to 7th M.G. Coy., 12/9/16
116	...	Lyden, W.	K. in A., France, 29/7/16.
737	...	McArdell, L. C.	M.Gr. Ivalided 11/4/16.
1130	...	McAuliffe, D.	T. to 7th L.T.M. Bty. 1916. Ptd. Cpl. M.M. and Bar. D. of Wds., France, 12/3/17.
1093	...	McCabe, M.	T. to I.C. Corps 1/2/16. Ptd. T/-Cpl.
738	...	McCaig, C.	
739	...	McCaig, C.	K. in A., France, 29/7/16.
1211	...	McCarthy, J. P.	T. to 51st Bn. 2/4/16.
131	L/Cpl.	McCarthy, M.	K. in A., France, 21/5/18.
901	...	McCleery, R. L.	Reg. Sig. T. to 2nd Div. Sig. Coy. 14/3/16. Ptd. E.R. Sgt.
1062	...	McColl, A.	K. in A., France, 29/7/16.
671	...	McCooke, D.	T. to 2nd F. Coy., Eng., 16/3/16.
489	...	McCorry, J.	Ptd. L/Cpl. K. in A., France, 29/7/16.
482	...	McDonald, A.	Wdd. 1915. Apptd. Dr.
894	...	Macdonald, B. M.	Apptd. 2nd Lieut. 22/10/17. Ptd. Lieut. Wdd. 2 occ.
132	...	McDonald, D.	T. to H.T.M. Bty. 11/6/16. Ptd. Bombadier. Wdd.
341	...	McDonald, D.	
334	...	McDonald, F. R.	
133	...	McDonald, J. A.	K. in A., France, 29/7/16.
343	...	McDonald, W.	T. to Army Corps Ammunition Park 19/11/15.
483	...	McDonnell, F. L.	Ptd. T/-Cpl. Wdd.
339	...	McDowall, J.	K. in A., France, 29/7/16.
1027	...	McEnroe, F.	Ptd. L/Cpl. K. in A., France, 3-6/11/16.
335	...	McErlain, J.	Ptd. L/Cpl. Invalided 4/8/15.
742	...	McEvoy, A.	Ptd. L/Cpl. K. in A., France, 16-18/11/16.
1101	...	McGavin, C. G.	Ptd. Cpl. Wdd. 2 occ. T. to Dental Unit, A.A.M.C., 30/10/18.

THE 28th: A RECORD OF WAR SERVICE, 1915-19.

Appendix H—continued.

28TH BATTALION.—NOMINAL ROLL OF ORIGINAL MEMBERS—continued.

Reg. No.	Rank on Embarkation.	Name.	Memoranda.
134	Dr.	McGeachie, D. ...	K. in A., France, 29/7/16.
1122	...	McGill, W. P. ...	K. in A., Gallipoli, 22/9/15.
1028	...	McGinnis, A.	
336	...	McGrath, T.	
1082	...	McGregor, C.	
1029	...	McGregor, F. A.	K. in A., France, 4-6/8/16.
1178	...	McIntosh, W. ...	Ptd. Sgt. K. in A., Belgium, 28/9/17.
968	...	McIntyre, D. H.	K. in A., France, 3-6/11/16.
337	Sgt.	McIntyre, J. ...	See Appendix E.
1115	Sgt.	McIntyre, K. M. G. ...	Apptd. 2nd Lieut. 16/8/16. Ptd. Captain. Wdd. M.C.
672	...	McIntyre, P. ...	Wdd. 2 occ.
1201	...	McKail, C. ...	T. to 7th M.G. Coy., 3/3/16. Ptd. L/Sgt.
1192	...	McKay, D. ...	T. to 48th Bn. 26/4/16.
660	...	Mackay, D. McK. ...	Pioneer. D. of Wds., Gallipoli, 26/9/15.
743	Sgt.	Mackay, S.	
744	...	McKenzie, A. ...	D. of Wds., Egypt, 30/11/15.
344	...	MacLean, J. ...	Wdd. 1915 and 2nd occ.
945	...	McLeod, D. D. ...	K. in A., France, 7/6/16.
484	...	McLeod, J. ...	Wdd. 2 occ.
135	Bgr.	McLernon, J. L. ...	Wdd. 1915 and 2nd occ.
488	...	McMahon, P. ...	Ptd. L/Cpl.
1131	...	McMahon, P.	
1077	...	McMillan, N. A. ...	Invalided, 1915.
922	...	McMorrow, P. C. ...	Wdd.
994	...	McNamara, J. ...	D. of Wds., Gallipoli, 3/10/15.
747	...	McNulty, H. R.	
136	...	McQueen, W.	
666	...	MacRae, J. W. ...	Wdd. 1915. T. to 2nd Pnr. Bn. Ptd. Sgt. Wdd. 2nd occ.
477	...	Madden, J. W. ...	Ptd. L/Cpl. Wdd. 1915.
931	...	Malatzky, L. ...	M.Gr. T. to 7th M.G. Coy. 3/3/16. Ptd. Cpl. Wdd. 2 occ.
658	...	Mandelzon, H. ...	K. in A., France, 29/7/16.
1088	...	Mann, J. H. ...	Ptd. L/Cpl. Wdd.
1196	...	Manson, G. ...	Ptd. L/Cpl. Wdd. 2 occ.
118	...	Marquand, C. J. ...	T. to 51st Bn. 2/4/16.
965	...	Marshall, J. C.	
119	...	Marshall, L. W. ...	Ptd. Sgt. Wdd.
345	...	Marshall, W. ...	Wdd. 1915. Invalided.
120	Dr.	Marsland, J. C. ...	K. in A., France, 3-6/11/16.
1121	...	Martin, D. ...	Apptd. 2nd Lieut. 1/5/17. Ptd. Lieut. Wdd.
121	...	Martin, G. E. ...	T. to 32nd Bn. 6/4/16. Apptd. 2nd Lieut. 1/6/18. Ptd. Lieut. Wdd. 2 occ.
478	...	Martin, H. ...	T. to 7th M.G. Coy. 13/11/16. Apptd. Dr.
122	...	Martin, J. M. ...	Ptd. Cpl. Wdd. 2 occ.
895	...	Mason, H. ...	K. in A., France, 24/6/16.
897	...	Mason, R.	
349	...	Mathers, J. E. ...	D. of Wds., England, 12/10/16.
668	...	Matson, R. P. ...	T. to 7th M.G. Coy. 3/3/16. Rejoined Bn. 24/12/16. D. of Wds., Belgium, 20/9/17.
123	...	Mawdesley, P. E. J.	
1090	...	May, H.	
346	...	Mayger, S. ...	T. to 2nd Pnr. Bn. 9/3/16. Ptd. Cpl.
896	Dr.	Mayger, W. J. ...	Wdd. K. in A., France, 18/4/18.
572	...	Mead, F. M. A. ...	Wdd. 1915.
1102	...	Meagher, E. J. G. ...	Wdd. K. in A., Belgium, 4/10/17.
573	...	Melsom, A. ...	Pioneer. Ptd. Sgt. Ment. in Despatches.
1135	Sgt.	Melville, B. W. G. ...	Ptd. C.S.M. K. in A., Belgium, 20/9/17.
124	...	Merrick, J. ...	K. in A., Gallipoli, 30/9/15.
661	Cpl.	Metcalfe, W. M.	

Appendix H—continued.

28TH BATTALION.—NOMINAL ROLL OF ORIGINAL MEMBERS—continued.

Reg. No.	Rank on Embarkation.	Name.	Memoranda.
471	Dr.	Mewha, J.	Ptd. Cpl.
574	...	Mighall, R.	Ptd. Cpl. T. to 2nd M.G. Bn. 20 3/18.
966	...	Milburn, J.	Wdd.
1141	...	Mill, W. L. S.	K. in A., France, 29/7/16.
355	Dr.	Millea, A. G.	Ptd. L/Cpl. T. to 7th M.G. Coy. 3 3/16.
353	...	Milligan, D.	T. to 51st Bn., 2/4/16.
127	...	Mills, A.	
472	...	Mills, O.	Wdd.
354	...	Milner, G.	
128	...	Milroy, M. R.	T. to 32nd Bn. 6/4/16. Wdd. 2 occ.
933	...	Minchin, H. d'E.	Ptd. Cpl.
473	...	Mineter, M.	T. to 48th Bn. 26/4/16. K. in A., France, 5/8/16.
1091	...	Minett, W. H.	K. in A., France, 29/7/16.
1185	...	Mitchell, F. T.	Wdd. 1915 and 2nd occ.
656	...	Mitchell, T. P.	Wdd. 1915 and 2 occ. later.
999	...	Molloy, H.	St. Bearer. Ptd. Cpl. D.C.M.
350	...	Moloney, J. V.	Wdd.
662	...	Monck, E. C.	Ptd. A/Sgt. Wdd. 1915 and 2nd occ.
1136	...	Monger, F. E.	
577	...	Moore, G.	Wdd. 1915. T. to 7th M.G. Coy. 11 8/16, and to Australian Flying Corps 27/8/17. Ptd. A/Sgt.
1066	...	Moore, H. J.	Wdd.
357	...	Moore, J. J.	
347	...	Moore, W.	T. to 1st Pnr. Bn. 9/3/16. Wdd.
352	...	Moore, W. J.	Wdd.
129	...	Morey, L.	Ptd. L/Cpl. Wdd.
356	Cpl.	Morris, H.	Ptd. Sgt. K. in A., France, 1/6/18.
469	...	Morrison, J.	St. Bearer. Ptd. Cpl. Wdd. 2 occ.
578	...	Mortimer, F.	Ptd. E.R. Sgt.
944	...	Morton, L. J.	T. to 27th Bn. Wdd. 2 occ.
655	...	Mountjoy, C.	Invalided 31/8/15.
654	...	Mountjoy, R. C.	Apptd. Dr.
663	...	Moxham, J.	T. to 5th F. Coy., Eng., 18/8/15. Apptd. Dr.
348	...	Moyle, E. T.	K. in A., France, 3–6/11/16.
1151	...	Mullen, C. G.	Ptd. Cpl. Wdd.
1111	...	Munro, N. A.	K. in A., Gallipoli, 16/12/16.
1161	...	Murdock, A.	Ptd. L/Cpl. T. to 5th F. Coy., Eng., 11/3/16.
909	Dr.	Murray, C. G.	Wdd. 2 occ.
940	Bgr.	Murray, H. J.	Wdd. 1915. T. to 10th Light Horse 10/6/16. Wdd. 2nd occ.
902	...	Murray, S.	Reg. Sig. Wdd.
1059	...	Naughton, R. D.	
492	...	Neale, T. A.	Ptd. T/Cpl.
748	...	Neilson, G. B.	T. to 7th M.G. Coy. 3/3/16. Ptd. A/Sgt.
799	Sgt.	Neumann, H. P.	Evacuated 1915. T. to 44th Bn., 1916. Apptd. 2nd Lieut. 30/6/17. Ptd. Lieut.
1051	...	Newman, G. C.	Apptd. Dr. Wdd. T. to 7th M.G. Coy. 25/7/17.
1177	...	Newnes, M. F.	M. Gr. T. to 2nd Pnr. Bn. 11/3/16. Apptd. 2nd Lieut. 26/8/16. Ptd. Captain. Wdd. 2 occ.
673	...	Nicholson, T.	
749	...	Nielsen, O. S.	Ptd. Cpl. K. in A., France, 4–6/8/16.
192	...	Nolan, R. A.	T. Ptd. 2nd Cpl.
1113	...	Norman, E. H.	T. to 2nd Pnr. Bn. 12/3/16.
674	...	North, H. J.	
1189	...	O'Brien, T.	K. in A., France, 29/7/16.

THE 28th: A RECORD OF WAR SERVICE, 1915-19.

Appendix H—continued.

28TH BATTALION.—NOMINAL ROLL OF ORIGINAL MEMBERS—continued.

Reg. No.	Rank on Embarkation.	Name.	Memoranda.
359	...	O'Connor, D. ...	T. to 7th M.G. Coy. 8/3/16. Ptd. Cpl. Wdd.
675	...	O'Dea, P.	
1184	...	O'Dell, A. R. ...	T. to Australian Cyclist Bn. 1916.
358	...	O'Doherty, F. J.	Apptd. Dr.
138	...	O'Donnell, M. ...	T. to I.C. Corps 1/2/16. Wdd.
139	...	O'Driscoll, M. J.	T. to H.T.M. Bty. 17/6/16.
993	...	O'Dwyer, W. ...	Medical Officer's Orderly. T. to 7th Fld. Amb. 15/8/16.
494	...	Ogilvie, A. E. ...	T. to 48th Bn. 26/4/16.
921	...	O'Keefe, W. ...	Wdd. 1915.
360	...	Okely, E. J.	
1103	...	O'Loughlin, D. F.	Wdd. 1915. T. to 7th L.T.M. Bty., 11/10/16. D. of Wds., France, 26/11/16.
910	Dr.	Olson, H. W.	
140	...	O'Neill, C. ...	D. of Wds. whilst Prisoner of War, Germany, 5/10/16.
952	...	O'Neill, J. ...	K. in A., France, 29/7/16.
141	...	O'Neill, J. B. ...	Ptd. L/Cpl. Wdd.
1030	...	O'Sullivan, J. M.	Ptd. Sgt.
495	...	Owen, G. J. ...	Wdd.
1007	Bgr.	Owen, V. R.	
679	...	Page, A. H. ...	T. to 2nd Pnr. Bn. 9/3/16.
143	...	Pannell, G. G. ...	Wdd.
751	...	Park, J. H.	
367	...	Parker, W. R. ...	Ptd. Sgt. Wdd.
752	Cpl.	Parry, E. ...	Invalided 15/8/15.
936	...	Partington, J. L.	St. Bearer. K. in A., France, 29/7/16.
677	...	Patterson, A. ...	Wdd. 1915. T. to 7th M.G. Coy. 3/3/16. Ptd. T/-Cpl.
144	...	Pattison, L. A.	Pioneer. Ptd. Sgt.
496	Sgt.	Pead, S. W. ...	D. of Wds., at sea, 22/9/15.
753	...	Pearce, C. ...	Reg. Sig. T. to 2nd Div. Sig. Coy. 12/8/15. Ptd. Cpl.
680	...	Pearson, A. ...	D. of Wds., France, 18/8/16.
1174	Dr.	Peek, H. E. L.	T. to 7th M.G. Coy. 3/3/16. Apptd. 2nd Lieut. 23/9/18.
900	...	Peers, G. S. ...	Reg. Sig. T. to 2nd Div. Sig. Coy 14/3/16. Ptd. C.Q.M.S.
1079	...	Pengelly, F. E.	Wdd.
145	...	Penney, A.	
1133	...	Pennycuick, E. H.	Wdd.
676	...	Peterson, A. ...	T. to 7th M.G. Coy. 3/3/16.
361	...	Phillips, J. N. ...	T. to 5th F. Coy, Eng., 18/8/15. Apptd. Dr.
1058	...	Phillis, W.	K. in A., France, 29/7/16.
1031	...	Pickering, S. ...	Wdd.
365	...	Pickthorn, A. E.	Ptd. L/Cpl. K. in A., France, 3-6/11/16.
976	...	Pierce, M. R.	
755	...	Piggott, W. C. ...	Reg. Sig. Apptd. 2nd Lieut., 23/9/18. Ptd. Lieut. M.M.
1032	...	Pike, H. J. ...	Wdd. 2 occ. Ment. in Despatches.
916	Bgr.	Pilgrim, J.	
780	C.Q.M.S.	Piper, C. J. ...	Wdd. and Invalided in 1915. Apptd. 2nd Lieut., 1/10/16 and returned with 5th/44th Rfts. Ptd. Lieut. Wdd. 2nd occ.
800	Sgt.	Piper, G. H. W.	Wdd. 1915. K. in A., France, 21/5/16.
147	Cpl.	Pitt, W. H.	
756	...	Plant, H. S. ...	Wdd. Ptd. E.R. Sgt.
362	...	Podesta, A.	
363	...	Pollard, J. ...	St. Bearer. Wdd. 2 occ.

Appendix H—continued.

28TH BATTALION.—NOMINAL ROLL OF ORIGINAL MEMBERS—continued.

Reg. No.	Rank on Embarkation.	Name.	Memoranda.
1132	...	Portch, W.	
369	...	Powell, A.	K. in A., France, 29/7/16.
368	...	Powell, G. E.	Wdd. 1915 and 2nd occ. Ment. in Despatches. *M.M.* Appt. 2nd Lieut. 24/1/17. K. in A., France, 26/3/17.
497	...	Powell, J.	Invalided, 3/9/15.
757	...	Pratt, W.	Ptd. Cpl. Wdd.
678	...	Preece, R.	Wdd.
148	...	Price, H. A. E. ...	K. in A., France, 29/7/16.
1085	...	Price, H. G.	T. to 2nd M.G. Bn., 20/4/17. Ptd. Cpl.
364	...	Price, J. L.	Wdd. 1915. T. to A.A.V.C., 10/8/17.
758	...	Price, J. W.	Wdd. 3 occ. T. to 4th M.G. Coy., 18/4/18.
500	...	Pritchard, F. C. ...	Ptd. Sgt. Wdd.
149	Cpl.	Pritchard, T.	Wdd.
681	...	Pryce, W. O.	T. to Aust. Cyclist Bn., 16/4/16.
498	...	Pugh, H.	Wdd. 1915. Ptd. Cpl. T. to A.A.S.C., 3/7/17.
370	...	Purdue, A.	St. Bearer. Ptd. L/Cpl. T. to 7th Fld. Amb., 29/9/16.
371	...	Quick, J. K.	Ptd. Cpl. D. of Ill., Egypt, 14/8/15.
580	Dr.	Quick, J. R.	Wdd.
686	...	Randle, C.	
581	...	Randle, P.	K. in A., France, 16-18/11/16.
582	...	Rasmussen, A. C. ...	D. of Ill., Egypt, 4/9/15.
509	...	Raymond, H.	Wdd.
508	...	Raynor, L.	Wdd.
583	...	Read, P. E.	M. Gr. Ptd. Cpl. K. in A., France, 29/7/16.
1033	...	Reay, J.	Wdd.
510	...	Redford, W. E. ...	Wdd. K. in A., France, 1/6/18.
682	...	Reed, A. J.	Ptd. Sgt. Wdd.
1179	...	Reed, W. J.	Reg. Sig. Wdd.
584	...	Reen, C. F.	K. in A., Gallipoli, 11/10/15.
1035	...	Reeves, D. G.	Wdd.
373	...	Reilly, E. J.	T. to 5th F. Coy., Eng., 18/8/15. Wdd.
374	...	Richardson, R.	K. in A., France, 29/7/16.
972	...	Ricketts, H.	Wdd.
507	...	Rickman, F. O. ...	T. to Australian Cyclist Bn., 12/5/16. Ptd. R.Q.M.S.
1061	...	Ridley, H. B. W. ...	Apptd. 2nd Lieut. 1/6/18. Ptd. Lieut.
512	...	Roach, J.	K. in A., France, 3-6/11/16.
376	...	Robb, J.	Wdd.
151	...	Robe, T.	St. Bearer. Wdd. K. in A., France, 19/5/18.
687	...	Roberts, W. H. ...	Wdd. 2 occ.
585	...	Robertson, A.	
1191	...	Robertson, A. S. ...	Reg. Sig.
970	...	Robins, A.	Wdd. Invalided, 21/1/16. Rejoined 2/5/17.
1034	...	Robinson, F. E.	
372	...	Rodd, S. H.	T. to 7th M.G. Coy. 3/3/16. Ptd. Sgt. Wdd.
955	...	Rogers, W. J.	T. to 51st Bn. and later to 13th M.G. Coy. K. in A., France, 30/3/17.
1209	...	Rolfe, C. E. C. ...	Ptd. Cpl. Wdd. 2 occ.
152	...	Rosenow, A. A.	
505	...	Ross, J.	
1206	...	Rowe, A. J. J. ...	T. to 5th F. Coy., Eng., 18/8/15. Apptd. Dr.
760	...	Rowe, T. R.	Ptd. Sgt. Wdd.
761	...	Rowles, R. L.	T. to 7th M.G. Coy. 24/9/16. Ptd. T/-Cpl.

Appendix H—continued.

28TH BATTALION—NOMINAL ROLL OF ORIGINAL MEMBERS—continued.

Reg. No.	Rank on Embarkation.	Name.	Memoranda.
683	...	Russell, W. E.	
1097	...	Rust, J. D.	K. in A., France, 16-18/11/16.
1087	...	Ruthven, G.	Wdd. 1915.
1036	...	Sage, J.	K. in A., France, 29/7/16.
377	...	St. George, M.	Ptd. Cpl.
762	...	Salter, A.	K. in A., France, 4–6/8/16.
763	...	Salter, F.	
1125	...	Sandercock, J.	Ptd. Sgt. Wdd. 2 occ.
1064	...	Satterthwaite, W.	T. to 5th F. Coy., Eng., 18/8/15. Mentioned in Despatches.
991	...	Sayer, W. R.	
1123	...	Scanlan, J. A.	
1134	...	Schilling, G. H.	T. to 17th A.A.S.C. 2/9/15.
527	...	Schleicher, J.	Wdd.
528	...	Schleicher, W. J.	Wdd. 1915.
533	...	Scorer, A.	Wdd.
765	...	Scott, J.	T. to 2nd Div. Sig. Coy. 12/8/15. Ptd. L/Cpl. *M.M.*
767	...	Scullin, J. J.	K. in A., France, 29/7/16.
691	...	Seal, E.	Ptd. L/Cpl. K. in A., France, 3/5/17.
692	...	Seal, H.	Ptd. L/Cpl. Wdd.
1000	Cpl.	Sears, F.	*See* Appendix E.
1107	...	Self, T. A.	K. in A., France, 29/7/16.
694	...	Selleck, F. P.	Invalided 18/9/15. Rejoined 23/10/17.
768	...	Sennett, P. F. A.	
378	...	Sewell, J.	
776	R.Q.M.S.	Sexty, R. G.	*See* Appendix E.
155	...	Seymour, H. L.	Ptd. L/Sgt. Wdd. *M.M.*
697	...	Seymour, W. J.	Ptd. L/Cpl. K. in A., France, 3–6/11/16.
734	...	Shapcott, D. W.	
530	L/Cpl.	Sharland, N. L.	Ptd. Cpl. Wdd. 2 occ.
695	...	Sharp, S. H.	K. in A., France, 11/8/18.
531	...	Sharpe, L. J.	K. in A., France, 4–6/8/16.
156	Sgt.	Shaw, M. C. A.	Invalided 1916. Returned with 21st Rfts. Apptd. 2nd Lieut. 1/10/16. Rejoined 22/1/18 Ptd Lieut. Previously served in South African War.
1167	...	Shaw, R. G. G.	K. in A., France, 29/7/16.
1108	...	Shelley, R. P.	T. to 7th M.G. Coy. 3/3/16. Apptd. 2nd Lieut. 9/2/17. Ptd. Lieut. K. in A., France, 4/7/18.
517	...	Shenfield, E. A.	St. Bearer. K. in A., Gallipoli, 22/9/15·
769	...	Sheppard, G.	
770	...	Sherrit, E.	Wdd.
1076	Bgr.	Shipway, A. J.	
1038	...	Sholl, H. E.	
696	Cpl.	Shorrock, J.	Apptd. 2nd Lieut. 1/6/18. Ptd. Lieut. Wdd. Ment. in Despatches. *D.S.O.*
157	...	Simm, G. H.	Ptd. Cpl. K. in A., France, 29/7/16.
514	...	Simmonds, H.	Apptd. Dr. *M.S.M.*
688	...	Simpson, A.	Wdd. 1915 and 2nd occ. T. to 2nd M.G. Bn. 27/8/18.
984	...	Simpson, D.	Wdd.
807	Sgt.	Simpson, J.	Ptd. R.S.M. K. in A., France, 29/7/16.
519	Cpl.	Simpson, S. L.	Wdd. T. to 32nd Bn. 6/4/16.
158	...	Sissons, J. E.	K. in A., France, 29/7/16.
771	...	Siva, A.	
772	...	Skerry, R. C.	K. in A., France, 29/7/16.
1075	Sgt.	Skipworth, C. J.	
160	...	Smart, J. L.	T. to 48th Bn. 26/4/16. Wdd.
1002	...	Smiley, H. F.	Apptd. 2nd Lieut. 24/7/17. Ptd. Lieut. Wdd. 1915 and 2nd occ. *M.C.*
1073	...	Smith, D. J.	Invalided 3/9/15. Rejoined 27/3/17.

Appendix H—continued.

28TH BATTALION—NOMINAL ROLL OF ORIGINAL MEMBERS—continued.

Reg. No.	Rank on Embarkation.	Name.	Memoranda.
773	...	Smith, E. A.	Ptd. T/- Cpl. D. of Ill., France, 19/4/16.
939	...	Smith, H.	
693	...	Smith, J.	Invalided 29/1/16. Rejoined 18/1/17.
524	...	Snudden, A.	K. in A., Gallipoli, 14/9/15.
520	...	Southey, J. W.	T. to I.C. Corps, 31/1/16. Wdd.
526	...	Spratt, C.	K. in A., France, 3-6/11/16.
973	...	Spring, F. R.	Ptd. Cpl. K. in A., France, 29/7/16.
515	...	Stables, W.	Ptd. Sgt.
161	...	Stapleton, W. W.	Wdd. 2 occ. K. in Ac., France, 27/3/17.
162	...	Starr, H.	Apptd. 2nd Lieut. 24/1/17. Ptd. Lieut. Mentioned by the Secretary of State for War.
1067	...	Stein, J. F.	Wdd.
163	...	Stephens, A.	K. in A., France, 29/7/16.
525	...	Stephenson, L.	
1154	...	Stewart, A.	T. to 59th Bn. Ptd. L/Sgt. Wdd. M.M.
518	...	Stewart, J.	K. in A., France, 16-18/11/16.
522	...	Stewart, R.	T. to 5th F. Coy., Eng., 18/8/15. Ptd. 2nd Cpl.
698	...	Stiepelman, W. L.	Wdd.
1037	...	Still, S. C.	
164	...	Stokes, A.	T. to I.C. Corps 1/2/16.
165	Cpl.	Stranger, A. T.	T. to 32nd Bn., 6/4/16. K. in A., France, 20/7/16.
690	...	Street, O. D. T.	
166	...	Strong, J.	K. in A., France, 29/7/16.
516	...	Stubbs, W.	Wdd. 1915.
379	...	Sullivan, W. J.	Ptd. Cpl. Wdd.
1124	...	Sutton, D.	T. to I.C. Corps, 30/1/16. Ptd. L/Cpl. Wdd.
956	...	Sweeting, A. J.	Wdd. Belgian *Croix de Guerre*.
535	...	Tacey, E.	St. Bearer.
1042	...	Tapscott, E. E.	
987	...	Tarrant, O. F.	
1040	...	Tassicker, F. S.	Ptd. L/Cpl.
702	...	Taupin, L.	
1057	...	Taylor, E.	
168	...	Taylor, F. C.	Reg. Sig. Ptd. Cpl.
1041	...	Terrell, C.	Apptd. Dr.
386	...	Terry, A.	
382	...	Terry, G. H.	
1626	...	Thetford, H.	Ptd. L/Sgt.
537	Dr.	Thomas, A. B.	T. to I.C. Corps. 1/2/16. Ptd. Sgt.
536	...	Thomas, A. L.	Wdd. T. to 2nd Pnr. Bn.. 5/11/17.
703	...	Thomas, F.	K. in A., France, 29/7/16.
1071	...	Thomas, H. C.	T. to 48th Bn., 26/4/16.
173	...	Thomas, H. G.	K. in A., France, 15/9/16.
380	...	Thomas, H. H.	
1043	...	Thomas, P. G.	Ptd. L/Cpl. Wdd.
540	Cpl.	Thomas, R. A.	
949	...	Thomas, S. B.	A.A.M.C. Detail. T. to 7th M.G. Coy., 16/3/17. Ptd. Cpl.
169	...	Thomas, W. D.	K. in A., France, 29/7/16.
170	...	Thomas, W. N.	Invalided to Australia 25/9/15. Returned and T. to 46th Bn., 20/4/16. Wdd. 2 occ. M.M.
1081	...	Thompson, A. H.	T. to 51st Bn., 2/5/18. K. in A., France, 10/6/18.
701	Sgt.	Thompson, S. S.	Orderly Room Sergt. Ptd. C.S.M. D. of Wds., France, 19/8/16.
980	...	Thomson, J. L.	K. in A., France, 3-6/11/16.
171	...	Thorley, F.	T. to 2nd Pnr. Bn., 13/3/16.

THE 28th: A RECORD OF WAR SERVICE, 1915-19. 199

Appendix H—continued.

28TH BATTALION—NOMINAL ROLL OF ORIGINAL MEMBERS—continued.

Reg. No.	Rank on Embarkation.	Name.	Memoranda.
538	...	Thorp, A.	Wdd.
383	...	Thorpe, W. W.	K. in A., France, 29/7/16.
699	...	Tolerton, D.	Ptd. L/Sgt.
700	...	Tomasini, J.	K. in A., France, 29/7/16.
539	...	Toolin, W.	
384	...	Trenorden, L. C.	Ptd. Cpl. M.M. K. in A., France, 3-6/11/16.
1006	Bgr.	Tucker, W. H.	
172	...	Tugby, S.	T. to 2nd A.G.H. 31/12/15.
174		Tully, J.	Ptd. Cpl. Wdd. K. in A., France, 29/7/16.
385	...	Tummel, G. E.	
1039	...	Tyson, H. H.	K. in A., France, 29/7/16.
705	...	Uren, R.	
706	...	Venton, A. R.	Wdd. 1915. Apptd. 2nd Lieut. 31/3/17. Ptd. Lieut.
707	...	Vincent, A. E.	
176	...	Vincent, W.	D. of Wds, France, 12/8/18.
1152		Waddingham, F. H.	M.Gr. T. to 7th M.G. Coy. 3/3/16. Apptd. 2nd Lieut. 13/12/16. D. of Wds., France, 10/3/17.
715	...	Walker, R.	Wdd. 2 occ. M.M.
716	Cpl.	Walker, R. E.	Apptd. 2nd Lieut. 24/1/17. T. to 3rd Aust. Rly Cov., 30/8/17. Ptd. Captain.
177	L/Cpl.	Walker, T. E. W.	Ptd. C.Q.M.S.
947	Bgr.	Wallace, E. A.	
387	...	Waller, E.	St. Bearer.
1110	...	Walsh, C. R.	Apptd. 2nd Lieut. 5/8/17. Ptd. Lieut. Wdd.
907	Dr.	Walsh, J. P.	Wdd.
712	...	Walsh, T. P.	
547	Cpl.	Waltham, R.	Invalided to Australia 31/8/15, Returned and T. to 8th Bn. 17/5/16. K. in A., France, 18/8/16.
542	...	Ward, J. H.	Ptd. Cpl. K. in A., Belgium, 28/10/17.
1048	...	Ward, W.	Ptd. L/Cpl.
1047	...	Watson, E.	
179	...	Watson, J. E.	T. to 4th Pnr. Bn. 18/5/16. Ptd. Sgt. Wdd. M.M.
1169	...	Watson, J. S.	D. of Wds., France, 18/7/18.
711	...	Watson, R. A.	K. in A., France, 29/7/16.
1044	...	Webb, A. G.	Ptd. Sgt.
724	...	Weir, J.	T. to 48th Bn. 26/4/16. Ptd. Cpl. Wdd. 2 occ.
725	...	Wellington, H.	Ptd. Cpl. Wdd.
550	...	West, C.	
1109	...	Whelan, J.	D. of Wds, France, 8/8/16.
545	...	White, M.	T. to 51st Bn. 2/4/16. K. in A., France, 25/4/18.
709	Bgr.	White, P.	T. to 16th A.A.S.C., 18/8/15. Apptd. Dr. Wdd.
181	...	Whiteaker, W.	K. in A., France, 29/7/16.
1012	Bgr.	Whitfield, E. A.	K. in A., France, 29/7/16.
182	...	Whittingham, J.	
1170	...	Whologan, T. L.	T. to 4th M.G. Coy. 27/5/16. Ptd. T/Cpl. Wdd. 2 occ.
1084	...	Williams, D. J.	Invalided 31/8/15. Rejoined 24/8/16.
1210	...	Williams, D. R.	
183	...	Williams, E. G.	
184	Sgt.	Williams, J. Z.	Wdd.
728	...	Williams, L. G.	

Appendix H—continued.

28TH BATTALION—NOMINAL ROLL OF ORIGINAL MEMBERS—continued.

Reg. No.	Rank on Embarkation.	Name.	Memoranda.
723	...	Williams, R. H.	K. in A., France, 29/7/16.
185	...	Williams, R. J. G.	T. to 46th Bn., 10/7/16. Wdd 2 occ.
549	...	Williams, T.	
548	...	Williams, W. R.	Pioneer. T. to 10th Light Horse, 5/3/16.
186	...	Williamson, W. F.	Wdd.
722	...	Wilson, A.	D. of Wds., Gallipoli, 12/10/15.
546	...	Wilson, B. B. R.	Ptd. L Cpl. K. in A., France, 3–6/11/16.
187	...	Wilson, E.	Reg. Sig. D. of Ill., Australia, 11/7/16.
388	Cpl.	Wilson, L. G.	Ptd. Sgt. K. in A., France, 3–6/11/16.
929	Dr.	Wilson, N. S.	Ptd. Sgt. K. in A., France, 29/7/16.
718	...	Wilson, T.	T. to 2nd M.G. Bn., 3/3/16. Ptd. Sgt. *D.C.M.*
719	...	Wilson, T.	
1181	...	Wilson, W. H.	Wdd. 2 occ.
389	Cpl.	Wilson, W. L.	Ptd. Sgt. Wdd. *M.M.*
717	...	Wingrove, A.	K. in A., France, 29/7/16.
1099	...	Winters, B.	Wdd. Invalided 9/2/16. Rejoined 18/1/17. Ptd. Cpl. *M.M.*
188	...	Wintle, E. A.	T. to A.A.S.C., 15/11/15, and afterwards to 5th M.G. Bn., 6/9/18. Appt. 2nd Lieut. 1/6/18. Ptd. Lieut.
713	...	Wise, T.	Wdd.
1045	...	Wishart, W. J.	
541	...	Withers, G.	
783	Sgt.	Wolstenholme, R.	Ptd. C.S.M. D. of Ill., Egypt, 24/2/16.
189	...	Wood, G. B.	Wdd. 2 occ.
190	...	Woodford, E. L.	Wdd. 3 occ.
899	Cpl.	Woodrow, H. W.	Ptd. Sig. Sgt.
552	...	Woodward, E.	Wdd. 1915.
710	...	Woodward, T. J.	T. to 48th Bn., 25/4/16.
544	...	Wright, A. E.	T. to 58th Bn., 29/2/16.
727	...	Wright, F.	D. of wds., Malta, 28/11/15.
191	...	Wright, L.	Invalided to Australia, 4/8/15. Returned and T. to 5th Pnr. Bn. *M.M.*
911	...	Yeldon, R. A.	Reg. Sig. Wdd.
1153	...	Yelverton, M. W.	M. Gr. T. to 7th M.G. Cov., 11/8/16. Apptd. 2nd Lieut., 18/11/16. Ptd. Lieut. Wdd.

SUMMARY.

Number of Names on the Roll (Officers not included)	997
Actual Strength of Battalion on Embarkation—	
Officers	34
Warrant Officers	10
Staff Sergeants and Sergeants	35
Corporals and Lance-Corporals	40
Privates	912
Total	1,031

Casualties amongst Original Members during the War—

	Officers.	Other Ranks.
Killed in Action	4	216
Died of Wounds	4	60
Died of Illness	2	14
Died from Other Causes	...	2
Total Deaths	10	292

Percentage of Casualties (Deaths) to Strength—
    Officers ... 29·4   Other Ranks ... 29·3

N.B.—The exact figures in regard to the wounded are not available. The percentage was very high.

Number of Original Members who gained Commissions in the Field	63
Number of Honours conferred on Original Members for Gallant Conduct and Distinguished Service	80

Appendix I.

28TH BATTALION, AUSTRALIAN IMPERIAL FORCE.

NOMINAL ROLL of Members of Reinforcements who joined the Battalion in the Field prior to the 21st March, 1916.

NOTES.
1. The abbreviations used in Appendix H. apply to this Roll.
2. The number of the Reinforcement to which the Member belonged is indicated by the first figure which occurs in the column headed "Memoranda."
3. The date on which the Member joined the Battalion in the Field is shown thus—"J.18/8/15."

Reg. No.	Rank on Embarkation.	Name.	Memoranda.
1506	...	Akers, J. G. A.	1. J.18/8/15. T. to 2nd Pnr. Bn. 13/3/16. Apptd. Dr.
2338	...	Alderman, C.	5. J.19/1/16. T. to 2nd Pnr. Bn. 11/3/16. Wdd. 2 occ.
2339	...	Allan, A.	5. J.19/1/16. T. to 2nd Pnr. Bn. 11/3/16.
1888	Prov. Cpl.	Allanson, C.	3. J.12/10/15. K. in A., France, 4-6/8/16.
1805	...	Allen, N.	2. J.12/10/15. T. to 4th Pnr. Bn. 24/11/16.
1889	...	Allen, W. L.	3. J.12/10/15. T. to A. Army Ordnance Corps 1/9/17. Ptd. E.R. Warrant Officer, Cl.2.
2113	...	Alletson, J. C.	4. J.19/1/16. Ptd. Cpl. Wdd.
2114	...	Anderson, A.	4. J.19/1/16.
1662	...	Anderson, G.	2. J.12/10/15.
3003	Prov. Sgt.	Anderson, H. M. M.	7. J.15/3/16. Wdd. 2 occ. T. to A.A. Pay Corps 21/10/16.Ptd.T/-Sgt. Ment. by the Secretary of State for War.
3006	Prov. Sgt.	Anderson, J. T.	7. J.15/3/16. K. in A., France, 29/7/16.
1891	...	Anderson, S.	3. J.12/10/15. Wdd.
1890	...	Anderson, W.	3. J.12/10/15. Wdd.
3030	...	Andrews, E. C.	7. J.6/3/16. T. to 15th Bn. 7/3/16. Wdd.
1664	...	Annesley, F.	2. J.19/1/16. Wdd.
2115	...	Arcus, G. A.	4. J.19/1/16. K. in A., France, 6/8/16.
1666	...	Armstrong, H. J.	2. J.12/10/15.
2340	...	Armstrong, R.	5. J.19/1/16. K. in A., France, 4-6/8/16.
2342	...	Arundell, R. T.	5. J.19/1/16. Wdd.
1668	...	Atkins, E. R.	2. J.29/12/15. K. in A., France, 5/11/16.
2116	...	Attwood, C. S.	4. J.19/1/16. Wdd.
2343	...	A'Vard, W. H.	5. J.19/1/16.
1508	...	Ayling, H. E.	1. J.18/8/15. K. in A., Belgium, 2/11/17.

Appendix I—continued.

28TH BATTALION.—NOMINAL ROLL OF REINFORCEMENTS—continued.

Reg. No.	Rank on Embarkation.	Name.	Memoranda.
1634	...	Bailye, J.	1. J.18/8/15. Wdd.
1509	...	Baker, F.	1. J.18/8/15. Wdd. 3 occ.
1670	...	Bannister, G.	2. J.12/10/15. Wdd.
1513	...	Barnaby, G.	1. J.18/8/15. D. of Wds., France, 4/8/16.
2344	...	Baron, B. E.	5. J.19/1/16. Apptd. Dr. Wdd. 3 occ.
1517	...	Barrett, H. W.	1. J.18/8/15.
1892	...	Barron, J.	3. J.19/1/16.
1672	...	Bateman, C. E.	2. J.29/12/15. T. to 2nd Pnr. Bn. 10/3/16. Wdd. K. in A., France, 5/10/18.
2117	...	Bayliss, J.	4. J.19/1/16. K. in A., France, 3-6/11/16.
2119	...	Beaton, R.	4. J.19/1/16.
1673	...	Beckley, A. J. A.	2. J.12/10/15. Ptd. L/Sgt. Wdd.
1893	...	Beckwith, J. M.	3. J.12/10/15. T. to 7th F. Coy., Eng., 7/3/16. Ptd. Cpl.
1883	Prov. Cpl.	Bedford, H.	3. J.12/10/15. Ptd. Cpl. K. in A., France, 4-6/8/16.
1874	...	Beeton, F.	2. J.12/10/15.
1512	...	Bell, J. L.	1. J18/8/15. T. to 51st Bn. 2/4/16.
2347	...	Bell, T.	5. J.19/1/16.
2348	...	Bell, W.	5. J.19/1/16. D. of Wds., Belgium, 22/9/17.
2346	...	Bennett, A. T.	5. J.19/1/16. Wdd. 2. occ.
1675	...	Bennett, H. C.	2. J.12/10/15. Wdd.
1622	...	Bennett, R. W.	1. J.18/8/15. K. in A., France, 3-6/11/16.
1894	...	Bernard, A.	3. J.19/1/16. T. to 2nd M.G. Bn. 23/3/18. K, in A., France, 4/7/18.
1807	...	Berndt, F. J.	2. J.29/12/15. T. to 2nd Div. Salvage Coy. 24/1/17.
1895	...	Bickford, A.	3. J.12/10/15. T. to I.C. Corps, 1/2/16. Apptd. 2nd Lieut. 1/71/6. Ptd. Captain. Adjutant 3rd Camel Bn. 1917–18. Wdd. 1915 and 2 occ. later. M.C.
1896	...	Billings, J. V.	3. J.12/10/15. Wdd. K. in A., France, 3/5/17.
1897	...	Bishop, F. J.	3. J.12/10/15. T. to 32nd Bn. 10/3/16. Ptd. Sgt. Wdd. 2 occ. K. in A., France, 23/6/18.
2349	...	Blackham, F. M.	5. J.19/1/16. Ptd. Cpl. Wdd.
2020	...	Blaikie, W.	3. J.19/1/16. T. to 2nd Pnr. Bn. 3/5/16. Ptd. Cpl. Wdd.
1898	...	Blaikie, W. B.	3. J.12/10/15. T. to 2nd Pnr. Bn. 10/3/16. Apptd. Dr.
1516	...	Blatchly, C. D. C.	1. J.18/8/15. T. to 51st Bn. 2/4/16. Wdd. 2 occ.
1899	...	Blechynden, A. W.	3. J.12/10/15. Wdd.
1900	...	Bodinner, C.	3. J.12/10/15.
1906	...	Bolt, J. W.	3. J.12/10/15. Wdd.
2118	...	Bond, F.	4. J.19/1/16. Apptd. 2nd Lieut. 22/10/17. Ptd. Lieut.
2350	...	Boothby, A.	5. J.19/1/16. K. in A., France, 4-6/8/16.
1515	...	Bowman, W.	1. J.18/8/15. T. to A.A.S.C. 4/1/18. Apptd. Dr.
2120	...	Bowron, T.	4. J.19/1/16. Wdd. 2 occ.
2105	A/–Sgt.	Brady, E. W.	4. J.19/1/16. Ptd. T/-Cpl. D. of Wds., France, 3/3/17
2110	A/–Cpl.	Brady, F.	4. J.19/1/16.
2121	...	Brankstone, H.	4. J.19/1/16.
2352	...	Breakell, S.	5. J.19/1/16. K. in A., France, 3-6/11/16.

THE 28th: A RECORD OF WAR SERVICE, 1915-19. 203

Appendix I—continued.

28TH BATTALION.—NOMINAL ROLL OF REINFORCEMENTS—continued.

Reg. No.	Rank on Embarkation.	Name.	Memoranda.
2122	...	Brealey, J. W. ...	4. J.19/1/16. T. to H.T.M.Bty. 22/4/16. Ptd. Sgt.
2353	...	Brindley, R. ...	5. J.19/1/16. T. to 12th F.A.Bde., 6/2/18. Apptd. Dr. Wdd.
1905	...	Britt, N. W. ...	3. J.12/10/15. Wdd. 1915. K. in A., France, 29/7/16.
2125	...	Britten, L. ...	4. J.19/1/16. D. of Wds., England, 13/6/16.
2124	...	Britten, W. H.	4. J.19/1/16.
2332	Prov. Cpl.	Bromilow, J. L.	5. J.19/1/16. K. in A., France, 29/7/16.
1676	...	Bromley, T. H.	2. J.12/10/15. Wdd. 2 occ.
1901	...	Brooks, A. W. ...	3. J.12/10/15. Wdd. 1915.
1514	...	Broomfield, F. ...	1. J.18/8/15. T. to 7th F. Coy., Eng., 7/3/16. Apptd. 2nd Lieut. 26/3/17. Ptd. Lieut. Wdd.
1511	...	Brown, A.	1. J.18/8/15. Wdd. 1915.
1677	...	Brown, A. J. ...	2. J.12/10/15. Ptd. L/Cpl. K. in A., France, 29/7/16.
2126	...	Brown, E. M. ...	4. J.19/1/16. T. to 2nd Div. Hqrs., 24/1/16. Ptd. S.Q.M.S.
1904	...	Brown, H.	3. J.12/10/15. Wdd.
1610	...	Brown, J.	1. J.25/10/15.
1902	...	Brown, T.	3. J.29/12/15. Wdd.
1903	...	Brown, T. A.	3. J.12/10/15. D. of Wds., France, 8/11/16.
1510	...	Brown, W.	1. J.18/8/15.
1678	...	Brown, W.	2. J.12/10/15.
1679	...	Bruce-Drayton, G. A. H.	2. J.29/12/15. Ptd. E.R.Cpl. Wdd.
3057	...	Butler, J.	7. J.15/3/16.
2133	...	Cadd, C. A.	4. J.19/1/16. T. to 7th L.T.M.Bty. 26/7/16.
2134	...	Cadd, G.	4. J.19/1/16. Ptd. Sgt. Wdd. M.M.
2354	...	Cadden, J. J. ...	5. J.10/3/16. T. to Aust. Provo. Corps 9/7/16. Apptd. 2nd Lieut. 6/10/17. Ptd. Lieut. D. of Ill., England, 31/10/18.
2331	Prov. Cpl.	Callaghan, J. ...	5. J.19/1/16.
2355	...	Campbell, G. W.	5. J.19/1/16. Ptd. Cpl.
1681	...	Carlsen, T. E. ...	2. J.12/10/15. K. in A., France, 29/7/16.
1682	...	Carr, J. ...	2. J.12/10/15. Wdd.
2357	...	Carrington, V. J.	5. J.19/1/16. T. to 2nd Pnr. Bn. 13/3/16. Wdd. 3 occ.
1683	...	Carson, W.	2. J.12/10/15. D. of Wds., Belgium, 20/9/17.
1907	...	Carter, H.	3. J.29/12/15. K. in A., France, 4-6/8/16.
2111	A/-Cpl.	Carter, T. A. ...	4. J.19/1/16. T. to 7th L.T.M.Bty. 4/6/16. Ptd. Cpl. D. of Wds., France, 1/6/18.
2358	...	Carter, W. G. C.	5. J.19/1/16.
1684	...	Casey, W. P. ...	2. J.12/10/15.
1908	...	Castle, A. E.	3. J.12/10/15. Ptd. Sgt. Wdd. D.C.M.
2128	...	Castle, A. V.	4. J.19/1/16. K. in A., France. 29/7/16.
1609	...	Chalmers, W. R.	1. J.18/8/15. D. of Wds., France, 30/7/16.
2359	...	Chandler, E. A.	5. J.19/1/16. K. in A., France, 29/7/16.
1632	...	Chandler, H. ...	1. J.18/8/15. Ptd. Cpl. D. of Wds., Belgium, 12/3/18.

Appendix I—continued.

28TH BATTALION.—NOMINAL ROLL OF REINFORCEMENTS—continued.

Reg. No.	Rank on Embarkation.	Name.	Memoranda.
1686	...	Cheeseman, J.	2. J.25/10/15. Invalided 13/3/16. Rejoined 2/5/17. Ptd. L/Cpl. K. in A., France, 3/10/18.
1687	...	Chivers, H.	2. J.12/10/15. Ptd. Sgt. *M.S.M.*
2129	...	Clancy, J. M.	4. J.29/12/15. T. to I.C. Corps, 30/1/16. Rejoined Bn. 18/11/17.
1885	...	Clark, R. W.	3. J.12/10/15. T. to 2nd M.G. Bn. 20/3/18. Wdd.
1688	...	Clarke, W. J. A. ...	2. J. 12/10/15. T. to 7th F. Coy., Eng., 7/3/16. Wdd.
2130	...	Clausen, H. W. ...	4. J.19/1/16.
1689	...	Clayton, T. G.	2. J.12/10/15. Ptd. Sgt. K. in A., France, 8/8/18.
2360	...	Cliff, S. F. ...	5. J.22/1/16. T. to 11th Bn. 4/3/16.
1525	...	Clohessy, S.	1. J.18/8/15. Invalided 29/8/15.
1909	...	Coffey, E. J.	3. J.12/10/15.
1520	...	Coleman, G. A. ...	1. J.18/8/15. Ptd. Cpl. Wdd. *M.S.M.*
1523	...	Coll, E. A.	1. J.18/8/15. K. in A., France, 29/7/16.
1690	...	Collins, J. G.	2. J.12/10/15. Wdd. 1915. Invalided.
1911	...	Collins, R. J. R. ...	3. J.12/10/15.
1691	...	Connelly, G.	2. J.12/10/15.
2132	A/- Cpl.	Connolly, M.	4. J.19/1/16. Ptd. L/Cpl. K. in A., France, 29/7/16.
1910	...	Connolly, R. P. ...	3. J.29/12/15. Wdd.
1692	...	Cook, J. A.	2. J.12/10/15. T. to 2nd Pnr. Bn., 14/3/16. Ptd. Sgt.
2361	...	Cook, O.	5. J.19/1/16. K. in A., France, 29/7/16.
2136	...	Coomber, F. H. G. ...	4. J.19/1/16. Wdd.
1882	Prov. Cpl.	Corboy, E. W. ...	3. J.12/10/15. Wdd. 2 occ.
1914	...	Cornell, A. S.	3. J.29/12/15.
1521	...	Cornish, E. C. ...	1. J.18/8/15. T. to 2nd Pnr. Bn. 13/3/16. Wdd.
1693	...	Coskry, J. G.	2. J.29/12/15. Ptd. Cpl. Wdd. *M.S.M.*
1694	...	Costello, F. P. ...	2. J.12/10/15. Ptd. L/Cpl. Wdd. 1915.
2131	...	Cottage, L.	4. J.19/1/16. D. of Wds., France, 6/11/16.
1913	...	Courtis, W.	3. J.12/10/15. T. to 51st Bn. 2/4/16.
1695	...	Cowden, J. A.	2. J.12/10/15.
1912	...	Cox, G. L.	3. J.12/10/15. T. to 3rd Echelon, G.H.Q. 1/12/17. Ptd. Sgt.
2362	...	Cramb, F. B.	5. J.19/1/16. Ptd. Sgt. Wdd. 2 occ. D. of Wds., France, 10/7/18.
2363	...	Criddle, D.	5. J.19/1/16.
1916	...	Crisp, S.	3. J.12/10/15. T. to 7th L.T.M. Bty. 15/8/16. Ptd. L/Cpl.
1522	...	Crossman, A. R. ...	1. J.18/8/15. Wdd.
2364	...	Cullen, C. E.	5. J.19/1/16. K. in A., France, 29/7/16.
2024	...	Cuming, A. M. ...	3. J.12/10/15.
1524	...	Cuming, J. M.	1. J.18/8/15. Wdd.
1696	...	Curtin, E.	2. J.12/10/15. T. to I.C. Corps 1/2/16.
1915	...	Cusack, M. P.	3. J.29/12/15. Ptd. Cpl. Wdd. 3 occ.
2139	...	Dalton, W. H.	4. J.19/1/16. Wdd.
1917	...	Dalziell, R. J.	3. J.12/10/15. Wdd.
2137	...	Daniels, C. A.	4. J.19/1/16. Ptd. L/Cpl. K. in A., France, 26/3/17.
1878	Prov. Sgt.	Davey, P.	3. J.12/10/15. T. to 2nd Div. Salvage Coy. 24/1/17. Ptd. L/Cpl.
2366	...	Davies, I. D.	5. J.19/1/16. K. in A., France, 29/7/16.

THE 28th: A RECORD OF WAR SERVICE, 1915-19.

Appendix I—continued.

28TH BATTALION.—NOMINAL ROLL OF REINFORCEMENTS—continued.

Reg. No.	Rank on Embarkation.	Name.	Memoranda.
1528	...	Davis, E.	1. J.18/8/15. T. to 7th F. Coy., Eng., 7/3/16. K. in A., France, 8/1/17.
2365	...	Davis, T. J.	5. J.19/1/16. T. to 2nd Pnr. Bn. 12/3/16. Wdd.
1919	...	Davis, W. P.	3. J.25/10/15. Invalided 21/1/16. Rejoined 23/1/17. K. in A., France, 10/6/18.
2102	A/– Sgt.	Dawkins, O.	4. J.19/1/16. Ptd. Cpl.
1918	...	Dawson, A.	3. J.12/10/15. Ptd. L/Cpl. Wdd. 1915 and 3 occ. later.
2255	...	Dawson, H. E.	4. J.19/1/16.
2140	...	Dean, W. J.	4. J.19/1/16. Wdd. 2 occ.
2329	Prov. Sgt.	Decke, H.	5. J.19/1/16. Ptd. Cpl. Wdd.
1920	...	Dedman, H. T.	3. J.12/10/15. K. in A., France, 3-6/11/16.
1529	...	D'Emarchi, H. C.	1. J.18/8/15. Wdd.
2367	...	Dench, G. H.	5. J.19/1/16. K. in A., France, 29/7/16.
1526	...	Dent, E. A.	1. J.18/8/15. Invalided 28/1/16. Rejoined 19/2/17. K. in A., France, 10/3/17.
1921	...	Denton, H. J.	3. J.12/10/15. Ptd. L/Sgt. Wdd.
2141	...	Digwood, C. J.	4. J.19/1/16. Wdd.
2021	...	Dixon, A. A.	3. J.29/12/15. K. in A., Belgium, 20/9/17.
1922	...	Dixon, W. A.	3. J.12/10/15. T. to 7th M.G. Coy. 22/11/17. Apptd. Dr.
1923	...	Dodds, J.	3. J.12/10/15. Wdd.
2142	...	Doherty, B. L.	4. J.19/1/16. K. in A., France, 29/7/16.
2368	...	Douglas, P. A.	5. J.19/1/16. T. to 2nd Pnr. Bn., 12/3/16.
1527	...	Douglas, T. L.	1. J.5/11/15. D. of Wds., France, 4-6/8/16.
1699	...	Dovell, H. J.	2. J.12/10/15. K. in A., France, 29/7/16.
1698	...	Dovell, L.	2. J.12/10/15. Wdd.
1924	...	Downey, W. J.	3. J.12/10/15. Apptd. Dr.
2369	...	Drury, A.	5. J.19/1/16. Wdd. 2 occ.
2143	...	Dudley, F.	4. J.19/1/16. K. in A., France, 29/7/16.
2144	...	Duncan, G.	4. J.19/1/16. Wdd.
1530	...	Dunkley, I. E.	1. J.18/8/15. Apptd. 2nd Lieut. 16/8/16. Ptd. Captain.
2370	...	Dunn, R. H.	5. J.19/1/16. Ptd. Cpl. Wdd. 3 occ. M.M.
2145	...	Eastwood, A. G.	4. J.19/1/16. Wdd. K. in A., France, 26/3/17.
1607	...	Edmonds, E.	1. J.18/8/15. K. in A., Belgium, 20/9/17.
2371	...	Edwards, E. C.	5. J.19/1/16. K. in A., France, 28-29/7/16.
1532	...	Edwards, E. M.	1. J.18/8/15. D. of Ill., Egypt, 12/2/16.
1926	...	Edwards, H. J.	3. J.29/12/15. Wdd.
2372	...	Edwards, M. C.	5. J.19/1/16. Wdd. M.M.
1925	...	Edwards, R. G.	3. J.12/10/15.
1700	...	Edwards, S. R.	2. J.29/12/15. Wdd.
2016	...	Egan, T. W.	3. J.12/10/15. Ptd. Sgt.
1930	...	Ellement, H. A.	3. J.12/10/15. Wdd. 1915.
1630	...	Elliott, D. L.	1. J.18/8/15. T. to Aust. Provo Corps, 9/9/17. Ptd. E.R. 2nd Cpl.
1533	...	Elliott, G.	1. J.18/8/15.
2373	...	Elliott, W.	5. J.19/1/16.

Appendix I—continued.

28TH BATTALION.—NOMINAL ROLL OF REINFORCEMENTS—continued.

Reg. No.	Rank on Embarkation.	Name.	Memoranda.
1927	...	Elsegood, E. R. ...	3. J.29/12/15. T. to 22nd M.G. Coy. 18/12/17. Wdd.
1701	...	Emery, H. V. ...	2. J.12/10/15. Wdd. 4 occ. D.C.M.
2146	...	Emery, J. W. ...	4. J.29/12/15. Ptd. C.S.M. Wdd. 3 occ.
1928	...	Evans, A. W. ...	3. J.3/11/15. K. in A., France, 29/7/16
2375	...	Everett, J. ...	5. J.19/1/16. K. in A., France, 3/8/16.
1929	...	Evetts, P. V. ...	3. J.12/10/15. Wdd. 2 occ.
1931	...	Farrell, J. A. ...	3. J.29/12/15. Wdd. 2 occ.
1534	Cpl.	Ferguson, H. K. ...	1. J.18/8/15. T. to 51st Bn. 2/4/16. K. in A., France, 24/4/18.
2376	...	Feutrill, T. W. ...	5. J.19/1/16. T. to 11th Bn., 4/3/16. K. in A., France, 22-25/7/16.
1703	...	Fairns, C. G. ...	2. J.12/10/15. Wdd.
1704	...	Firth, A. ...	2. J.29/12/15. Ptd. Sgt. Wdd. 2 occ.
1932	...	Fitzgerald, E. ...	3. J.12/10/15. Wdd. 1915.
2377	...	Fitzgerald, N. F. ...	5 J.19/1/16. T. to 7th M.G. Coy., 8/2/18. Ptd. L/Cpl. Wdd.
1933	...	Fitzpatrick, F. M. ...	3. J.12/10/15. T. to 7th M.G. Coy., 3/3/16. Ptd. T/C.S.M. Wdd. 3 occ. D.C.M., M.M.
1706	...	Fitzpatrick, J. M. ...	2. J.29/12/15. T. to 2nd Pnr. Bn., 14/3/16. Ptd. L/Cpl. Wdd.
2378	...	Fleming, S. J. ...	5. J.19/1/16.
2150	...	Foley, A. ...	4. J.19/1/16. Wdd.
2148	...	Foot, J. ...	4. J.19/1/16. Wdd. 2 occ.
2153	...	Ford, R. H. ...	4. J.19/1/16.
1535	...	Fordham, C. T. ...	1. J.18/8/15. K. in A., Belgium, 10/10/16.
2151	...	Forrest, A. J. ...	4. J.19/1/16. Wdd.
2379	...	Forrest, J. C. ...	5. J.19/1/16. Wdd.
1617	...	Forrester, R. E. ...	1. J.22/8/15. Ptd. T/Sgt. Ment. in Despatches.
2381	...	Forth, A. ...	5. J.19/1/16. D. of Wds., France, 30/5/16.
1935	...	Foster, G. ...	3. J.12/1/15. Wdd. 2 occ. K. in A., Belgium, 20/9/17.
2152	...	Foster, L. N. ...	4. J.19/1/16. Wdd. D. of Wds., France, 13/11/16.
2154	...	Foster, R. T. ...	4. J.19/1/16. Wdd. 2 occ.
1707	...	Foster, W. G. ...	2. J.12/10/15.
2149	...	Fox, J. A. ...	4. J.19/1/16. Ptd. Sgt. Wdd. 2 occ. French *Croix de Guerre*.
2382	...	Freddy, G. ...	5. J.19/1/16. Ptd. Sgt. Wdd.
1887	Prov. Cpl.	Freeman, V. S. ...	3. J.12/10/15. Ptd. Sgt. Wdd. 3 occ.
2383	...	Fry, J. ...	5. J.19/1/16. Wdd.
1936	...	Gardner, H. C. ...	3. J.12/10/15. T. to 2nd Pnr. Bn., 9/3/16. Ptd. Staff Sgt.
1709	...	Gaston, D. J. L. ...	2. J.12/10/15. Ptd. L/Cpl. Wdd. K. in A., France, 3/5/17.
2157	...	Gatenby, G. H. ...	4. J.19/1/16. K. in A., France, 29/7/16.
1537	...	George, S. ...	1. J.18/8/15.
1539	...	Gibb, D. ...	1. J.18/8/15. T. to 2nd Pnr. Bn. 12/3/16.
1937	...	Gibbs, J. W. ...	3. J.12/10/15. Wdd.
2156	...	Gibbs, L. ...	4. J.19/1/16. Wdd. 2 occ.
1710	...	Gilbert, P. G. ...	2. J.12/10/15. T. to 48th Bn. 26/4/16. K. in A., France, 14/8/18.

THE 28th: A RECORD OF WAR SERVICE, 1915-19. 207

Appendix I—continued.

28TH BATTALION.—NOMINAL ROLL OF REINFORCEMENTS—continued.

Reg. No.	Rank on Embarkation.	Name.	Memoranda.
1938	...	Gillies, J.	3. J.12/10/15. T. to A.A. Postal Corps 9/9/16. Rejoined Bn. 20/10/17. Wdd.
1711	...	Gleeson, S. J.	2. J.12/10/15. K. in A., Gallipoli, 15/10/15.
1540	...	Glew, G. A.	1. J.18/8/15. Wdd. D. of Wds., England, 19/11/17.
1712	...	Golden, J.	2. J.12/10/15. Wdd.
2386	...	Golding, A.	5. J.19/1/16. T. to 2nd Pnr. Bn. 12/3/16. Ptd. Cpl. Wdd.
1939	...	Golding, G. B.	3. J.12/10/15. Ptd. Cpl. D. of Wds., Belgium, 4/11/17.
1713	...	Goodisson, A.	2. J.12/10/15. Wdd.
2388	...	Gould, A. J.	5. J.19/1/16. K. in A., France, 7/6/16.
2390	...	Graham, M.	5. J.19/1/16. K. in A., France, 29/7/16.
2158	...	Gray, F.	4. J.19/1/16. Wdd.
3113	...	Gray, J. J.	7. J.15/3/16. Ptd. L/Cpl. K. in A., Belgium, 4/10/17.
1942	...	Green, F. L.	3. J.29/12/15. T. to 7th F. Coy., Eng., 7/3/16. K. in A., France, 27/5/18.
2155	...	Green, G.	4. J.19/1/16. Wdd. T. to Y.M.C.A. Ptd. Hon. Lieut. 1/5/18.
1714	...	Green, J. H.	2. J.12/10/15. Wdd. 2 occ.
1943	...	Green, P. I.	3. J.12/10/15. T. to 2nd Pnr. Bn. Ptd. Cpl.
2159	...	Green, R.	4. J.19/1/16.
1940	...	Greenwood, W.	3. J.12/10/15.
2391	...	Grigsby, W. E.	5. J.19/1/16. T. to 51st Bn. 2/4/16. Wdd.
1941	...	Groat, D.	3. J.12/10/15. K. in A., France, 3–6/11/16.
1715	...	Hadden, A.	2. J.12/10/15. K. in A., France, 29/7/16.
1716	...	Hale, F. L.	2. J.12/10/15. D. of Wds., France, 23/8/16.
2392	...	Hall, R.	5. J.19/1/16. Wdd.
1544	...	Hall, R. V.	1. J.18/8/15. T. to 10th L. Horse, 23/10/15.
1545	...	Hallam, E. J.	1. J.18/8/15. D. of Ill., at Sea, 24/10/15.
2160	...	Halls, J. A.	4. J.19/1/16.
2163	...	Halton, P. J.	4. J.19/1/16. Wdd. 2. occ. Apptd. Hon. Sgt.
1877	Prov. Sgt.	Hammond, A. P.	3. J.12/10/15. Ptd. Cpl. K. in A., France, 27–29/8/16.
2162	...	Hann, E. F.	4. J.19/1/16. K. in A., France, 29/7/16.
1719	...	Hannan, F. O.	2. J.12/10/15. Wdd.
3134	...	Hardie, A.	7. J.15/3/16. Ptd. C.S.M. Wdd. 2 occ.
1949	...	Hardwick, A. E.	3. J.29/12/15. Wdd.
2161	...	Hargrave, W.	4. J.19/1/16. T. to 7th M.G. Coy. 17/7/16. Apptd. 2nd Lieut. 12/2/17. Ptd. Lieut. Wdd. 2 occ.
2250	...	Harper, F. W.	4. J.19/1/16. T. to Aust. Provo. Corps 16/9/16. Apptd. 2nd Lieut. 1/1/17. Ptd. Lieut.
3127	...	Harper, R. H.	7. J.15/3/16. K. in A., France, 29/7/16.
1944	...	Harrington, F. L.	3. J.12/10/15. K. in A., France, 27–29/8/16.
1542	...	Harris, A.	1. J.18/8/15. Ptd. Sgt. Wdd. 3 occ.
1721	...	Harris, E.	2. J.12/10/15. Wdd. 2 occ.
2403	...	Harrison, J.	5. J.19/1/16. Wdd. 2 occ.

Appendix I—continued.

28TH BATTALION.—NOMINAL ROLL OF REINFORCEMENTS—continued.

Reg. No.	Rank on Embarkation.	Name.	Memoranda.
1547	...	Hart, H. J.	1. J.18/8/15.
1722	...	Hart, M.	2. J.12/10/15. K. in A., France, 29/7/16.
1653	A/Cpl.	Hartshorn, A. H. E.	2. J.12/10/15. T. to I.C. Corps, 30/1/16. Ptd. Sgt.
1724	...	Harvey, T. J.	2. J.12/10/15. Apptd. Dr.
2393	...	Harwood, W.	5. J.19/1/16. Wdd. 2 occ.
1543	...	Hawkins, F. W.	1. J. 18/8/15. T. to 16th Bn. Ptd. L/Cpl. Wdd.
1654	A/Sgt.	Hawkins, G. O.	2. J.12/10/15. T. to 12th F. Coy., Eng., 25/7/16. Ptd. T/Sgt. Wdd.
1945	...	Hawkins, J.	3. J.12/10/15.
2164	...	Hay, C. H.	4. J.29/1/16. T. to 2nd Pnr. Bn. 14/3/16. Wdd.
1725	...	Healey, A. P.	2. J.19/1/16. Ptd. Sgt. Wdd.
1951	...	Helm, W.	3. J.12/10/15. K. in A., France, 10-16/18.
1726	...	Henderson, F. G.	2. J.19/1/16. K. in A., France, 29/7/16.
2394	...	Henkel, H. W.	5. J.19/1/16. T. to A.A. Pay Corps 13/4/17. Ptd. Sgt. Wdd. 2 occ.
2395	...	Hepburn, C. J.	5. J.19/1/16. Ptd. L/Cpl.
2165	...	Herbert, F. W.	4. J.19/1/16. Wdd.
1727	...	Herdsman, A. J.	2. J.12/10/15. K. in A., France, 29/7/16.
1548	...	Herron, R.	1. J.18/8/15. K. in A., France, 29/7/16.
2166	...	Hewitt, H.	4. J.19/1/16. Wdd. 3 occ. Ment. in Corps. Orders.
1728	...	Hicks, W. H.	2. J.12/10/15. Ptd. T/Cpl. K. in A., Belgium, 4/10/17.
1729	...	Hill, A. J.	2. J.12/10/15. K. in A., France, 29/7/16.
2167	...	Hines, A.	4. J.19/1/16. D. of ill., England, 16/8/16.
1946	...	Hobbins, S. J.	3. J.12/10/15.
2396	...	Hobbs, R. C.	5. J.19/1/16. Ptd. Sgt. Wdd.
2168	...	Hodges, F. G.	4. J.19/1/16. T. to H.T.M. Bty. 22/4/16. Wdd. 2 occ.
1732	...	Hodsdon, L.	2. J.12/10/15. Wdd.
1947	...	Hoey, A.	3. J.29/12/15. Ptd. L/Cpl. Wdd. 2 occ.
1633	...	Hoffman, J.	1. J.18/8/15. Wdd. 2 occ.
1948	...	Holden, T. G.	3. J.12/10/15. K. in A., France, 4-6/8/16.
1733	...	Holgate, W. R.	2. J.12/10/15. K. in A., France, 29/7/16.
1734	...	Houston, H. J.	2. J.12/10/15. Wdd.
2169	...	Howarth, W.	4. J.19/1/16. Wdd. 3 occ. *M.M.*
3148	...	Howe, W. J.	7. J.15/3/16. D. of Wds., Germany, whilst prisoner of war, 17/10/17.
2170	...	Howells, J. W.	4. J.19/1/16.
2399	...	Howes, F. W. P.	5. J.19/1/16. T. to 48th Bn. 26/4/16.
3152	...	Hubbard, H.	7. J.15/3/16. Wdd.
2400	...	Hughes, W. R.	5. J.19/1/16. *M.M.*
2401	...	Hunt, C. R.	5. J.19/1/16. Ptd. L/Cpl. Wdd. 2 occ.
2402	...	Hunton, S.	5. J.19/1/16. T. to 7th Fld. Amb. 29/12/17. Wdd.
3156	...	Hutchison, C. T.	7. J.19/1/16. K. in A., France, 28-29/7/16.
1736	...	Ing, G. L.	2. J.12/10/15. T. to 14th M.G. Coy. 24/4/16. Apptd. 2nd Lieut. 26/8/16. Ptd. Lieut. Ment. in Despatches. Wdd.

THE 28th: A RECORD OF WAR SERVICE, 1915-19.

Appendix I—continued.

28TH BATTALION.—NOMINAL ROLL OF REINFORCEMENTS—continued.

Reg. No.	Rank on Embarkation.	Name.	Memoranda.
1737	...	Inkpen, L. H. ...	2. J.12/10/15. Wdd. 2 occ.
2171	...	Inwood, W. T. ...	4. J.19/1/16. Wdd.
1738	...	Jackson, J. T. ...	2. J.12/10/15. Wdd.
1953	...	Jackson, W. B.	3. J.12/10/15. Apptd. 2nd Lieut. 7/4/17. D. of Wds., France, 3/5/17.
1952	...	Jackson, W. J.	3. J.12/10/15. K. in A., France, 16-18/11/16.
1954	...	Jefferies, F. ...	3. J.12/10/15. Wdd. 2 occ.
2172	...	Jellings, S. ...	4. J.19/1/16. Ptd. L/Sgt. Wdd.
1955	...	Jenkins, O. ...	3. J.12/10/15. T. to 13th Light Horse 7/12/15.
2173	...	Jenyns, A. C. ...	4. J.19/1/16. Wdd.
2174	...	Job, E. E. ...	4. J.19/1/16. Wdd.
1956	...	Johnson, A. E.	3. J.12/10/15. T. to I.C. Corps, 1/2/16.
2405	...	Johnson, J. W.	5. J.19/1/16. T. to A.A. Ordnance Corps 1/9/17. Ptd. L/Cpl. Wdd.
1957	...	Johnson, W. B.	3. J.19/1/16. Wdd. 2 occ. K. in A., France, 3/5/17.
1550	...	Johnston, E. C.	1. J.18/8/15. T. to 10th Light Horse, 22/1/16. Apptd. Dr.
1958	...	Jones, A. C. ...	3. J.12/10/15. K. in A., France, 29/7/16.
1961	...	Jones, E. H. ...	3. J.12/10/15. K. in A., Belgium, 20/9/17.
2175	...	Jones, F. ...	4. J.19/1/16. D. of Wds., France, 12/3/17.
1960	...	Jones, L. F. ...	3. J.12/10/15.
1740	...	Joyce, G. ...	2. J.12/10/15. K. in A., France, 3-6/11/16.
2176	...	Keals, D. P. ...	4. J.19/1/16. T. to 2nd Div. Hqrs., 14/8/17. Ptd. L/Sgt. Wdd.
2177	...	Keals, F. L. ...	4. J.19/1/16. K. in A., France, 21/5/16.
2406	...	Keillor, D. ...	5. J.19/1/16.
3164	...	Kelly, F. M. ...	7. J.15/3/16. K. in A., France, 3-6/11/16.
1742	...	Kenworthy, D. W. ...	2. J.12/10/15. Ptd. L. Cpl. Wdd. 2 occ M.M.
1743	...	King, G. H. ...	2. J.29/12/15.
1552	...	Kirkham, W. E. ...	1. J.18/8/15. Apptd. Dr.
1963	...	Knight, F. C. ...	3. J.12/10/15.
1554	...	Lee, R. ...	1. J.18/8/15. Ptd. L/Cpl. Wdd. K. in A., France, 26/3/17.
1502	Sgt.	Leeds, J. M. ...	1. J.18/8/15. Invalided 21/1/16. Rejoined 5/10/17. Apptd. 2nd Lieut. 1/1/19. Ptd. Lieut.
3174	...	Leigh, C. T. ...	7. J.15/3/16. K. in A., France, 10/5/16.
1744	...	Leonard, R. J. ...	2. J.12/10/15. Wdd. 2 occ.
2407	...	Lewis, H. G. ...	5. J.19/1/16.
2017	...	Liardet, V. G. ...	3. J.29/12/15. T. to 2nd Div. Sig. Coy. 2/4/17.
1624	...	Lindahn, J. ...	1. J.18/8/15. K. in A., France, 29/7/16.
1555	...	Long, C. R. ...	1. J.18/8/15. Wdd.
1964	...	Lord, W. E. ...	3. J.12/10/15. Ptd. Cpl. Wdd.

Appendix I—continued.

28TH BATTALION.—NOMINAL ROLL OF REINFORCEMENTS—continued.

Reg. No.	Rank on Embarkation.	Name.		Memoranda.
2180	...	Louder, W. J.	...	4. J.19/1/16.
1965	...	Lovell, J. B. ...	...	2. J.12/10/15. Wdd.
2410	...	Lucas, S. R. ...	...	5. J.19/1/16. Wdd.
1745	...	Lukin, H. W. ...	...	2. J.29/12/15. Ptd. T/Sgt. K. in A., France, 29/7/16.
1966	...	Lund, R. J. ...	...	3. J.12/10/15. Ptd. Cpl.
2408	...	Lyons, R. ...	...	5. J.19/1/16. Wdd.
2414	...	McCahon, H. A.	...	5. J.19/1/16. Ptd. Cpl. Wdd. 2 occ.
1968	...	McCallum, M. ...	...	3. J.12/10/15. Ptd. L/Cpl. K. in A., France, 3-6/11/16.
2415	...	McCarthy, B. J.	...	5. J.19/1/16. Wdd.
3207	...	McCaskill, M. ...	...	7. J.15/3/16. Ptd. L/Cpl. Wdd. D. of Wds., Belgium, 2/1/18.
2251	...	McDermott, V. F.	...	4. J.19/1/16.
2193	...	MacDonald, A. ...	...	4. J.19/1/16. Wdd.
2185	...	McEnroe, P. T.	...	4. J.19/1/16. K. in A., France, 29/5/16.
2417	...	McGinnis, F. W.	...	5. J.19/1/16. K. in A., France, 3-6/11/16.
1751	...	McGregor, J. ...	...	2. J.19/1/16.
1752	...	McHugh, J. ...	...	2. J.10/1/16. Ptd. Sgt. Wdd. D. of Wds., Belgium, 4/10/17.
2418	...	McInnes, I. ...	...	5. J.19/1/16. K. in A., France, 29/7/16.
1070	...	McKeown, P. J.	...	3. J.12/10/15. Wdd.
1971	...	McKinnon, D. S.	...	3. J.12/10/15. K. in A., France, 29/7/16.
1558	...	MacLachlan, J. J.	...	1. J.18/8/15. K. in A., France, 29/7/16.
1754	...	McLaughlin, W.	...	2. J.12/10/15. Wdd.
1969	...	McLean, G. J. ...	...	3. J.12/10/15. Ptd. Sgt. Wdd.
1504	Sgt.	McTaggart, G. S.	...	1. J.18/8/15. Apptd. 2nd Lieut. 16/8/16. Ptd. T/Captain. D.C.M. D. of Wds., France, 9/8/18.
2181	...	Maddern, W. T.	...	4. J.19/1/16. Ptd. L/Cpl. M.M Wdd. D. of Wds., Belgium, 28/10/17.
1747	...	Madigan, W. ...	...	2. J.12/10/15. D. of Wds., France, 14/8/15.
2411	...	Maitland, J. M.	...	5. J.19/1/16. Ptd. Cpl.
1967	...	Marshall, J. W.	...	3. J.29/12/15. Wdd.
1748	...	Masters, F. D. ...	...	2. J.12/10/15. Wdd.
1749	...	May, A. ...	...	2. J.12/10/15. T. to 51st Bn. 3/3/16. K. in A., France, 14-16/8/16.
1750	...	Mayes, W. J. ...	...	2. J.12/10/15. T. to 51st Bn. K. in A., France, 15/8/16.
2412	...	Meredith, A. F.	...	5. J.19/1/16.
2334	Prov. Cpl.	Meredith, I. H.	...	5. J.19/1/16. Ptd. T/- Sgt. Wdd. D.C.M.
1755	...	Merifield, W. T.	...	2. J.12/10/15. Ptd. E.R. Sgt.
1756	...	Messenger, J. T.	...	2. J.12/10/15. K. in A., France, 4-6/8/16.
1757	...	Meyer, A. C. ...	...	2. J.12/10/15. T. to 2nd Div. Sig. Coy. 7/5/17. Wdd. D. of Ill., France, 5/12/18.
1758	...	Meyer, W. L. ...	...	2. J.12/10/15. K. in A., France, 29/7/16.
2182	...	Middleton, D. ...	...	4. J.19/1/16.
1505	Cpl.	Miller, J. B. ...	...	1. J.18/8/15. Ptd. Cpl.
1975	...	Miller, O. ...	...	3. J.29/12/15.
1976	...	Miller, T. ...	...	3. J.29/12/15. T. to 2nd Div. Sig. Coy. 15/11/17. Rejoined Bn. 29/4/18.
2183	...	Milligan, F. D.	...	4. J.19/1/16. Wdd.

THE 28th: A RECORD OF WAR SERVICE, 1915-19. 211

Appendix I—continued.

28TH BATTALION.—NOMINAL ROLL OF REINFORCEMENTS—continued.

Reg. No.	Rank on Embarkation.	Name.	Memoranda.
3205	...	Minett, S. J. ...	7. J.15/3/16. K. in A., France, 29/7/16.
1760	...	Moller, H. A. ...	2. J.12/10/15. K. in A., France, 26/3/17.
2184	...	Moore, G. S. ...	4. J.19/1/16. K. in A., France, 5/9/18.
1974	...	Moore, H. ...	3. J.12/10/15. K. in A., France, 3--6/11/16.
3198	...	Moran, B. J. ...	7. J.15/3/16. Ptd. Sgt. K. in A., Belgium, 20/9/17.
2188	...	Moran, R. J. ...	4. J.19/1/16. Wdd. Ment. in Corps Orders.
2022	...	Morgan, R. ...	3. J.29/12/15. T. to A.A. Postal Corps 12/10/18. Wdd. *M.M. and Bar.*
2187	...	Morgan, S. H. S. ...	4. J.19/1/16. Ptd. Sgt. Wdd. 3. occ.
1972	...	Morphett, H. H. ...	3. J.12/10/15. T. to H.T.M. Bty 22/4/16, and to 51st Bn. 21/7/17. Ptd. L/Cpl. K. in A., France, 25/4 18.
1561	...	Morris, R. ...	1. J.18/8/15. Apptd. Dr.
1762	...	Morrison, J. D. D. ...	2. J.29/12/15. K. in A., France, 29/7/16.
1557	...	Morrow, A. ...	1. J.18/8/15. K. in A., Gallipoli, 16/12/15.
1556	...	Morrow, E. ...	1. J.18/8/15. Ptd. Cpl. Wdd. 2 occ.
2328	Prov. Sgt.	Mullen, F. S. H. ...	5. J.19/1/16. Apptd. 2nd Lieut. 16/8/16. Ptd. Lieut. Wdd.
2189	...	Mullins, J. ...	4. J.19/1/16. D. of Wds., Belgium, 5/11/17.
2186	...	Mullins, V. H. ...	4. J.19/1/16. D. of Wds., France, 5/11/17.
1876	Prov. Sgt.	Munro, R. C. ...	3. J.12/10/15. Ptd. T/- Sgt. K. in A., France, 26/2/17.
1764	...	Murphy, B. F. ...	2. J.12/10/15. Ptd. Sgt. D.C.M. Belgian *Croix de Guerre.* Detached for special duty with Dunsterville's Force through Mesopotamia and Persia to Baku. *Bar to D.C.M.*
2252	...	Murphy, E. ...	4. J.19/1/16. Wdd.
2190	...	Murphy, H. O. ...	4. J.19/1/16. Wdd. 2 occ.
2258	...	Murphy, P. J. D. ...	4. J.19/1/16. K. in A., France, 29/7/16.
2413	...	Murray, D. ...	5. J.19/1/16. Wdd.
2191	...	Murray, F. ...	4. J.19/1/16. T. to I.C. Corps 1/2/16. Ptd. L/Cpl.
1765	A/- Cpl.	Murray, R. ...	2. J.12/10/15.
1562	...	Murray, T. ...	1. J.18/8/15. Ptd. T/- Cpl. Wdd. 1915 and 2nd occ.
2420	...	Nalder, R. B. ...	5. J.19/1/16. Wdd.
2253	...	Neville, S. ...	4. J.19/1/16. K. in A., France, 3-6/11/16.
1567	...	Newman, W. C. F. ...	1. J.18/8/15. K. in A., France, 29/7/16.
1977	...	Nicholls, J. F. H. ...	3. J.12/10/15. Wdd.
2194	...	Nicholls, W. G. P. ...	4. J.19/1/16. T. to 16th Bn. 10/3/16.
2422	...	Nichols, R. H. ...	5. J.19/1/16.
2195	...	Nicol, H. R. ...	4. J.19/1/16. Ptd. Sgt.
1978	...	Nicol, W. C. ...	3. J.29/12/15. T. to I.C. Corps, 1/2/16.
2196	...	Oakey, G. A. V. ...	4. J.19/1/16. K. in A., France, 29/7/16.
2197	...	O'Boyle, J. ...	4. J.19/1/16.
1569	...	O'Brien, H. ...	1. J.18/8/15. D. of Wds., France, 4-6/8/16.
1979	...	O'Connor, D. E. ...	3. J.12/10/15. K. in A., France, 29/7/16.
2025	...	O'Donnell, L. ...	3. J.29/12/15.
1980	...	O'Donnell, R. ...	3. J.21/1/16.

Appendix I—continued.

28TH BATTALION.—NOMINAL ROLL OF REINFORCEMENTS—continued.

Reg. No.	Rank on Embarkation.	Name.	Memoranda.
2112	A/- Cpl.	O'Grady, G. C.	4. J.19/1/16. Apptd. 2nd Lieut. 1/8/16. Ptd. Lieut. Wdd. 2 occ.
6343	...	O'Grady, S. de C.	T. from 16th A.A.S.C. 4/3/16. Ptd. Sgt. Wdd. 3 occ.
2018	...	O'Loughlin, L. ...	3. J.29/12/15. K. in A., France, 29/7/16.
2423	...	Olsen, E. H.	5. J.19/1/16. Ptd. L/Cpl. K. in A., France, 29/7/16.
1981	...	O'Neill, J. C. ...	3. J.12/10/15. T. to 2nd M.G. Bn. 26/5/18. Wdd. 2 occ.
1982	...	Osborne, T. S. ...	3. J.12/10/15. Wdd.
1616	...	Parker, F.	1. J.18/8/15. Apptd. Dr.
2424	...	Parker, P. H.	5. J.19/1/16. Wdd.
1608	...	Parkinson, T. ...	1. J.18/8/15. T. to 7th M.G. Coy. 3/8/16.
2198	...	Parkyn, A.	4. J.19/1/16. K. in A., France, 29/7/16.
1571	...	Parnell, C.	1. J.18/8/15. Ptd. Sgt. Wdd.
1768	...	Parsons, C. W. G.	2. J.12/10/15. Ptd. Cpl. K. in A., France, 3-6/11/16.
2426	...	Pascoe, F. J. ...	5. J.19/1/16. Ptd. Sgt. Wdd. D. of Wds., Belgium, 23/9/17.
2199	...	Passmore, A. C.	4. J.19/1/16. K. in A., France, 29/7/16.
1659	A/Sgt.	Paterson, A. M.	2. J.12/10/15. T. to I.C. Corps, 1/2/16. Ptd. Sgt.
2427	...	Payne, A. E. ...	5. J.19/1/16. Wdd. 2 occ.
1983	...	Peach, G. H. ...	3. J.12/10/15. Wdd. 2 occ.
1802	...	Phillips, E. C. ...	2. J.29/12/15. Wdd.
2202	...	Phillips, H. ...	4. J.19/1/16. Wdd.
2429	...	Phillips, T. L. ...	5. J.19/1/16 K. in A., France, 3-6/11/16.
2027	...	Philpott, A. ...	3. J.29/12/15. Wdd.
1627	...	Pickard, H. ...	1. J.18/8/15. K. in A., France, 29/7/16.
2203	...	Plumb, F. A. ...	4. J.19/1/16. Wdd.
1574	...	Pollard, J. H. ...	1. J.18/8/15. T. to 2nd Pnr. Bn., 12/3/16. Wnd. 2 occ.
1984	...	Pratt, F. B. ...	3. J.29/12/15. Ptd. L/Cpl. Wdd. 2 occ.
1573	...	Prentice, T.	1. J.18/8/15.
2200	...	Price, C. W. ...	4. J.19/1/16. K. in A., France, 29/7/16.
1985	...	Price, S. F. ...	3. J.12/10/15. Ptd. Sgt. Wdd. 3 occ. D.C.M. M.M.
2434	...	Priest, G.	5. J.19/1/16. Ptd. L/Cpl. Wdd.
1986	...	Probert, C. G.	3. J.19/1/16. Wdd.
2204	...	Quarrell, C. ...	4. J.19/1/16. Ptd. L/Cpl. D. of Wds., France, 17/11/16.
1988	...	Raby, H. C. ...	3. J.12/10/15. D. of Wds., France, 30/7/16
1578	...	Rainsden, A. ...	1. J.18/8/15. Drowned at sea, 6/10/15.
1580	...	Raitt, E. W. ...	1. J.18/8/15. K. in A., France, 29/7/16.
2207	...	Ramsay, W. J. C.	4. J.19/1/16.
1620	...	Randell, N. ...	1. J.18/8/15.
1771	...	Rankin, G. ...	2. J.29/12/15. T. to 2nd Div. Salvage Coy., 24/1/17. Ptd. E.R. Cpl.
1772	...	Rankine, S. C. ...	2. J.12/10/15. T. to I.C. Corps and later to 14th Light Horse 1/7/18. Ptd. T/Cpl.

THE 28th: A RECORD OF WAR SERVICE, 1915-19.

Appendix I—continued.

28TH BATTALION.—NOMINAL ROLL OF REINFORCEMENTS—continued.

Reg. No.	Rank on Embark- ation.	Name.	Memoranda.
2208	...	Rawnsley, E. R. ...	4. J.19/1/16. T. to 4th Pnr. Bn. 30/12/16. Wdd.
2435	...	Reidy, J. T. ...	5. J.19/1/16. Wdd.
2205	...	Rickard, L. G. ...	4. J.19/1/16. Wdd.
2254	...	Rillstone, L. J.	4. J.19/1/16. Ptd. Cpl.
2327	Prov. Sgt.	Riva, C. S. ...	5. J.19/1/16. Wdd. T. to 3rd Echelon, G.H.Q.,22/12/16. Ptd. E.R. Staff Sgt.
1989	...	Roberts, H. W.	3. J.12/10/15.
1575	...	Roe, J. A. ...	1. J.18/8/15. Wdd. 1915. T. to Aust. Provo. Corps 10/6/17. Ptd. E.R. Sgt. Ment. in Despatches.
1991	...	Rolls, A. L.	3. J.12/10/15. Wdd. 2 occ. K. in A., France, 10/6/18.
1773	...	Rosser, O. ...	2. J.12/10/15.
1503	Sgt.	Rourke, J. J. ...	1. J.18/8/15. Ptd. C.S.M.
2211	...	Rowe, C. C. ...	4. J.19/1/16. Invalided 11/4/16. Re- joined 4/1/18. Wdd. 2 occ.
1613	...	Rowe, T. F. ...	1. J.18/8/15. Ptd. Sgt. Wdd.
1993	...	Roxburgh, S. D.	3. J.12/10/15. Ptd. Sgt. Wdd.
1576	...	Roy, J. H. ...	1. J.12/10/15. Ptd. L/Cpl. D. of Wds., Egypt, 28/11/15.
1774	...	Rudler, J. H. ...	2. J.12/10/15. Wdd.
2206	...	Rushton, L. ...	4. J.29/12/15. K. in A., France, 29/7/16.
1995	...	Sainsbury, N. G.	3. J.29/12/15. K. in A., France, 29/7/16.
1583	...	Sandells, S. W.	1. J.18/8/15. T. to 7th M.G. Coy. 15/9/16. Wdd.
1586	...	Sanders, C.	1. J.18/8/15. T. to 7th M.G. Coy, 3/3/16. Wdd.
1994	...	Sands, F. S. ...	3. J.12/10/15. Wdd. 2 occ.
1775	...	Saunders, J. ...	2. J.12/10/15. Wdd. 1915. D. of Ill., Egypt, 18/2/16.
1588	...	Savill, A. W. ...	1. J.18/8/15. Wdd. 2 occ.
2214	...	Sawyer, N. B. ...	4. J.19/1/16. Wdd. M.M.
2256	...	Scott, F. ...	4. J.19/1/16. Ptd. L/Cpl.
1884	Prov. Cpl.	Scott, F. A. ...	3. J.19/1/16. Ptd. E.R. Cpl.
1629	...	Scott, J. ...	1. J.18/8/15. T. to I.C. Corps, 30/1/16. D. of Wds., Palestine, 21/4/17.
2216	...	Selkirk, D. ...	4. J.19/1/16. Ptd. Cpl. Wdd. 2 occ.
2215	...	Seymour, G. H.	4. J.19/1/16. Wdd.
2220	...	Sharp, E. ...	4. J.19/1/16.
2446	...	Shaw, R. H. ...	5. J.19/1/16. Ptd. L/Cpl. Wdd.
2001	...	Sheldrake, W. G.	3. J.12/10/15. T. to Aust. Provo. Corps, 3/4/16.
1879	Prov. Sgt.	Shellabear, S. A.	3. J.12/10/15. T. to 2nd Div. Hqrs. 24/1/16. Apptd. 2nd Lieut. 1/4/19. M.S.M.
2221	...	Shepherd, G. ...	4. J.19/1/16. Wdd.
1635	...	Silvester, R. ...	1. J.18/8/15. Ptd. Cpl. Wdd. Ment. in Despatches.
1776	...	Simmers, F. ...	2. J.12/10/15. Ptd. Sgt. D. of Wds., France, 27/3/17.
1780	...	Sinclair, L. R. R.	2. J.29/12/15. K. in A., France, 29/7/16.
1781	...	Sinclair, W. H.	2. J.19/1/16. Ptd. L/Cpl. Wdd.
1782	...	Skinner, P. J. ...	2. J.12/10/15. K. in A., France, 29/7/16.
1582	...	Smart, E. S. ...	1. J.18/8/15. T. to 7th M.G. Coy. 3/3/16. Wdd.
1998	...	Smith, C. H. C.	3. J.12/10/15. T. to Aust. Flying Corps 3/8/17. Apptd. 2nd Lieut. 17/5/18. Wdd. 2 occ.

214   THE 28th: A RECORD OF WAR SERVICE, 1915-19.

Appendix I—*continued.*

28TH BATTALION.—NOMINAL ROLL OF REINFORCEMENTS—*continued.*

Reg. No.	Rank on Embark- ation.	Name.	Memoranda.
1587	...	Smith, E. E.	1. J.18/8/15. K. in A., France, 29/7/16.
2222	...	Smith, F.	4. J.19/1/16. T. to H.T.M.Bty. 11/6/16.
2218	...	Smith, G.	4. J.19/1/16. Wdd. K. in A., Belgium, 20/9/17.
2023	...	Smith, H. A.	3. J.29/12/15. D. of Wds., France, 30/6/16.
1907	...	Smith, H. D.	3. J.29/12/15.
2223	...	Smith, J.	4. J.19/1/16.
2224	...	Smith, S.	4. J.19/1/16. Wdd.
1783	...	Spencer, A.	2. J.19/1/16. Ptd. Sgt. Wdd. 3 occ.
2226	...	Spencer, E.	4. J.19/1/16.
2225	...	Spencer, H. J.	4. J.19/1/16. Apptd. 2nd Lieut. 27/9/17. Ptd. Lieut. Wdd. 2 occ.
1619	...	Spencer, T. W.	1. J.18/8/15. T. to 7th M.G.Coy. 14/3/16.
2104	A/-Sgt.	Stansfield, A.	4. J.19/1/16. T. to 2nd Pnr. Bn. 13/3/16. Ptd. Sgt. Wdd. 3 occ.
1996	...	Steele, P.	3. J.12/10/15. T. to Aust. Flying Corps 18/7/17. Ptd. L/Cpl. Wdd. 2 occ.
2227	...	Stent, A. G.	4. J.19/1/16. Ptd. Cpl. Wdd. 2 occ.
1660	A/-Cpl.	Stewart, C.	2. J.12/10/15. Ptd. L/Cpl. K. in A., France, 29/7/16.
1618	...	Stewart-Payne, E. C. S. F.	1. J.18/8/15.
2228	...	Strike, W. E.	4. J.19/1/16. Ptd. L/Cpl.
2219	...	Stuart, J. A. C.	4. J.19/1/16. T. to Aust. Provo. Corps, 5/8/17. Ptd. E.R. 2nd Cpl. Wdd.
1999	...	Stuart, V. O.	3. J.12/10/15. K. in A., France, 29/7/16.
2103	...	Stutchbury, H.	4. J.19/1/16. Ptd. T/-Sgt. Wdd. 2 occ.
2456	...	Summers, H. P.	5. J.19/1/16. Ptd. T/R.Q.M.S. Ment. in Despatches.
1623	...	Sumner, R.	1. J.18/8/15.
1585	...	Swindell, N.	1. J.18/8/15. Wdd.
2230	...	Tapper, N.	4. J.19/1/16. Ptd. Sgt.
1785	...	Tate, E. A. B.	2. J.12/10/15. T. to 10th Light Horse 29/1/16. Wdd. 1915.
1593	...	Taylor, D. P. E.	1. J.18/8/15. Wdd. 1915. T. to H.T.M. Bty. 11/6/16. Ptd. Bombardier.
2232	...	Taylor, J.	4. J.19/1/16. Wdd.
1560	...	Taylor, P. W.	1. J.18/8/15. K. in A., Belgium, 20/9/17.
2257	...	Templeman, J. W.	4. J.19/1/16.
2003	...	Terry, D. K.	3. J.12/10/15. Wdd.
2002	...	Terry, M. R.	3. J.12/10/15. K. in A., France, 29/7/16.
1786	...	Thomas, C.	2. J.29/12/15. K. in A., France, 29/7/16.
2005	...	Thompson, W. F.	3. J.19/1/16. Wdd.
2236	...	Thorn, L.	4. J.19/1/16. K. in A., France, 29/7/16.
2235	...	Thorns, A. J. V.	4. J.19/1/16. K. in A., France, 29/7/16.
1788	...	Thorp, H. H.	2. J.12/10/15. K. in A., France, 29/7/16.
2004	...	Tickle, F. R.	3. J.12/10/15. Wdd.
1789	...	Tilbury, G. V.	2. J.12/10/15. D. of Wds., France, 30/7/16.

THE 28th: A RECORD OF WAR SERVICE, 1915-19. 215

Appendix I—continued.

28TH BATTALION.—NOMINAL ROLL OF REINFORCEMENTS—continued.

Reg. No.	Rank on Embarkation.	Name.	Memoranda.
1804	...	Tindall, W. H. A.	2. J.29/12/15. Ptd. L/Cpl. Wdd. 2 occ.
2006	...	Tolland, F.	3. J.12/10/15. T. to 2nd Div. Sig. Coy., 14/8/16.
1790	...	Touzel, C. N.	2. J.12/10/15. T. to 16th Bn., 12/11/15. K. in A., France, 11/4/17.
1791	A/Cpl.	Townsend, W. G.	2. J.12/10/15. Invalided 2/1/16. Rejoined 4/12/16. Ptd. T/Sgt. Wdd.
1886	Prov. Cpl.	Tozer, H. J. H.	3. J.12/10/15. Apptd. 2nd Lieut. 7/4/17. Ptd. Lieut. Wdd. M.C. M.M.
1792	...	Tucker, W. H.	2. J.12/10/15. Apptd. T/Dr.
2234	...	Turner, C.	4. J.19/1/16. T. to 7th M.G. Coy. 13/11/16. Wdd.
2229	...	Turner, H. D.	4. J.19/1/16. Wdd.
1592	...	Turner, J.	1. J.18/8/15. Ptd. L/Cpl. Wdd. 1915 and 3 occ later.
2459	...	Turner, J.	5. J.19/1/16. D. of Wds., France, 22/8/16.
2238	...	Vallentine, V. G. J.	4. J.19/1/16. Wdd.
2239	...	Van Den Bosch, W.	4. J.19/1/16. T. to 48th Bn., 26/4/16. Wdd. 2 occ.
2237	...	Van-Ooran, C.	4. J.19/1/16. Ptd. Sgt.
2240	...	Vaughan, D. J.	4. J.19/1/16. Wdd.
2241	...	Vessey, E. R.	4. J. 19/1/16. Wdd.
2242	...	Vickers, W.	4. J.19/1/16. T. to 32nd Bn. 6/4/16. Ptd. Cpl. Wdd. K. in A., France, 16/3/18.
2019	...	Vickrage, T.	3. J.18/8/15. K. in A., France, 29/7/16.
2326	Prov. Sgt.	Walker, G. A.	5. J.19/1/16. Ptd. C.S.M. Wdd. K. in A., France, 1/6/18.
1803	...	Wallis, F. C.	2. J.18/8/15. T. to 2nd Div. Sig. Coy. 14/3/16. Wdd.
2243	...	Wallis, S.	4. J.29/12/15.
1602	...	Wardlaw, A. C.	1. J.18/8/15. T. to Aust. Provo. Corps 5/8/17. Ptd. E.R. 2nd Cpl. Wdd.
2007	...	Warner, S. E.	3. J.12/10/15. T. to 7th M.G. Coy. 3/3/16. Ptd. Cpl. Wdd.
2333	Prov. Cpl.	Warrington, A. V.	5. J.19/1/16. T. to 51st Bn. 3/3/16. Apptd. 2nd Lieut. 19/12/17. Ptd. Lieut. Wdd. 3 occ.
1599	...	Watson, J.	1. J.18/8/15. T. to 2nd · Pnr. Bn. 12/3/16. Apptd. Dr.
2008	...	Watson, T. D.	3. J.12/10/15. Wdd. 1915 and 2nd occ. D. of Ill., England, 30/10/17.
2247	...	Webb, S. A.	4. J.19/1/16. Ptd. Sgt. Wdd.
1631	...	Webb, W. J.	1. J.18/8/15. T. to 2nd Div. Sig. Coy. 14/3/16.
2029	...	Webster, W. D.	3. J.29/12/15. Apptd. T/Dr.
2330	...	Wedd, C. G.	5. J.19/1/16. T. to 51st Bn. 3/3/16. Ptd. Sgt. K. in A., France, 3/9/16.
1794	...	Weeks, E. S.	2. J.2/10/15. Wdd.
2010	...	Weir, J.	3. J.12/10/15. Wdd. 1915.
2009	...	West, C. H. G.	3. J.12/10/15. K. in A., France, 29/7/16.
1795	...	White, C.	2. J.12/10/15. Ptd. L/Cpl. Wdd. D. of Wds., Belgium, 2/11/17.
1597	...	White, G. M.	1. J.18/8/15. Ptd. Cpl. Wdd. 2 occ.

Appendix I—*continued.*

28TH BATTALION.—NOMINAL ROLL OF REINFORCEMENTS—*continued.*

Reg. No.	Rank on Embarkation.	Name.	Memoranda.
2011	...	Whittaker, F. F.	3. J.29/12/15.
2246	...	Wicks, F. C. ...	4. J.19/1/16. K. in A., France, 29/7/16.
1604	Cpl.	Williams, A. B.	1. J.18/8/15. T. to I.C. Corps 30/1/16.
2244	...	Williams, C. A.	4. J.19/1/16. T. to Aust. Wireless Signal Squadron 4/1/18. Wdd.
1596	...	Williams, C. H.	1. J.18/8/15.
1797	...	Williams, E. A.	2. J.12/10/15.
2012	...	Williams, J. M. H.	3. J.29/12/15. Ptd. L/Sgt.
1799	...	Williams, S. ...	2. J.12/10/15. K. in A., France, 4-6/8/16.
1601	...	Williams, S. H.	1. J.18/8/15. Wdd.
1614	...	Wilson, C. H. ...	1. J.18/8/15.
1615	...	Wilson, T. H. R.	1. J.18/8/15. Ptd. Cpl.
2013	...	Withnell, J. E.	3. J.29/12/15.
1605	...	Wood, J. J. ...	1. J.18/8/15. Wdd. 2 occ.
1800	...	Woodcock, L. N.	2. J.12/10/15.
1628	...	Woods, J. M. ...	1. J. 18/8/15. Ptd. Cpl. Wdd.
2014	...	Wragg, D. D. ...	3. J.12/10/15. T. to 11th Bn. 24/1/16. Wdd.
1801	...	Wright, I. R. ...	2. J.12/10/15. T. to 17th Fld. Amb. 16/6/17. Rejoined Bn. 28/10/17. Ptd. Cpl. Wdd. K. in A., France, 9/4/18.
2015	...	Wrighton, A. F.	3. J.12/10/15. D. of Wds., France, 6/8/16.
2248	...	Young, T. L. ...	4. J.19/1/16. D. of Wds., France, 2/1/17.

Appendix I—*continued.*

SUMMARY.

Number of Reinforcement.	Date Embarked.	Port of Embarkation.	Name of Transport.	Strength on Embarkation.		Number absorbed by parent unit prior to 21/3/1916.	
				Officers.	Other Ranks	Officers.	Other Ranks.
First	5/6/15	Fremantle	A2. " Geelong "	1	100	1	97
Second	23/7/15	do.	A64. " Demosthenes "	2	150	1	111
Third	2/9/15	do.	A68. " Anchises "	2	150	2	142
Fourth	1/10/15	do.	A20. " Hororata "	2	151	...	135
Fifth	13/10/15	do.	A32. " Themistocles "	2	150	...	87
Sixth	2/11/15	do.	A38. " Ulysses "	3	309	...	...
Seventh	18/1/16	do.	A7. " Medic "	3	301	3	15

Total of Reinforcements Nos. 1 to 7 = 15 Officers 1,311 other Ranks.
Total of Reinforcements absorbed prior to 21/3/16 = 7 ,, 587 ,,
Add transfers from other Units 1 ,, 1 ,,
Total additions to strength ... 8 ,, 588 ,,

Appendix J.

Honours conferred on Original Members of the 28th Battalion.

THE MOST DISTINGUISHED ORDER OF ST. MICHAEL AND ST. GEORGE.
Companion (C.M.G.):
Colonel H. B. Collett.

THE DISTINGUISHED SERVICE ORDER.
Companions (D.S.O.):
Brown, Major A.
Collett, Colonel H. B.
Denson, Major H. R.
Read, Lieut.-Colonel G. A.
Shorrock, Lieut. J.

THE ORDER OF THE BRITISH EMPIRE.
Officers (O.B.E.):
Davies, Lieut.-Colonel C. R.
Gunn, Hon. Captain J. R.

THE MILITARY CROSS (M.C.)
Allen, Captain L. G.
Brown, Major A.
Brown, Captain R.
Casey, Lieut. R.
Coburn, Lieut. A. P.
Foss, Captain C. M.
Graham, Lieut. N.
Hammond, Captain M. G.
King, Captain H. C.
Lamb, Major C. H.
Leaver, Lieut. W. A.
McIntyre, Captain J.
McIntyre, Captain K. M. G.
Nicholls, Captain T. O.
Phillips, Major R. C.
Shaw, Captain G. D.
Smiley, Lieut. H. F.
Sundercombe, Captain N. W.

BAR TO THE MILITARY CROSS.
Hammond, Captain M. G.
Phillips, Major R. C.

DISTINGUISHED FLYING CROSS (D.F.C.)
Phillips, Major R. C.

DISTINGUISHED CONDUCT MEDAL (D.C.M.)
Ahnall, 2nd Lieut. K.
Ballingall, Bty. Sgt.-Major C. T.
Clark, Coy. Sergt.-Major A. W.
Cooper, Private H. W.
Farmer, Lance-Corpl. H.
Farris, Private R. P.
Hall, Lance-Corpl. J.
Molloy, Corporal H.
Wilson, Sergeant T.

Appendix J—continued.

THE MILITARY MEDAL (M.M.)

Acres, Lance-Corpl. J. J.
Anderson, Sergt. W.
Bourne, Bty. Sergt.-Major R. F.
Broadbent, Private H. F.
Brown, Lance-Sergt. G. J. R.
Brown, Private W. T.
Cottingham, Private D.
Cross, Sergt. M.
Dunne, Corpl. M.
Fitzpatrick, Sergt. M. M.
Franco, Private H. A.
Hammond, Captain M. G.
Hendrick, Sergt. T. J.
Hill, Lieut. A. N.
Hopkins, Lieut. J.
Jerry, 2nd Lieut. A.
Jones, Driver G. B.
Keeley, Sergt. W. J.
Leaver, Lieut. W. A.
Lenegan, Private J. W.
McAuliffe, Corpl. D.
Piggott, Lieut. W. C.
Powell, 2nd Lieut. G. E.
Scott, Private J.
Seymour, Lance-Sergt. H. L.
Stewart, Lance-Sergt. A.
Thomas, Private W. N.
Trenorden, Corpl. L. C.
Walker, Private R.
Watson, Sergt. J. E.
Wilson, Sergt. W. L.
Winters, Corpl. B.
Wright, Private L.

BAR TO THE MILITARY MEDAL.
McAuliffe, Corpl. D.

MERITORIOUS SERVICE MEDAL (M.S.M.)
Brown, Lance-Sergt. J. W.
Goffin, Sergt. J.
Simmonds, Driver H.

BELGIAN CROIX de GUERRE.
Major E. G. Glyde.
Private A. J. Sweeting.

FRENCH CROIX de GUERRE.
Captain J. J. S. Scouler.

MONTENEGRIN ORDER OF DANILLO, 5th Class.
Lieut.-Colonel G. A. Read.

SERBIAN SILVER MEDAL.
Private H. A. Franco.

COMPILER'S NOTE.

The Compiler will be grateful if readers will point out to him, *in writing*, any errors in the narrative or inaccuracies and omissions in the personal records of members.

The completion of this volume was delayed considerably through difficulty in obtaining the required information. For the second volume a good deal of material is already in hand, but success cannot be ensured unless ex-members will co-operate with the 28th Battalion Association Committee and the Compiler.

In the many actions in which the Battalion fought, no single person could possibly observe all that happened. To give a complete picture it is therefore necessary that the stories should be set down by as many individuals as care to contribute. From their accounts a full and accurate narrative can be constructed. Lengthy writings are not required, nor need any contributor worry about style. It will be sufficient to merely set down actual occurrences and give the names of persons and places, also the dates and times. Anecdotes with reference to any Member of the Battalion are valuable and serve to lighten the story.

The following notes are made for the purpose of assisting the memories of those who are willing to help :—

    I. FRANCE, 1916.—Marseilles to Thiennes. Steenbecque, Morbecque, Hazebrouck, Erquingham, Armentieres, Rue Marle, Bois Grenier, Lille Post, l'Epinette, First Raid, Rue Dormoire, Red Lodge, Messines, La Plus Douve Farm. Move to Somme. Bertangles, Amiens, Warloy, The Brickfields, La Boisselle, Pozieres, Ypres, Flers, Geudecourt, Waterlot Farm.

    II. FRANCE, 1917.—Le Sars, Warlencourt, Malt Trench, Lagnicourt, Bapaume, Bullecourt, Noreuil, Senlis, Renescure, Passchendaele, Reninghelst, Swan Area, Broodseinde Ridge, Dickebusch, Albert Redoubt, Fletre, Steenvoorde, Aldershot Camp, Red Lodge, Neuve Eglise, Warnieton Sector, Romarin Camp.

    III. FRANCE, 1918.—Warneton Sector, Kortepyp Camp, Romarin, Loore, Le Waast. Return to Somme, Ville-sur-Ancre, Morlancourt, Monument Wood, Villers-Bretonneux, Herleville Ridge, Mt. St. Quentin, Haut Allaines, Beaurevoir. The Armistice. Move to and stay at Charleroi. Demobilising. Quotas. Journey to England.

    IV. Waiting for transports. Voyage to Australia.

    V. Incidents in Billets. The French and Belgian peasantry.

    VI. Schools of Instruction in France and England.

    VII. Tours of duty in Training Camps in England.

    VIII. Description and incidents of Hospital life.

    IX. Occurrences and places visited whilst on leave.

    X. Happenings to officers and men who, after enlisting in the 28th Battalion, were transferred to other units.

    XI. Experiences of Prisoners of War.

The Compiler would welcome any spare photographs of persons, places, and events, which are likely to be of general interest. It is particularly desirable to secure portraits of all those Members who were decorated for gallant service or were, for other reasons, well known in the Unit.

www.ingramcontent.com/pod-product-compliance
Lightning Source LLC
Chambersburg PA
CBHW031139160426
43193CB00008B/192